A RHETORIC OF
ELECTRONIC COMMUNITIES

New Directions in Computer and Composition Studies

Gail E. Hawisher and Cynthia L. Selfe, Series Editors

Computers and the Teaching of Writing in American Higher Education, 1979-1994: A History
Gail E. Hawisher, Paul LeBlanc, Charles Moran, and Cynthia L. Selfe

The Rhetoric of Electronic Communities
Tharon Howard

Nostalgic Angels: Rearticulating Hypertext Writing
Johndan Johnson-Eilola

The Computer and the Page: Publishing, Technology, and the Classroom
James Kalmbach

in preparation:

Opening Spaces: Critical Research Practices
Patricia Sullivan and James Porter

A Rhetorical Ethics for Electronic Writing/Publishing
James Porter

A RHETORIC OF
ELECTRONIC COMMUNITIES

Tharon W. Howard
Clemson University

 Ablex Publishing Corporation
Greenwich, Connecticut
London, England

Printed in the United States of America

Library of Congress Cataloging-in-Publication Data
Howard, Tharon W.
    A rhetoric of electronic communities / by Tharon W. Howard.
        p.   cm. — (New directions in computers and composition studies)
    Includes bibliographical references (p.) and index.
    ISBN 1-56750-294-6. — ISBN 1-56750-295-4. (pbk.)
    1. Information society. 2. Communication—Social aspects.
  3. Computer networks—Social aspects. 4. Computer bulletin boards—
Social aspects. 5. Electronic publishing—Social aspects.
  6. Community. I. Title. II. Series.
HM221.H68 1996
303.48'33—dc20   96-32727
                                                  CIP

Ablex Publishing Corporation
55 Old Post Road # 2
P.O. Box 5297
Greenwich, Connecticut 06830

Published in the U.K. and Europe by:
JAI Press Ltd.
38 Tavistock Street
Covent Garden
London WC2E   7PB
England

To my father, Darold Howard,
who taught me the value
of asking good questions,
and to my sons,
Bryce and Logan, who
keep those questions new

Contents

About the Author

Dr. Tharon W. Howard teachers in the Master of Arts in Professional Communication program at Clemson University. Howard directs the Document Design Laboratory where—in addition to producing fliers, brochures, scholarly journals, and books for the College of Arts, Architecture, and the Humanities—he teaches MAPC graduate students to create and maintain electronic publishing systems like Gopher, WWW, and LISTPROC servers.

Howard is also Director of the Clemson University Usability Testing Facility where he conducts research aimed at improving and creating new interface and document designs. He also designed and directs Clemson's Multimedia Authoring Teaching and Research facility where faculty and graduate students in architecture, arts, and the humanities learn to develop multimedia productions and have an opportunity to experiment with emerging instructional technologies.

Currently serving as the Chair of the Instructional Technology Committee for the National Council of Teachers of English and as Co-Director of the Carolinas Alliance for Computers and Writing, Howard has a commitment to the integration of instructional technologies into the classroom.

Acknowledgments

Even before I began studying the influence of communities on individuals, I was keenly aware of my own debt to all of those special people who made this project possible. I wish that I could acknowledge them all individually; unfortunately, this is not feasible. Nevertheless, I would like to express my gratitude to the members of the electronic discussion group PURTOPOI, to the graduate students and faculty in the Department of English at Purdue University, and to my colleagues at Clemson University. By unselfishly sharing their thoughts, concerns, experiences, and ideas, these individuals exemplified for me all that is best about communal life.

In addition to all these people, there are, of course, individuals whose particular contributions must not go unmentioned here. James Berlin, a superlative scholar and teacher, helped me develop both an understanding of cultural critique and more importantly, the commitment required to engage in it. Although I miss him very much, his influence is very much alive in this book. Janice Lauer—the person perhaps most responsible for creating, maintaining, and nurturing that wonderful community of rhetorical scholars at Purdue—has been my constant model of a concerned professional and contributed prompt and productive criticism throughout this project. Patricia Sullivan, my co-listowner on PURTOPOI and a distinguished researcher of computers and writing, is responsible for introducing me to electronic mail, for encouraging me to start PURTOPOI, and for helping to fill many of the fundamental gaps in my research plan. Also, James Porter—my dissertation Chair, my mentor, and friend—has sustained and guided me throughout this project, stimulating me to new insights when my interest flagged, tempering my sometimes over-exuberant naiveté as a graduate student, helping me remove "the stink of a dissertation" when I had to revise the work for publication as a book, and, most of all, giving me the space and the courage to try.

I would also like to recognize Gail Hawisher and Cynthia Selfe for the unselfish guidance they have provided so many young,

naive researchers of computers and composition like myself. As
the editors of this Ablex series, the sponsors of Hugh Burn's
Dissertation Award, the editors of the journal *Computers and
Composition*, the editors of the NCTE series on research in computers and composition, and, finally, as authors of many vision-
ary works in the field, they have done more to legitimate the kind
of study this project represents than any other two individuals I
know.

I would also be remiss if I did not recognize my colleagues from
the MA in Professional Communication program at Clemson
University. This book has benefitted from the revision suggestions
Susan Hilligoss graciously provided, even though she was deeply
involved in her own book projects. Dixie Goswami's remarks on
early versions of the manuscript were also extremely valuable and
much appreciated. I have also been fortunate to have been able to
profit from discussions about the work with Beth Daniell, Martin
Jacobi, Stuart Selber, Elisa Sparks, and Art Young. My thanks
also for all those late night conversations on the MOOs with
Wayne Butler, Eric Crump, Michael Day, Lester Faigley, Traci
Gardner, Fred Kemp, and Becky Rickly.

Finally, I wish to acknowledge my personal indebtedness to my
family who have sacrificed so much for this project. My youngest
son Logan has given me those ebullient diversions I needed to
keep me centered. And my oldest son Bryce has given me his self-
less, unassailable loyalty—never once questioning me when I used
"work" as a rationale for ignoring him. Lastly, my wife, my collab-
orator, and my best friend, Wendy has given me her love; sacrific-
ing her career, giving up a decent house, and putting her dreams
on hold in order to help me achieve my selfish goals. She is the
person without whom this project would have been unthinkable.

chapter one

Introduction

In today's information society, few would argue that computer technologies haven't influenced many of our most fundamental social relationships. Researchers are only just beginning to understand how radically those relationships have been altered. Today, the computers that evolved from the pulleys and gears of Babbage's mechanical "difference machine"[1] touch virtually every aspect of our daily lives and make McLuhan's (1968) "global village" realizable. Wherever there are satellites, microwave towers, radio packets, fiber optic cables, or plain copper wires to carry the data, people use computers to communicate with other people.

This kind of global connectivity engenders power. Indeed, an individual anywhere in the world can find out (with a modem, a PC, and the right passwords) how much money I make; who I talk to regularly; what kinds of food, books, and movies I like; what my political affiliations are; whether my credit rating is any good; and much, much more. For some, like Burnham (1984), Cronkite (1983), Bowers (1988), and Zuboff (1988), this kind of surveillance capability makes Orwell's nightmare or Foucault's panopticon society a "virtual" reality. For others, like Rheingold (1993), Deward (1988), Hiltz and Turoff (1978), Lipnack and Stamps (1986), Kinneavy (1991), or Cooper and Selfe (1990), the computer's connectivity offers freedom to people whose voices have been silenced by oppressive, exclusionary

---

[1] See Chapter One of Burnham's (1994) *The Rise of the Computer State* for an interesting history of early computers.

social forces and political hegemonies. The problem is that both these views are right and wrong.

But this book isn't really about computer hardware, databases, networks, or software. Technological issues are interesting, even seductive, and, of course, some understanding of how computers actually operate is required if we wish to thoroughly explore their potential effect on social relationships. Yet, the mechanics of computer technology change so rapidly that even the computer science journals can't keep up with them. Published discussions of technological developments are often *passé* by the time they appear in print because of the lengthy publication process.[2] Consequently, this project is about something far less transient and even more pervasive than the mechanics behind computer technology. *This is a study of power*, the power to monitor what is said, to authorize who can speak, and even to censor what they are saying. But even more important, it is a study of the power to determine what is and is not thinkable or knowable—that is, the power to shape and maintain the communities that shape and maintain us. To put this somewhat less dramatically, this book engages in a rhetorical analysis of the concept of *community*, utilizing the unique qualities of the writing that occurs on wide-area electronic networks to better understand both what existing theories of community may be able to explain in this important new medium and how, in turn, this new medium challenges and problematizes those existing theories. What explanatory power does existing notions of community offer us in the new electronic medium? And can "electronic publishing" or writing on wide-area networking systems (WANS) really produce radically new forms of communities that will enable the formation of resisting subjectivities as many of its proponents now claim?

At this point, I should note that I prefer to use the term "network text" to describe writing that occurs on WANS rather than the terms "computer-mediated communication" (CMC), "computer-mediated writing," "electronic text," "network communication," or "video text." The major reason for this is that, though these latter terms may be more common, they also tend to imply

---

[2] There are several interesting effects of the extremely short half-lives of such articles. One of these is the speculative, future-oriented nature of articles on computer technology that writers seem to adopt in order to increase the lifespan of their work. Another is the absence of formal, published histories; instead, a kind of folklore of computer technology has emerged, as evidenced by network discussion groups like COMP.FOLKLORE on USENET. This has tended to increase the value of insider knowledge, deifying those who have it. It is only now becoming available through works like Quarterman's (1991) *The Matrix*.

that the discourse that takes place on WANS like the Internet does not really represent a new medium but is actually little more than print or oral discourse repackaged in a computer-based delivery system. Most researchers using the term computer-mediated communication, for example, tend to focus on the ways that network texts resemble a conversation, conferences, or electronic dialog, thereby tacitly imposing standards and metaphors from oral media on this new medium. Similarly, the term computer-mediated writing implies that we are dealing with printed texts that happen to appear on computers. I believe, however, that researchers and users of this new medium should eschew the dominant "conversation" metaphor. As we shall see in Chapter Six, computer conferences are *not* like oral conversations or dialogs. They are, instead, more like the discourse that occurs in improvisational theaters (cf. Laurel, 1993). They may "sound" like face-to-face conversations, but they aren't, and researchers and users who fail to recognize this are at risk. On MOOs and IRC channels (see Appendix B), for example, where users participate in real-time communications across the network, there are cyber-rapists who take advantage of the fact that many networkers at all levels of experience consider the communication on MOOs and IRC channels to be virtually the same as an oral conversation or chat. The victims of cyber-rape assume, erroneously, that their electronic discourse will have the same status as their oral discourse. Because they come to the event with the conversation metaphor, they assume that the same standards for privacy and privilege exist in both media. They don't—at least not yet. At this stage, the networked text medium is still too new for many standards to have become widely shared both in and across electronic discourse communities. As a result, cyber-rapists are able to take the text of revealing MOO and/or IRC conversations and redistribute them in professional settings in ways that seriously damage the victims' reputations.

The term electronic text or "e-text" comes closer to avoiding this problem of imposing the metaphors of other media on network text; however, the potential range of discourses covered by e-text is too broad. A HYPERCARD stack or a multimedia document could be and has been called an electronic text or electronic writing, and since the focus of this book is on WANS discourse, another, more descriptive term is required. Network communication also proves inadequate because it refers to television and radio network broadcasts. The same logic applies to the term video text, which is used to describe the writing that appears on many cable television channels, particularly those announcing local community events, news, weather, etc.—that is, one-way print communication that uses the television screen like a piece of paper. Of all the terms that might be used to signify the discourse that occurs on WANS, only the term network text (NT) seems to avoid these problems because it hasn't been used to describe types of discourse in other media. Also, due to the work of many contemporary rhetoricians and literary theorists, the term "text" has become sufficiently broad enough to be applied to a variety of media. It's not unusual today to speak of a painting's "subtexts" or "to read the text" of an architectural experience.

In general, this book is an attempt to construct a theory of community adequate, not only for the new medium of network text, but also for traditional media. Although computer networking adds new considerations and challenges to existing theories of community, many of the issues facing students of electronic publishing at least have their analogs in traditional media. Thus, as researchers go forward fascinated by this new medium, they must still "do so knowing full well that this 'new' electronically mediated communication or mode of information is in many ways not new at all, but has been anticipated in social developments and theoretical initiatives for decades, even centuries" (Poster, 1990, p. 19).

Indeed, even the concept of a networked community itself is not new, as Lipnack and Stamps (1986) have observed:

> Almost 300 years ago, in the then "new world," local groups calling themselves Committees of Correspondence formed a network, a communications forum where homespun political and economic thinkers hammered out their ideological differences, sculpting the form of a separate and independent country in North America. Writing to one another and sharing letters with neighbors, this revolutionary generation nurtured its adolescent ideas into a mature politics. Both men and women participated in the debate over independence from England and the desirable shape of America's future. . . . The concepts of independence and government had been debated, discussed, discarded and reformulated literally hundreds of times by the time people in the revolutionary network met in Philadelphia. (p. 61)

Examples of networked communities like the American revolutionary network can be found throughout human history. Caesar's letters during his campaign in Gaul are evidence of similar communities in Roman times. Obviously then, such communities do not depend on NT for their existence.

Nor can one argue that the emergence of NT is necessary for the study of networked communities. Sociologists have long studied scientific communities or what Crane (1972) calls "invisible colleges" without having recourse to NT. Crane and other researchers working in the 1960s and early 1970s were able to show how the "growth of a research area reflects a social interaction process in which contact between scientists contributes to the cumulative growth of knowledge" by examining other media than computer networks (Crane, 1972, p. 34). In fact, Crane argued that the failure to form or join a community of researchers who communicated by "correspondence, telephone, meetings, conferences" or other interpersonal means seriously reduced the number of publications researchers experienced (p. 24), thereby demonstrating that computer networks are neither necessary for the formation of such communities nor for their study.

This of course raises the question, "Why bother to study writing on electronic networks at all?" Does this new medium really force us to reconsider and reconstruct current notions of community? The answer, as with any such all-or-nothing formulation, is once again both yes and no.[3] The relationship between one medium and another is not an ontological binary but, rather, is an analytical one. It is possible to distinguish between oral, print, and NT media for analytical purposes, but that should not be taken to mean that each medium represents a sutured totality or a unified whole. Rather, like the petals of a flower or the tiles of a roof, there are overlaps; each division is unavoidably imbricated in a whole system of other/Other relations. Furthermore, to use another metaphor popular with poststructuralists, the boundary between print and NT, for example, "plays" across a free floating space of indeterminacy in the same way that the "play" in a guitar string describes a space as it vibrates. Thus, the argument that wide-area networks simply make the transmission of the print medium more efficient and economical is as overstated and *other*-directed as is the argument that NT represents a radical departure from oral or print media and therefore requires its own, distinctive rhetoric(s).

To argue that electronic writing is just the same old print transmitted electronically rather than on the page is to operate from a outdated and retrograde view of language. When we adopt this efficiency approach to electronic writing, it suggests that language

---

[3] Vitanza (1990) has a useful way of answering questions based on binary formulations; when Vitanza is asked such a question, his playful answer is "Nes/Yo." I interpret Vitanza's "Nes/Yo" response to binaries as a means of saying that the answers to such questions can be found only in the play of oppositions—that is, in the space created between two poles.

is transparent and that technology is just a neutral tool for transmitting language. Such a perspective does not acknowledge that
form and medium play a role in shaping meaning, or, to borrow
one of McLuhan's (1972) famous maxims, it fails to recognize that
"the medium is the message." However, there is a more important
problematic at stake here than the old form/content binary. What
concerns me here is the way discursive structures "interpellate" or
"hail" language users into particular subject positions and social
relationships.[4] Language is a system of shared social relations,
and communication imbricates us in those relations. Given then
that medium does affect meaning and that discursive acts call us
into subject positions, researchers must consider the meanings
and subjectivities invoked by electronic publishing. If, as
researchers, we view electronic writing simply as an efficient and
neutral vehicle for the transmission of content, then we have no
control over the ways it may victimize or empower us. We will have
no way to make informed decisions about the kind of society
WANS can help us shape or about the ways we can use networks
in our classrooms. Thus, as Carolyn Marvin (1988) makes clear,
the study of NT is less about efficiency "than a series of arenas for
negotiating issues crucial to the conduct of social life; among
them, who is inside and outside, who may speak, who may not,
and who has authority and may be believed" (p. 4). The study of
writing on WANS, therefore, is critical if researchers are to negotiate these issues in an informed and effective manner.

On the other hand, the argument that NT represents a radical
departure from other media forms and therefore deserves its own
rhetoric(s) goes too far. In the first place, as I have already pointed
out, the analytical boundaries or frames theorists put around a
medium have no ontological basis; they float free and play so that
there is overlap between media forms. It is therefore difficult to
conceive of a radically new and distinct form that does not in some
way participate in the old.

But there is another problem with this separatist view of NT.
The constructed nature of boundaries doesn't mean that analytical frames don't have an effect—they do. As Derrida (1987) points
out in "Parergon," "There is no natural frame. *There is* frame, but
the frame *does not exist*" (p. 81). In other words, frames and signifiers may not be tied to metaphysical truths and referents, but
there are still frames and signifiers, and both are still necessary

---

[4] See Chapter Four for a discussion of Althusser's (1971) concept of interpellation.

for communication. We can't speak without making differentiations between things—in saying, "I am talking about X," one concomitantly says, "I'm not talking about Y, or A, or B, or C, etc." Frames thus create objects for study by dividing what is inside the frame from what is outside. In terms of the separatist view of electronic writing, this objectification process has become a problem because it makes it easy to overlook exclusionary practices found in other media that are nevertheless replicated in NT. For example, a line of argument popular among NT proponents goes: in a classroom environment, only one person can speak at a time because of the limitations of the oral medium. However, NT is a different medium and therefore does not suffer from this feature of oral discourse; thus, NT enables greater participation in classroom discussions. In other words, according to this logic, speech and print have exclusionary practices, but, because NT is not speech or print, it is not exclusionary.

One result of this kind of logic has been a tendency toward a euphoric excess among NT researchers. As Hawisher and Selfe (1991a) have pointed out in their review of research on computers and composition, the research on computers and writing has tended toward the extremely positive (p. 56). Indeed, in their efforts to validate NT in the composition community, NT proponents have tended to make overly enthusiastic claims in order to counterbalance the "many faculty members in English departments [who] view computer-assisted composition with indifference, disdain, or outright hostility" (Gerrard, 1991, p. 5). James Kinneavy, for example, loudly proclaimed at the 1991 Conference on College Composition and Communication that "I won't teach again without computers" since, without the support of computer technology in his classroom, he would be forced to revert to the authoritarian and exclusionary practices found in traditional classroom formats.

This kind of enthusiastic support for networked classrooms and electronic writing may seem natural for a group that sees itself as marginalized, but it has at least two serious consequences. First, as feminists like Cixous (1965) have made clear, this kind of separatist logic merely reinscribes the violence of marginalization in a vicious cycle where each side seeks to privilege its preferred medium over the others'. Consider, for example, King's (1991) bold proclamation that "we cannot foresee them now, but just as radio weaned itself from the habits of the newspaper and as TV weaned itself from radio, so the networks must wean themselves from print" (p. 31). Obviously, such a "kill the parent" attitude will force many traditional literary scholars to "circle the wagons" against this new threat.[5] Indeed, one can already see attacks against computer networks in the same way that television or citizen-band radio media have been attacked as vulgar or faddish and not worthy of serious scholarly use or attention.[6] The popularity and polyphony of the Internet has already led some to claim that "it's an open-ended invitation to waste time on the job or at home because of the all-you-can-eat-for-free nature of e-mail and the unfettered ability to browse ALT.TRIVIA everywhere" (Howard, 1994, p. 107).

The second problem with this privileging of NT is an extension of the first. The problem here is that it may prevent network researchers from exploring important areas related to WANS usage. Because frames create an inside and an outside, issues believed to be outside the frame are ignored; they belong to some other (and usually less favored) discipline or methodology. Thus, just as many scholars of literature and rhetoric tend to devalue studies of television and other forms of mass media because they are "outside the boundaries of traditional scholarship," there is a danger that electronic writing researchers will undervalue the theories, methodologies, and experiences of the other fields and disciplines. Or to put this another way, there's a danger that electronic writing researchers will find themselves trying to reinvent the wheel. And already, there is a strong movement in this direction, particularly among people who wish to promote electronic citizenship.

In this broad-based movement on the networks and in the NT literature, "the term 'electronic citizen' points out the growing significance of free speech based on electronic media" (Connolly, et al, 1991a, p. 37).[7] Proponents of electronic citizenship (myself

---

[5] Winterowd's (1990) book *The Rhetoric of the "Other" Literature* offers a useful analysis of this marginalization process where the distinction between discursive and presentational texts is made by scholars. See also Bourdieu's (1984) *Distinctions* for a discussion of how class divisions are made based on an individual's aesthetic appreciation of different media.

[6] For arguments on the value of studying such "vulgar" media see Barthes' (1972) analysis of professional wrestling in *Mythologies*, Hodge and Kress' (1988) analysis of graffiti in *Social Semiotics*, and Fiske's (1987) analysis of television programs in *Television Culture*. I would also note, anecdotally, that new users often compare e-mail to CB radio.

[7] Deward (1988) similarly defines "electronic citizenship" as a "term for using a personal computer and telecommunications to become more effective in influencing public policy" (p. 13).

included) wish to make NT a technology of freedom or a means of encouraging greater participation in the democratic process and in the composition classroom. However, in their attempts to validate NT, they sometimes go too far. Consider the implications of the following assertion from Connolly, et al's essay "A Bill of Rights for Electronic Citizens:"

> Historically, the promise of new technologies and knowledge formats has been stunted by the habits and concepts based on the use of familiar tools. In the first stage of technological innovation, new technologies are often used only as more efficient means to achieve traditional ends. (1991a, p. 38)

The difficulty is not with the authors' criticism of those who would use computer networks as a more efficient means of transmitting print; I also criticized this position earlier. The difficulty is with the implication that all familiar tools will stunt the future uses of electronic writing and the suggestion that electronic writing has *inherent* goals that differ from the traditional ends of other media. NT is certainly not neutral or value-free as I have already argued, but the goal of increasing the number of voices heard in a participatory democracy and in the classroom is neither inherent in the electronic medium nor limited to it. And network researchers clearly don't need to discard and then reinvent concepts like community, discursive practices, polyphony, or intertextuality just because they are familiar tools developed through the study of media other than NT, particularly given the kind of play that exists in media frames. Rather, theorists need to create a space where like Janus, the two-faced Roman god of doors and gateways, we can examine what these familiar tools can tell us about writing on WANS and what writing on WANS can tell us about these familiar tools.

In this book therefore, I propose to situate myself in the spaces where the boundaries between media play in order to gain a Janusian perspective on the concept of community, for I wish to understand *both* what existing notions of community can tell us about writing for computer networks and how electronic writing challenges and forces us to revise those notions of community. For those accustomed to scholars who speak with a monological voice from the Olympian ground of higher reason, this Janusian perspective may seem hypocritical or "two-faced;" it may appear that I am trying to occupy an apolitical site where I can critique all other theories without remaining loyal to any particular theory.

However, my main goal in this study is not deconstructive but, rather, revisionary.[8] I do not seek to eliminate existing theories of community by situating them in some kind of forever-expanding, constantly changing, or even frameless frame, and I certainly would not claim that I am inscribing them within the only natural or all-encompassing frame capable of suturing all the possible manifestations of community. Rather, I seek to (re)construct one theory of community that will yield explanatory power across traditional media frames. Hence, like the Roman statues of Janus, I wish to stand in the doorway, at the interface between inside and outside, for it is there that meaningful differences are most clear.

To achieve this goal, I will engage in analyses of theoretical concepts of community and rhetorical analyses of texts produced in particular electronic communities, and these analyses will be distributed across seven chapters. Chapter Two explores the social, political, and rhetorical significance of the new NT medium. Furthermore, because I am situating myself on the boundaries between the oral and print media and the NT medium, Chapter Two explores the play in various framings of media, and particular attention is given to the role media assumes in subject formation. In other words, is a medium a neutral tool or vessel for the transmission of content, or does it have a constitutive function in the construction of meaning?

Chapter Three continues the discussion of the relationship between print and NT media begun in Chapter Two, examining the emerging definitions of electronic writing and electronic publishing and (to help further demonstrate how NT forces rhetoricians to re-examine assumptions that may be taken for granted in rhetoric theory) it addresses the question of what factors control the production and consumption of meaning in electronic publishing. Additionally, the chapter reviews some of the major foundations that have been used to claim that the NT medium is itself an agency of communal change—arguments that are directly challenged in Chapter Six.

Chapters Four and Five begin the rhetorical analyses of theoretical conceptions of community, building the analytical framework for the examination of a specific electronic community in Chapter Six. Chapter Four, in keeping with the multimodal, Janusian approach, examines how theorists from fields outside

---

[8] For a discussion of revisionary approaches in historiography, see Berlin's (1987) "Revisionary History: The Dialectical Method" and Vitanza's "'Notes Towards Historiographies of Rhetoric" in the 1987 Spring/Summer issue of *PRE/TEXT*.

rhetoric have tried to define or develop taxonomies of community. Several important concepts are introduced in this review, including the limitations of spatial approaches to community, the definition of a "communitarian theorist," the concept of "reciprocity," and the roles of "common sense" and "ideology" in theories of community. In addition, several recurring issues are posed in this review; the most important of these being the binary between what Sandel (1982) calls "individualistic" and "constitutive" theories of community. Finally, this binary is exemplified through an examination of Althusser's (1971) concept of "interpellation" and Kant's (trans. 1988) "subjective necessity."

Chapter Five continues to explore the framework begun in the previous chapter and offers a review of community as it has been used by social constructionists in the field of rhetoric. Building on the individualistic and constitutive binary developed in Chapter Four, this chapter shows how this binary has been expressed as an epistemological gap between foundationalism and antifoundationalism or what has also been called rhetorics of resistance and rhetorics of accommodation. This chapter develops the view that taking an agonistic stance toward one or the other side of these binaries has tended to lead theorists into the trap of determinism. In other words, proponents of either side of the binary ultimately end up promoting a view of rhetoric that can no longer be defined as a process of adjudicating between competing knowledge claims.

Chapter Six moves from community-wide discussions to the level of a particular electronic forum (Porter, 1992, p. 107). Chapter Six focuses mainly on the birth and subsequent evolution of a group entitled "PURTOPOI: The Rhetoric, Language, and Professional Writing Discussion Group." This chapter explores the ways PURTOPOI members have been forced to negotiate a particular kind of "netiquette," or network etiquette, as a result of the immaturity of the NT medium. Issues addressed here include, for example, how individuals become members of the group and how disruptive individuals are excluded from it. What sorts of topics are introduced for discussion, what authorizing strategies are deployed in their introduction, and what topics are ignored or rejected as unsuitable? In general, this chapter investigates the ways members resist and accommodate the group in order to better understand the explanatory power offered by both the individualistic and constitutive communitarian approaches to electronic communities.

Based on the observations resulting from Chapter Six's analysis of PURTOPOI, Chapter Seven offers a "Janusian" revision of the individualistic and constitutive binary. This chapter discusses how the inside/outside problematic frustrates attempts to revise the individualistic constitutive binary and utilizes feminist standpoint theorists' concept of "positionality" and LaClau and Mouffe's (1985) concept of the "articulatory moment" as means of dealing with the inside/outside problematic. Ultimately, this chapter describes how it is possible for individuals both to resist and accommodate interpellation into a discourse community by arguing for a revised view of discourse communities. As previous chapters have shown, it is impossible for individuals to avoid the discursive practices of particular communities; yet, resistance and conflict are, paradoxically, required to maintain group unity. Thus, this chapter argues for a view of communities that sees them both as unified *and* as sites of struggle, a view expressed in the concept of Janusian synthesis. Chapter Seven argues that groups negotiate a space in which certain kinds of struggle are permitted; indeed, the *ethos* of community membership requires that individuals within a group constantly challenge the boundaries that pre-exist their membership. Communities are never unities because as soon as they become unified or as soon as they realize total consensus, they cease to function as communities; there's no communication within them any longer, so that the forces that bind their members together into a community are gone. Thus, there can never be a community that is completely successful in forcing its members to accommodate its discursive practices, nor can there ever be a community that is completely without hegemony. *Both* resistance and accommodation must be present in order for a community to exist.

chapter two

The Social, Political, and Rhetorical Significance of Networked Text

SOCIOLOGICAL CHANGE

The actual reasons an individual might choose to participate in WANS are no doubt locally determined and extremely complex. Nevertheless, one of the reasons often given for the increasing popularity of NT on WANS is empowerment.

Few media offer individuals the ability to have a voice in social, economic, political, and/or pedagogical change as does NT. Today, wherever there are satellites, fiber-optic cables, radio packets, telephone lines, or plain copper wires to connect computers together, discourse occurs between ordinary people in ways that seem to eliminate and subvert the hegemonic mediation of government, educational, and corporate institutions. With today's WANS technology, ordinary individuals have access to publication, distribution, and consumption systems that rival and often exceed newspaper, television, and radio publication methods. Before CNN or CBS can put a video camera on the scene with reporters who basically tell us what we are seeing, ordinary people are communicating with other ordinary people through NT and WANS, interpreting events that shape our world. For example:

- While the Tiananmen Square massacre was happening, Chinese college students were sending out eyewitness accounts of the event to other people all over the world via computer networks (Quarterman, 1991, p. xxiv).
- When Soviet hard-liners attempted their coup in August of 1991, news of the event "found its way from a computer-based communications network in the Soviet Union to Finland and, from there, to the Internet and other computer-based networks around the world." And later, with other media still in shambles or under hostile control, "the network was used by Boris Yeltsin and the constitutional powers in order to disseminate information abroad throughout the coup attempt" (Welsh, 1992, p. 42).
- When a Spanish journalist was shot down in the streets of Panama by American troops, readers of a USENET electronic discussion group known as NEWS.HEADLINES learned from people in Spain about shots fired in empty streets, while U.S. television viewers saw nothing of the event.
- Before American news organizations could see the news-worthiness of an invasion by Canadian troops into the sovereign territory of the Mohawk nation, computer-mediated discussion groups like NEWS.HEADLINES were already considering the international implications of Canada's actions.
- At the University of Texas, when the president of the university came under pressure from local right-wing conservative groups and subsequently suspended a freshman composition curriculum aimed at increasing students' awareness of cultural diversity, computer-mediated discussions groups responded. In fact, members of a LISTSERV discussion group named "Megabyte University" responded to the problem by collaboratively producing a letter of protest, thereby bringing national pressure to bear on the problem weeks before conventional methods of communication could have accomplished the same goal.

- During Desert Storm, students enrolled in my composition class at Purdue University in Indiana read, on the same day the messages were sent, about the personal terror felt by an Israeli citizen who, huddling over a computer keyboard in her basement, sent out e-mail messages while Iraqi scud missiles fell around her.

As these anecdotes illustrate, NT has the potential for dramatically impacting our academic practices, as well as our social, political, and economic lives. Indeed, in France, where almost the entire country has access to Minitel, these kinds of changes have already begun.[1] In France, people do their banking on the network, they get their news and weather reports from the network, and, more than anything else, they *talk to each other* over the network. Minitel, with over 4 million terminals, is part of their everyday experience; indeed, it is so much a part of the French experience that some observers have been able to describe the network's impact on the country's 1988 national elections (Quarterman, 1991, p. xxiii).

The French experience is not unique. Already in this country, similar experiments in NT are underway, and one of the best examples is the Cleveland FreeNet. As its name implies, FreeNet was created to give anyone with a personal computer and a modem free access to the power of international computer networks. Using the goals of National Public Radio as its model, the National Public Telecomputing Network (which developed and maintains the FreeNet system software) offers all citizens access to the information necessary for decision-making in an open participatory democracy. However, unlike NPR, the FreeNet's NT medium also allows citizens unparalleled access to each other and to information. Rather than listening to one of NPR's news correspondents describe and interpret the U.S. Supreme Court's decision on an important sex discrimination case, FreeNet users (as well as students in my composition classes) can read the actual majority and minority opinions that the Justices them-

---

[1] Much of Minitel's success was due to the fact that it was begun by the government telephone company, France Telecom. As Quarterman (1991) points out, France Telecom "gave the Minitel terminals away free as replacements for paper telephone directories, in hopes of eventually recouping their costs in increased telephone revenue. The strategy worked, and FT now gets $158 million more out of a total new industry of about a billion dollars a year" (pp. 451–452).

selves wrote about the case.[2] Furthermore, users can discuss the decisions and opinions *with each other*, negotiating various interpretations without the overt and hegemonic mediation of news correspondents.

The empowerment that results from such direct access to information and to other people has attracted tremendous attention in recent years. As Rheingold (1993) has pointed out, "The political significance of CMC [computer-mediated communication] lies in its capacity to challenge the existing political hierarchy's monopoly on powerful communications media, and perhaps thus revitalize citizen-based democracy" (p. 14). Yet, it's worth noting that, although many people tend to think of NT as a revolutionary new medium and wide-area computer networking as a new technology, both actually have existed for quite some time. As Lynch (1990) has pointed out, the NT medium started almost 50 years ago when "the first use of terminals (at that time, teletypes) to communicate with computers over telephone lines was demonstrated in the 1940s" (p. 270). Indeed, it could be argued that Edison's repeating telegraph also created a new kind of wide-area electronically-mediated networking system since the repeating telegraph removed the dependence on human mediation for both the storage and transmission of data across long distances.

Despite these early examples of networking, however, most researchers locate the beginnings of the large, public wide-area networks (WANS) in the early 1960s with the development of the ARPANET (Advanced Research Projects Agency Network), a network that was first designed by the Department of Defense in order to give other government agencies, contractors, and researchers time-sharing access to extremely expensive mainframe computing facilities. The ARPANET is seen by networkers as the original source for today's WANS (wide-area networking systems) because of two major architectural developments in the ARPANET which, for more than 30 years, have been and continue to be forces in WANS technologies. First, the ARPANET laid the foundations upon which future WANS could be built because it sponsored the development of standards or protocol suites that

---

[2] To connect to the Cleveland FreeNet via 300, 1200, 2400, or 9600 baud modem access, dial (216)368-3888. Internet access is available via telnet at FREENET-IN-A.CWRU.EDU (129.22.8.82). Supreme Court opinions are stored in the Project HERMES database. Once connected, either via modem or telnet, login as a visitor, type "go hermes". To learn more about NPTN, login as above, type "go admin", and select the menu entries for NPTN. Please note, however, that these details may have changed subsequent to the publication of this book.

governed the transmission and control of data. Without standardized protocols to tell each individual computer how to talk to other computers on a network, WANS would not have been possible. Hence the first important contribution of the ARPANET was the development of the TCP or "Transmission and Control Protocol" suite, which is still (though in a slightly different dialect) the *lingua franca* networked computers must speak on today's Internet.

The second major development in WAN architecture that the ARPANET introduced and that we still live with on the Net is a system of decentralized and distributed routers. A product of Cold War thinking in the RAND Corp. (Rheingold, 1993), the ARPANET was originally designed to survive a nuclear attack. The basic idea was to create a telecommunications system in which large sections of the network could be eliminated without significant effect on the remaining system; holes and gaps in the network's fabric would be bypassed automatically without significantly degrading the performance of whatever hadn't been destroyed in the attack. A logical consequence of this line of thinking was that there could be no centralized control systems that could easily be knocked out. The ARPANET and the Internet therefore were largely constructed without the command and control centers we would typically expect in a Dept. of Defense project. Instead, routers on the net (which are the network equivalent of an army private) were invested with the information access and power usually reserved by officers in a military hierarchy. So rather than waiting for a centralized authority to tell it how and where to move packets of information on the net, any router in the system is empowered automatically to move information around the net in whatever fashion it determines is best. And each router is able to determine the best route to use because it is constantly sending and receiving "rips" or "routing information packets" to and from other routers on the net. These rip exchanges between the net's privates enable every individual router on the net to know what every other router knows; thus, eliminating the privileged information that makes central control systems (or an officer corps for that matter) both possible and necessary.

The ARPANET's legacies are immediately clear to anyone who has ever tried to become a new Internet user. Before you can even get connected, you have to solve the enormous logistical problem of locating a computer that speaks TCP/IP (the Transmission and Control Protocol/Internet Protocol). Then assuming that you are able to find a way to create or connect to a TCP/IP-literate system that will allow you access to the Internet, you are still faced with the problem of locating network resources and facilities. Because there is no central control on the Internet, there is also no authorized central source that the new user can consult in order to gain access to services. Indeed, the quickest way for someone to get tarred with the sobriquet "newbie" or "net neophyte" is to ask the question, "Who's in charge?" Experienced networkers know that no single source of authority exists on the Net and that the locations of network services and facilities change daily. Indeed, experienced "net navigators" or "net surfers" know that most network services are almost never provided by any centralized government or commercial entity. In the main, today's network tools and services are really the products of volunteers and are gifts to the larger community. Thus, in the same way that the routers have to maintain a constant "rip exchange" to keep abreast of changes in the network, the experienced networker depends on other networkers to remain plugged into the Net.

Of course, in saying that most of the facilities on the Net today are the products of volunteers, I don't mean to suggest that there are no commercial services on the Net. As the ARPANET evolved into the Internet, a number of companies created and shared network utilities that are still in use today. Several commercial companies began developing WANS technology during the late 1970s and early 1980s, largely because giving remote users time-sharing access to powerful mainframe computing environments had and continues to have tremendous industrial and commercial potential. Indeed, as Quarterman (1991) points out, the government telephone company in France alone received approximately $158 million per year in increased revenues from France's famous national network, the Minitel (p. 452). Thus, given that this new networking industry could potentially generate billions of dollars for those companies willing to risk the research and development costs, a number of notable companies such as Xerox, General Motors, IBM, Digital Equipment, AT&T, and Burroughs became early commercial pioneers in WANS technology. As a result, these organizations developed many of the time, text and file sharing protocols in use today on the more popular WANS like Internet, UUCP, USENET, and BITNET (Quarterman, 1991, pp. 139–41).

Nevertheless, despite these early efforts at developing WANS technology, the WANS revolution and the information superhighway still had to wait (somewhat ironically) for the introduction of the personal computer. It really wasn't until personal computers and modems began to be purchased widely throughout the 1980s that interest in and access to WANS became the significant sociological phenomenon that it has become today (Aumente, 1987, p. 13). WANS technology was and, in fact, still is heavily dependent on mainframe computing environments so that, prior to the introduction of the modem and the personal computer, the only practical way to access WANS technology was to have a terminal with direct access to a mainframe computer. Modems and personal computers, however, allowed average, ordinary individuals to use their existing telephone lines to connect their personal computers to mainframe computers. Hence, since 1985 when personal computer sales really exploded, millions of people all over the world were suddenly able to use their computers to communicate via WANS, and the WANS revolution can truly be said to have begun.

Unfortunately, it is almost impossible to determine the exact number of people using WANS today, making it difficult for advocates of NT to argue that a real revolution is underway. One problem is that a single mainframe computer may support anywhere from a dozen to several hundred users, so that any estimate based on the number of computers is extremely unreliable. Furthermore, on a network like the Internet, you can't even figure out the exact number of computers since in 1993 the Internet was comprised of nearly 5,000 smaller subnetworks worldwide (Van Houweling, 1992, p. 5), and these regional subnetworks were themselves, as LaQuey (1990) points out, "further subdivided into hundreds and sometimes thousands of hosts at each site" (p. 194). Thus, back in 1991 the estimated number of computers on Internet ranged from 40,000 to 700,000 (Quarterman, 1991, p. 278; Welsh, 1992, p. 41). And finally, to make matters even more complicated, Internet is only *one* among an ever-increasing number of networks around the world.

Despite these difficulties in the collection of quantitative data, however, there are some measures and estimates regarding network growth that indicate the explosive interest in WANS since 1985. For example, according to Quarterman (1991), the number of smaller subnetworks connected to the Internet had increased from just under 100 in 1985 to almost 500 by 1988 (p. 282); by January 1990, LaQuey (1990) found that the number had grown to 2,218 (p. 194). And this incredible growth rate has yet to stop; in the Spring of 1991, Hall reported that network traffic at that time was increasing by 20 to 25 percent every month (p. 19), so that by February of 1992, Merit was reporting

3,738 subnetwork connections.[3] Twenty-nine months later in July of 1994, the number of subnets had grown to more than 36,000 with a new subnetwork coming online every 30 minutes (Rickard, 1994, p. 71). This exponential growth overwhelmed existing networks. In fact, the situation became so desperate that the U.S. government agreed to spend $2 billion for the NREN (National Research and Education Network) in order to subsume the overburdened Internet and to reduce the traffic surfeit.

Simply measuring subnetwork growth, however, doesn't really give a good sense of the extent of the WANS revolution. Perhaps a better way to get some sense of how much WANS are being used is to look at the number of bytes of information transferred across networks. According to Spafford (1990), in June of 1989, "the USENET was carrying almost 6 Mbytes of new traffic and more than 2700 articles *each day* (average) to more than half-million readers in more than 17 countries" (p. 385, emphasis added). And USENET, which is one of the oldest networks in existence, doesn't even support electronic mail messages. On networks that do support e-mail, the numbers are almost too big to comprehend. For example, the Internet, which does support e-mail, also maintains some data on its use. Although the Internet is actually a vast collection of smaller, regional networks, the backbone between the majority of these smaller nets is the National Science Foundation's NSFNet. In other words, messages that travel from one subnetwork to another travel across the NSFNet backbone. According to the March 1992 issue of *Boardwatch Magazine*, for the month of December 1990 alone, the NSFNet backbone handled over 573 billion bytes of traffic between subnets. One year later, in December of 1991, that number jumped to 1 trillion, 359 billion bytes, an increase of 137 percent (p. 43).

Put in more familiar terms, it could be said that by the end of 1991, the NSFNet backbone was carrying 45 billion bytes of data every day. Now, if we assume that the average e-mail message is 1000 characters long, *we "would be talking about 45 million e-mail messages" every single day* ("Internet Statistics," p. 43, emphasis

---

[3] NSFNet usage statistics are maintained by Merit Network, Inc., a not-for-profit organization established in 1966. Merit has managed the NSFNet backbone since 1987 when they were awarded a contractual agreement with the NSF and publishes the NSFNet usage statistics on a monthly basis. At the date of this publication, Merit's NSFNet statistics were available via anonymous ftp at NIS.NSF.NET (35.1.1.48) in the directory /nsfstats.

added). And that 45 million messages per day doesn't even begin to reflect the real amount of traffic on the Internet. It's only a measure of the messages that passed from one regional network to another. According to the NSF's Network Information Service, in February 1992 3,738 regional networks were connected to the NSFNet (see footnote 3). None of the internal traffic on these 3,738 regional networks is reflected in that 45 million messages per day number, and the Internet has been growing at a rate of about 20 percent every month since 1992. So the total amount of Internet traffic is, no doubt, considerably higher.

Obviously, these are only rough estimates, but it should still be just as obvious that a tremendous number of people are communicating with an awful lot of other people on wide-area networks. This raises the question "Why?" Why is it that the number of regional networks connected to the NSFNet alone increased from a mere 173 in 1988, to over 3700 in 1992, to more than 36,000 in 1994? Why did so many people find NT so compelling that in 1992 they sent the data equivalent of 45 million messages across one network alone?

One answer may be that WANS like FreeNet, FidoNet, Comserve, Internet, and BITNET expose citizens to voices traditionally silenced by homophobic, phallocentric media. In the immature micropolitical environment of today's networks, NT on WANS is still relatively free of the kinds of overt editing and censoring that occurs in print, television, or radio. WANS offer forums where the repressed voices of homosexuals, feminists, Marxists, and left-wing liberals can be heard alongside those of the homophobes, misogynists, neo-nazis, and right-wing conservatives. Juxtaposed to media that tend to offer the monological voice of a mythical, centered mainstream (see Fiske, 1987b), WANS can open us to a polyphony so diverse and centrifugal that it sometimes appears to lead to sheer anarchy. To those accustomed to the normal rationalist discourse of traditional, more mature media—a discourse produced according to the well-established "procedures of exclusion" Foucault (1981) describes in his "Order of Discourse" (p. 52)—the discourse of NT no doubt makes it seem like "the speech of the madman" has been released upon society. NT on WANS thus *seems* to hold tremendous potential for activists seeking all sorts of social, political, economic, and pedagogical change. But is it really possible for all those seeming potentialities to become actualized?

If it could be shown that electronic discussion groups that communicate by means of this new medium represent radical new sites for the formation of resisting subjects, of agencies capable of critiquing old, corrupt, and exclusionary discursive practices found in other media, then there would be solid foundation upon which to base arguments that call for the increased use of NT in our classrooms, our professional discourse, and society in general. However, before accepting these arguments for the increased use of NT, it is important to examine whether or NT does in fact allow for the formation of radical subjectivities.

SCOPE: THREE VOICES

Given that the use of NT is now growing at such an astonishing rate, given that so many people are beginning to use it, and given that its use seems to have the potential for such tremendous sociological impact, the medium clearly warrants scholarly attention. Indeed, in the area of business writing alone, NT is becoming so important that 98 out of 100 members of the American Business Communicators Association indicated that CMC was the business communication medium "of the next decade" (Mitchell, Crawford, & Madden, 1985, p. 11). Furthermore, with the increased use of instructional computing technology in traditional composition classrooms, along with the emergence of journals like *Computers and Composition* which are devoted to the study of computer-mediated writing instruction, more and more traditional rhetoricians are beginning to become aware of the potential importance of NT. As a matter of fact, more and more rhetoricians are turning to NT and to a growing number of electronic journals and discussion groups like MBU-L, HUMANIST, PURTOPOI, NCTE-TALK, and PMC-L in order to communicate with each other about current issues in rhetoric or related fields. More and more scholars are using information distribution systems like Gopher and the World Wide Web to connect to libraries and databases around the world, and more and more rhetoricians are meeting in virtual spaces like the "TechnoRhetorician's Bar and Grill" on MIT's MediaMOO where they can talk in real-time with colleagues from all over the world. All these teachers, researchers, and graduate students are doing a lot of communicating. For example, in the 816 days between February 28, 1990, and May 24, 1992, members of PURTOPOI, an electronic discussion group devoted to current issues in the field of rhetoric and composition, produced more than 2.4 million lines of text. Thus, there is a need for studies that introduce and explain how NT relates to the field of rhetoric *both* as an object of study generally and as a medium that may have

serious implications for the ways in which we will conduct rhetorical scholarship in the future.

As a researcher and advocate of NT, of course I would like to
justify the study of this new medium in the most positive terms.
Furthermore, as a teacher committed to helping my composition
students become productive members of our participatory democracy, citizens who are able to identify, resist, and change social
injustices, I would like very much to argue that NT is, in fact, free
of the exclusionary discursive practices found in more mature
media forms, that NT does release "the speech of the madman" so
that it may be heard. I would like to convince those rhetoricians
unfamiliar with NT that this new medium offers freedom to those
disenfranchised individuals whose voices have been silenced by
oppressive, exclusionary social forces and political hegemonies.
Unfortunately, however, I cannot argue for the importance of NT
in such unqualified terms.

Despite the fact that I originally began this project to celebrate
the liberating effects of NT and to show that this medium is what
Ithiel de Sola Pool (1983) calls a "technology of freedom," this book
is more often a cautionary tale for those researchers like myself
who have become fascinated with the potential of the medium. So
beyond the first goal of introducing the importance of this new
medium, a second major goal of this project is to show that the
discourse that goes on within what are variously referred to as
computer-mediated discussion groups, electronic bulletin boards,
or electronic conferences is often neither liberated nor liberating.
NT is *not* produced without the encumbrance of Foucault's (1972)
"discursive practices." Indeed, I will argue along with Laclau and
Mouffe (1985) that the demands of what they call "articulatory
moments" (p. 105) necessitate the employment of discursive formations "so fundamental that they remain unvoiced and
unthought" (Young, 1981, p. 48). Thus, my examination of electronic communities is firmly situated in the Althusserian observation that no discourse is free of ideology; it begins with the
assumption that, as Berlin so often pointed out to his students,
"all discourse has designs on us."

And yet, despite the fact that NT is "subject" to many of
Foucault's (1981) "procedures of exclusion," I would argue that
NT is still, relatively speaking, uninhibited by many of the same
oppressive discursive practices that inform well-established
media like print journals. This is not to say that NT is free of
oppressive practices; rather, it simply points out that many of the
practices found in print have yet to become so entrenched on NT
that they are almost invisible. NT is still so new that many of the

conventions and codes that seem transparent in print- and oral-based media are being explicitly negotiated by members of electronic communities. Indeed, as I discuss in Chapter Six, even such simple practices as whether or not it's acceptable to quote an e-mail message or whether or not individuals should "sign" their messages must be explicitly negotiated in groups that communicate via this new medium.

Furthermore, because NT is so new and because it exnominates and defamiliarizes conventions that can be taken for granted in more mature media, a study of NT has relevance for students of both print and oral discourse communities. In other words, rather than explaining and justifying the medium or cautioning other NT researchers about the limitations of the medium, the primary audience for this project is rhetorical theorists who hopefully will find value in this study since I will be viewing NT and the electronic communities it enables through the frameworks provided by rhetorical theories of discourse communities. Because I am interested in better understanding the ways individuals within electronic discussion groups are able to both accommodate and resist the ideologies of their groups, I will be working toward building an adequate theory of community for rhetoric. Consequently, I will be entering a theoretical problematic already well-established in the field—that is, what is the role of the subject in discourse communities? As I show in Chapters Four and Five, the issue of whether a member of a discourse community is an independent subject *in* the community or subject *to* the community has become a significant problem for rhetorical theorists since it threatens to divide the field into rhetorics "in which the 'subject' is construed as the unified and coherent bearer of consciousness" and rhetorics in which the subject is seen to be the "veritable product of ideological interpellation" (Smith, 1988, xxx-xxxi). Hence, a third major goal of this project is to offer an approach to the formation of subjects within communities that will allow members of communities to both resist and accommodate their communities.

A study of electronic discussion groups is critical to this understanding of subject formation within communities since it allows the examination of theories of discourse communities that were intended to explain print- or oral-based communities, followed by their application to similar phenomena in an alternative medium in order to see what explanatory power they might yield there as well as how they are challenged by the new medium. As Miller (1989) has pointed out in her book *Rescuing the Subject*, there is a danger when "we turn to an established oral model to explain all discourse events" (p. 9), and that danger is that we will allow observations based on oral models to become reified, to become the only framework through which we will allow ourselves to view discourse production. Thus, there is a need to find alternative mediums that we can use as models for comparison. We need to follow, for example, the precedents Fiske (1987a, 1987b) and Allen (1987) have set through their examinations of the television medium; examinations which, because they serve as analogs to the print medium, enrich our understanding of discourse communities. NT, I am arguing, is another such medium and is sufficiently different, as studies by Murray (1985) and Kiesler, et al. (1985) have shown, to offer insights into oral- and print-based models of communities, as well as the NT communities themselves. The study of NT is essential to this project since it allows researchers to situate themselves on the boundaries between various media where the meaningful play of differences becomes most clear.

NEUTRAL MEDIA AND VALUE-FREE TECHNOLOGIES

Throughout this study, I wish to maintain one constant premise, one foundation that stitches the sometimes contradictory voices in this book together. That premise is that a medium is *never* neutral and technological tools are *never* value-free.

There are two reasons why it is particularly important to foreground these propositions in a discussion of NT. First, although there have been numerous attacks on the Shannon-Weaver (1949) model of communication and its suggestion that anything that is not data or content is just noise,[4] the fact that this model uses the transfer of electronic information as an analog for all communication means that it has been extremely easy to offer it as an explanation for what goes on in the NT medium. Second, despite the fact that NT researchers like Kaplan (1991) warn that the "tools of inscription embody and construct ideological practices, redefining what exists, what is good, and what it is possible to do" (p. 21), many people, particularly those who have never actually used NT, tend to view e-mail as little more than a more efficient tool for disseminating what are essentially printed texts.

---

[4] See for example Porter's *Audience and Rhetoric* (1992, pp. 128–129); Poster's *Mode of Information* (1990, pp. 7, 28–30); Barton and Barton's "Communication Models for Computer-Mediated Information Systems" (1984, pp. 289–293).

Neither view is adequate because they fail to recognize the important roles that media and inscription devices[5] play both in shaping meaning and in the formation of subjectivities. Instead, these views see NT as just the neutral packaging of print, so that, from this perspective, form is divorced from content, and language is transparent. And of course, the consequence of making language and media transparent is that it's no longer possible to examine the social, economic, or political relationships upon which discursive structures depend and into which we are interpellated when we use them.

For example, consider that for most networkers protocols are transparent, in both the network architects' and the poststructuralists' sense of the term. To the network architect, something is transparent to users when a function is accomplished without the users' direct intervention. For example, networkers are seldom aware of the routes their e-mail messages must take in order to arrive at their final destination. Generally, users need to supply only the address of the site they wish to reach to send messages through the network; they don't need to specify each individual computer in the long chain of sites through which their messages must pass before arriving at their final destination. Instead, complex protocol suites or routing software automatically route the messages through a network or even through several networks, and usually they do this routing so efficiently that many networkers are unaware that their messages passed through any computers other than their host computer and the remote computer they addressed. It isn't until something goes wrong that networkers become aware of the limitations that protocols impose on network use; it's only when they are silenced by the protocols that users begin to see how much what can be said and who can say it are controlled by protocols.

And the effects of protocols go far beyond the simple routing of messages from point A to point B. In effect, a protocol suite represents an agreement among system administrators and network architects on the common languages and sets of behaviors that their computers use to talk to each other; without this agreement, no meaningful data exchange occurs. It is a common misconception that computers that are connected together form a network; a physical connection is only a necessary condition of

---

5 I am borrowing the term "inscription devices" from Latour & Woolgar's (1979) seminal work *The Social Construction of Scientific Facts* and from Latour's (1987) later work *Science in Action* (cf., pp. 64–70). The term "inscription device" and "black box" is discussed at greater length in Chapter Five.

networking,[6] *it is not a sufficient condition.* In fact, the individual computer sites or nodes of a network only represent the physical makeup of a network. For real networking to occur, for information to be exchanged electronically in a meaningful way, there must also be the same sharing of values, expectations, or mutual knowledge that are discussed by communitarian theorists like Hillery (1959), Effrat (1974), Taylor (1989), and Sandel (1982) in Chapter Four. For now, however, it is enough to say that protocols represent the electronic equivalent of *sensus communis* or "common sense."[7] In other words, protocol suites form the foundations that enable the production and interpretation of electronic texts.

The obvious point to be made here is that whoever controls WANS protocols controls what is possible on computer networks. It is largely for this reason that the Federal government authorized the expenditure of $2 billion for the NREN—despite an on-going recession, despite budget cuts in the Dept. of Defense and in domestic programs, despite a huge federal deficit, and despite the disastrous costs of the savings and loan bailout. As Senator Albert Gore put it in the "National High-Performance Computer Technology Act of 1989," "The nation which most completely assimilates high-performance computing into its economy will very likely emerge as the dominant intellectual, economic, and technological force in the next century" (S 5689). By taking the lead in the development and control of WANS protocols through the construction of the NREN, the U.S. clearly sought to emerge as that dominant force, just as, for example, it had once been the dominant force in the automobile and aerospace industries.

Unlike those manufacturing based industries, however, more is at stake here than just controlling modes of production. In today's information age, what's being sold is access to and ownership of information.[8] Indeed, the day is rapidly approaching when we may measure economic wealth not in terms of material

---

[6] Actually, a physical connection isn't even a necessary condition of networking if we take the position that infrared, laser, radio-packet, or microwave connections are not physical. However, for the purposes of this discussion, there is no need to put such a fine point on the matter.

[7] The term common sense is highly problematic, and, as seen in Chapter Four's discussion of Kant, it can be used to mean a natural sense common to all humans or it may mean a reified cultural sensibility that has been socially constructed. Here, I am using it in the latter sense.

[8] Mark Poster (1990) develops the term "mode of information" in recognition of the similar historical effects produced by owning a "mode of production" and the ownership of information (pp. 5–7).

products, but in terms of connectivity. Consider, for example, the economic effects of a computer virus that shut down the network between international stock markets in October 1987. As the *New York Times* reported then[9] and as Poster (1990) also observed later, the loss of connectivity resulting from the virus threatened "the world's financial hubs" with "instant economic collapse" (pp. 4–5). Denied access to their basic commodity, information, the New York, London, and Tokyo stock markets ground to a halt. Or to put this in terms of WANS, when a hostile force in the form of a virus assumed control of the protocols governing the network, it became, quite literally, the dominant force in the world's economy.

We can also see the importance of controlling protocols in the FBI's attempts to prevent Internet users from sending encrypted messages through the Net. The FBI and other government agencies have on several occasions sought legislation to make it illegal for private citizens to send messages across the network using codes that the government could not decode and translate. The proposed legislation would require that the step-by-step narratives required to decode a particular encryption scheme (i.e., a protocol suite) must be registered with the Federal government. The intelligence agencies want the ability to monitor communication on the network—in effect *to police* the network's use and to conduct surveillance activities. By preventing individuals from using unauthorized encryption systems (i.e., their own private language), the Federal government would be in a position to restrict what could and could not be said on the network. It's for this reason that debates over WANS protocol suites tend to become so acrimonious and highly politicized.

The upshot of this analysis of WANS protocols[10] then is that NT is not a transparent medium that utilizes a value-free technology merely to increase the efficient distribution of printed texts. The

---

[9] See a series of articles that appeared in the *New York Times*, October 18, 1987.

[10] Those interested in pursuing e-mail protocol standards further may wish to consult a series of electronic documents known as RFCs or "Requests for Comments." Of particular interest (though certainly not light reading) is RFC 822, which outlines the standards for handling 7-bit, ASCII e-mail messages. At the date of publication, RFC 822 and other RFCs are available via anonymous ftp at NIS.NSF.NET (35.1.1.48) or most other NICs (Network Information Centers). Other useful discussions also appear in Quarterman's *The Matrix* (1991, pp. 72–78) and Frey & Adams' *!%@:: A Directory of Electronic Mail Addressing & Networks* (1990, pp. 2–17).

differences between NT and print media are not simply quantita-tive; they are qualitative and represent fundamental shifts in the political, economic, and social relations that determine who has *power*. Even in academic disciplines that have (at least from a traditionalist point of view) remained relatively isolated from shifts in the stock market and international politics, the intro-duction of NT suggests that critical changes will occur in the practices of everyday academic life. As Kaplan (1991) has pointed out:

> The scope or field of action implied by the electronic redefinition of a text expands not just conceptually but spatially when it can be distributed quickly and widely through an electronic network. Networks expand an author's potential audience and, therefore, his or her power. Moreover, texts distributed electronically can bypass traditional publishers, and, therefore, bypass entrenched "gate-keeping" communities at least one of whose effects has been to silence or mute nontraditional voices and points of view. (p. 20)

The next chapter examines in more detail the role of the tradi-tional publisher and how that role may fundamentally be altered by the introduction of NT, so for now it is enough to observe that NT has the potential to qualitatively transform the economics of academic life. For example, in a world where keeping up with recent developments in the field is often a critical measure of suc-cess, those who are content to wait for the latest issue of a schol-arly journal in order to learn about new ideas and new trends in their fields put themselves as much as two years behind NT users. Hence, what at first glance may have appeared to be a simple mat-ter of differences in degrees of efficiency and speed becomes dif-ferences in kind; it becomes a qualitative distinction between the haves and the have nots.

The failure to see that media technologies are never value-free or to see that "the medium massages the message" (to use one of McLuhan's, 1972, famous maxims) is to remain blind to the role that NT might play in determining power relations. However, beyond the economics of NT, the work of both McLuhan and Ong (1982) suggests that the effects of this new medium may go much farther than simply preventing those with nontraditional argu-ments from being heard; it may even enable radical new forms of thought. In one of the seminal passages from his *Interfaces of the Word*, Ong both critiques the value-free view of media and asserts his own theory of media transformation as follows:

Unreflective reliance on models has generated the term "media" to
designate new technological ways of managing the word, such as
writing, print, and the electronic devices. The term is useful.... But
it can be misleading, encouraging us to think of writing, print, and
electronic devices simply as ways of "moving information" over some
sort of space intermediate between one person and another. In fact,
each of the so-called "media" does far more than this: it makes possible thought processes inconceivable before.... Writing and print
and the computer enable the mind to constitute within itself—not
just on the inscribed surface or on the computer programs—new
ways of thinking, previously inconceivable questions, and new ways
of searching for responses. (p. 46)

This suggestion that media have a significant role to play in
the formation of consciousness is extremely valuable if we wish
to understand how it is possible for individuals to resist interpellation into discourse communities—that is, how it is possible
to think outside the discursive practices of a community.
McLuhan's (1972) hot and cool media theory and Ong's (1982)
media transformation theory are important here because they
suggest that one means of resisting interpellation is to change
from the dominant medium of a community to a new medium.
In other words, if different media do in fact enable new ways of
thinking, allow us to ask previously inconceivable questions,
and encourage new ways of searching for responses, then one
way to think outside a community is to resituate the community's discussions in a new medium. Hence, if the traditional
classroom format is too oppressive since it privileges the
instructor's voice and only allows one person (who is usually
"authorized" by the instructor) to speak at a time, then perhaps
instructors should resituate the classroom discussion in the
virtual space offered by computer networks. Or if traditional
publishing methods are too exclusionary because "the publisher, in effect, authenticates the value of the text ... by guar-
anteeing the text's authoritative origins and its intrinsic value"
(Kaplan, 1991, pp. 20–21), then perhaps writers and scholars
should resituate the publication process in the NT medium.
Ong's (1982) and McLuhan's (1972) observations regarding the
role of media in the formation of consciousness are useful
because they allow researchers to posit hypotheses like those
above. They make it possible to ask whether or not electronic
classrooms and electronic publications do allow individuals to
resist the discursive practices of traditional classroom formats
and publication.

In spite of Ong's and McLuhan's useful contributions, however, I will not explore these issues in terms of their respective theories because each theory depends on a view of subjectivity that is problematic. For example, in the previous excerpt when Ong argues that media "enable the mind to constitute *within itself* ... new ways of thinking" (emphasis added, p. 46), he seems to suggest that consciousness is constituted by the mind itself (cf., Ohmann, 1985, p. 681). Although Ong (1982) makes it clear that he sees a phenomenological relationship between what he calls the "ontogenetic consciousness" of the individual and the "phylogenetic consciousness" of the social (pp. 42–43), ultimately it is always the ontogenetic that determines the limits of consciousness. In other words, Ong recognizes that we may in fact be born into media that precede our existence and alter our consciousnesses over time; yet, in terms of the growth of an individual, the potentialities of mind predate media. Or to use Ong's analogy, media are only catalysts for "releasing the energies" of the mind (p. 47). As a result, Ong finally ends up privileging the cognitive processes of the individual over the social.

Similarly, McLuhan's (1972) hot and cool media theory, as is suggested by the sensory nature of his terms, depends on the biological perceptions of individuals. For McLuhan, media forms stimulate the senses of observers, producing particular patterns of response, so that McLuhan's theory doesn't really explain how "the medium massages the message" so much as it describes how a medium massages the observer. In other words, for McLuhan, media reconfigure organs in the sensory mechanism, altering the complexion of the perceptual act. Consequently, as Poster (1990) also observes, "By focusing on the *sensorium* of the receiving subject he [McLuhan] preserves the subject as a perceiving, not an interpreting being" (p. 15).

Thus, because both McLuhan's and Ong's media theories ultimately depend on an individual's ability to perceive rather than on a subjected interpretation, they are incompatible with the Althusserian observation that no discourse is free of ideology upon which this project is based. Both offer valuable contributions to our understanding of the role of media/tion in the shaping of meaning, but I am seeking to develop a theory of mediation in which common sense can be seen as a social construct developed within a community rather than a self-evident biological given that all human beings must share (Perelman, 1969, p. 159). To develop this approach to mediation, it is important to understand better the ways in which theories of community influence what may be meant by the term common sense.

chapter three

What Is Electronic Publishing and Who Controls It?

THE INTRODUCTION OF ELECTRONIC WRITING

Most are familiar with the impact of the desktop publishing revolution. The developments in personal computing technology and particularly the introduction of laser printer technology in the 1980s have dramatically changed the traditional relationship between printers, authors, and readers. Traditionally, as Sullivan (1991) has observed, the author has had to give up "control" of the published page to commercial publishers because they owned the only appropriate means of production (pp. 43–44). Private individuals and even large corporations simply couldn't invest the capital necessary for the production quality consumers have come to demand of the printed page. Consequently, commercial printers occupied the space of an often unseen, seldom considered mediator or interface between writers and readers.

In terms of Shannon's (1949) information-transfer model, commercial printers served to actively filter the signal being transmitted by the sender/author to the receiver/reader. In effect, commercial printers served to complicate the simple production/consumption relationship upon which information-transfer models of language are based. However, the meaning-making role of commercial printers has been largely overlooked because the information-transfer model encourages researchers to view the author as the sole producer of meaningful texts; there is only room for one "presence" in the model's producer slot. Thus, commercial printers are often seen as little more than faithful scribes or "conduits" (Porter, 1992, p. 125).

The introduction of electronic writing technologies, however, has forced a recognition of the productive role of commercial publishers in the publication process. Far from neutral scribes, copyists, or conduits, commercial printers have long been secondary or even coproducers of meaning. However, the commercial printers' monopoly on the means of production and their coproducer role have been seriously undermined with the advent of software packages capable of integrating text and graphics and with the arrival of affordable laser printers capable of producing 300 dot-per-inch output, allowing font and image resolutions approximating that of commercial printers. As Sullivan (1991) points out:

> Desktop publishing became the rage in the corporate world because the entire page (text and graphics) could be reliably communicated to a printer and inexpensively produced in a form that looked nearly as good as commercial printing. Further, a desktop-publishing system could be paid for in a couple of months out of a savings in a commercial printing budget. (p. 51)

Sullivan goes on to observe that the elimination of the commercial printers' role as coproducers of meaningful texts has forced us to reconsider the factors we must examine when we teach writing. Before desktop publishing, "writers have not needed to think carefully about how the look of the page will affect the meaning of the text;" instead, the words themselves have been all that mattered (p. 43). As a result, writing instruction has tended to ignore the visual and other factors that are part of meaning production. But as electronic writing becomes more and more pervasive and as students are forced to take more and more responsibility for productive activities once performed by commercial printers, writing theorists will have to develop theories of language and pedagogies that can account for these activities.

Sullivan's analysis of the impact of desktop publishing technology is useful for a number of reasons. Certainly, it serves as an excellent example of how the introduction of new technologies and new media may force researchers to reconsider and problematize many long-standing, deeply entrenched theories of the writing process. Desktop publishing research like Sullivan's or like Fortune's (1991) "Visual and Verbal Thinking" essay has helped us to understand better how the visual has been devalued in contemporary writing theory. And other researchers, such as Wahlstrom (1989) in her "Desktop Publishing: Perspectives, Potentials, and Politics," have pointed out other factors in the writing process that desktop publishing technology calls into question, factors such as the *ethos* of the printed word—that is, the way readers automatically inseminate the printed word with reasonableness and rationality, making it pregnant with authentic meaning. As Wahlstrom points out, "We have burned and banned books we felt violated our trust in the printed word. As teachers of writing, we keep the tradition of reverencing print alive" (p. 175). However, just as Sullivan's (1991) work challenges the devaluation of the visual in contemporary writing theory, Wahlstrom goes on to question whether we can or, more importantly, whether we should maintain this reverence for print when "information can now be assembled in anyone's basement and will come out looking almost as authentic as anything coming from a typesetter" (p. 175).

Clearly, such research is valuable because it reveals new factors for consideration or because it recontextualizes issues researchers knew were there but didn't have to confront since they were outside the writing process that goes on in the traditional composition classroom. However, in terms of the discussion here, such research is particularly valuable because it forces a re-examination of notions of control. It provokes questions such as: How is electronic publishing different from traditional publishing? What's at stake in that control? And of course, who really does control or own the text in this new electronic environment?

WHAT IS ELECTRONIC PUBLISHING?

To understand how electronic publishing and electronic writing differ from traditional publishing, it is important to note that desktop publishing or other uses of the computer to produce *printed* texts may or may not be considered part of electronic publishing. I am using the term electronic publishing to refer to the practice of *distributing* texts *to audiences* solely through electronic means, particularly (though not exclusively) through WANS. Wahlstrom (1989), on the other hand, defines electronic publishing as the use of computers "to create documents which can be broadcast to home television screens as teletext or cablecast to televisions or computers as videotext or sent to a local printer who can use the electronic data to typeset them" (p. 174).

Although Wahlstrom's definition is certainly intelligible and clearly consistent with the term electronic, I want to distinguish between the scope of her definition and mine. To examine how electronic consumption may affect the electronic production of texts, researchers need to draw distinctions between the creation, distribution, and consumption of *electronic* texts, and it is difficult to make these distinctions in Wahlstrom's terms since her definition of publishing goes beyond distribution and includes the creation of texts that can be consumed either electronically or in print. Since electronic reading may be a factor in who controls electronic texts, WANS researchers need definitions of electronic publishing and electronic writing that recognize that writing for an electronic audience may be different than writing for readers of printed texts. Just as we differentiate between writing a speech and writing an article in order to understand better the ways the intended medium shapes the act of text production, we also need to differentiate between writing for print and writing for cathode ray tubes.

I do not consider the creation of documents in a computer environment to be part of electronic publishing *per se*. Rather, like Bolter (1991)[1], I would use the term "electronic photocomposition" (p. 5) to describe this process because, though some texts may be written on a computer using desktop publishing technology, they are often never intended to be distributed and consumed *by readers in an electronic medium*.[2] In other words, as Bolter (1991) has also pointed out, a "printed book can be about, but cannot be, an electronic book" (p. x). The following two examples may help illustrate this point.

---

[1] Bolter (1991) argues, as I do here, that desktop publishing technology is not part of electronic publishing when it is used to produce camera-ready copy for the printer, and uses the term "computer-assisted photocomposition" to distinguish this use of computers from electronic writing (p. 5).

[2] I realize that this definition of electronic writing will raise issues of intentionality for researchers of electronic publishing because it makes it extremely difficult to say that a text is the product of electronic writing if the researcher cannot speak to the author's intentions. Nevertheless, I maintain that writers *do* write for intended audiences, and we must therefore take this into consideration if we are to understand how those intended audiences—whether they are electronic or not— change the character of the composing process.

The journal *Publish*, according to its editor, Rosenzweig (1991), is produced entirely through electronic means: "We take every single page straight to film" (p. 10). Indeed, on the table of contents page for each issue of *Publish*, readers can find a list of the software used to create that particular issue. Similarly, Hawisher and Selfe's (1991b) anthology, *Evolving Perspectives on Computers and Composition Studies*, provides a list of the computer tools used to produce the book. On the final page of the book, readers will find the following:

> *Evolving Perspectives on Computers and Composition Studies* was composed on a Macintosh IIci using MICROSOFT WORD 4.0. The text was set up in 11/13 Palatino, with heads in Palatino and Avant Garde. Page Makeup was done with PAGEMAKER 4.0, and figures were created using FREEHAND 2.02. Proof pages were output from a LaserWriter II NTX at 300 dots per inch, and final pages were produced on a Linotronic 300 at 1270 dots per inch.

In both these cases, the texts were produced electronically on computers, but both were published and distributed *in print*. Indeed, Rosenzweig (1991) even takes pride in the fact that her journal looks like it was produced using traditional methods. She praises her staff's ability to "crank out issues that prove that producing a magazine electronically doesn't mean you must produce an electronic-looking magazine" (p. 10).

Wahlstrom's (1989) definition of electronic publishing would include both of the preceding examples since they both used "computers to create documents" and since they were "sent to a local printer who can use the electronic data to typeset them" (p. 174). However, I do not consider these to be electronic publications because they were not distributed electronically to readers. Furthermore, I do not believe these two publications are examples of electronic writing since the evidence would suggest that they were entirely produced for consumption in print (see footnote 2). As I stated earlier, I call the practice of creating texts for electronic readers electronic writing, and the production of camera-ready copy on a computer electronic photocomposition. Consequently, to be considered an electronic publication from the perspective taken here, a work must be *distributed to audiences* electronically. For example, articles submitted for publication in *The Journal of Postmodern Culture* (better known to networkers as PMC) or e-mail messages sent for redistribution by electronic discussion groups like PURTOPOI are considered electronic publications here because they are distributed publicly in electronic form. Yet, PMC

articles or PURTOPOI messages may or may not have been originally written electronically; they may, for example, have been
handwritten and then entered into the computer or they may have
been intended for publication in a book, magazine, newspaper, or
other printed publication and then later entered into an electronic
database so that they might be *re*-published electronically.
Furthermore, the readers may choose to print out the articles in
hardcopy form once they have been distributed. However, because
they are *distributed to readers through WANS*, they are electronic
publications.

The distinctions I am making between electronic writing, electronic photocomposition, and electronic publishing have several
important ramifications. One of the most obvious of these is that
electronic publications are most often read on the screen
(though, as previously stated, some readers may choose to
transform them into print later). And, as Haas (1989) and Daly
(1990) have pointed out, reading on the screen isn't the same as
reading hardcopy. Both Haas and Daly have found that e-readers (i.e., readers who read electronically published texts) tend to
make more "errors" in their reading. Certainly, there is a large
body of anecdotal evidence to support this since networkers frequently blame their misunderstandings or misreadings on their
computer interface. Haas (1989) suggests that one reason e-
readers may have trouble "getting a sense of the text" has to do
with the limitations of screen size and e-readers' ability to
remember what they've read. She suggests that, once there are
more than one or two screens full of text, "the size of the text
makes it difficult to hold an accurate representation in memory"
(p. 25).

Haas' analysis is important here because it suggests that control of the e-text may not belong solely to the author as traditional,
New Critical approaches would suggest. Haas' approach, like
Sullivan's (1991), suggests that the computer's visual interface
plays a role in controlling textual meaning. Furthermore, the e-
reader also plays a critical role in controlling e-text production.
And if one puts the electronic misreadings Haas observed in terms
of Iser's (1980) phenomenological approach to the reading process, it
may be possible to see the implications of this for communitarian
theorists more clearly.

For Iser, the reading process in print is always already "virtual;"
that is, "it is not to be identified either with the reality of the text
or with the individual disposition of the reader" (1980, p. 50).
Thus, like data in the virtual memory of a computer where e-texts
are located, the meaning of a text is a dynamic, temporal event

that occurs in and across a particular moment. Meaning is neither fixed in the text nor in the reader (just as data is not fixed in the computer's virtual memory); instead, textual meaning emerges from the virtual space where the reader and text come together. As Iser (1989) points out, "the reading process always involves viewing the text through a perspective that is continually on the move, linking up the different phases, and so constructing what we have called the virtual dimension" (p. 56).

The upshot of this phenomenological analysis is the now familiar position that meaning is constructed. For Iser, the text represents a set of fixed points, which he likens to the stars that assume the shapes of stellar constellation (p. 57). Between the stars in a constellation are "gaps" across which readers must draw lines as they read; until finally, remembering lines they've already drawn and anticipating lines that will come, the readers construct meaningful patterns. Thus, just as the stellar observer shapes the stars of the Big Dipper into a meaningful pattern, the reader of a novel or poem shapes disparate textual cues into a meaningful form.

Clearly then, Iser's theory of the reading process, like Haas', depends on the readers' memories to construct texts because they must be able to remember those lines they have drawn across textual gaps. This dependence on memory could suggest that a reader's mis-memory of a particular textual star will lead to the recreation of an inaccurate and specious "constellation" or textual meaning. We could also extrapolate from this that, because e-readers (particularly those in mainframe computing environments) often cannot backup and reread a previous screen, they are even more dependent on their memories than print readers and therefore much more likely to make an "error" in the construction of meaningful patterns.

Furthermore, if reading on the screen isn't the same as reading print, then writing for e-readers isn't going to be the same as writing for print readers. For example, one might argue that e-writers need to provide e-readers with more fixed points and fewer gaps in order to be intelligible. We might expect e-texts to be more repetitious than print for the same two reasons that Ong (1982) argues that oral cultures use "repetition, redundancy, [and] verboseness" (p. 114). As Ong points out, in oral discourse:

> Spoken words fly away. The reader can pause over a point he wants to reflect on, or go back a few pages to return to it. The inscribed word is still there. The spoken word is gone. So the orator repeats himself, to help his hearers think it over. Second, spoken words do

not infallibly carry equally well to everyone in the audience; syn-
onyms, parallelisms, repetitions, neat oppositions, give the individual hearer a second chance if he did not hear well the first time. (p.
114)

Thus, like Ong's orators whose words "fly away" from the lis-
teners' memories, e-writers must create e-texts that will similarly
vanish from e-readers' biological and virtual memories.

This recognition that words fly away in electronic publications
also suggests that e-texts may take more radical forms than simply the increased repetition of key ideas. For example, Ong
(1982), Bolter (1991), and Brent (1991) all have challenged the
systematic or periodic nature of these kinds of texts, suggesting
that just because print technology privileges linearity, we
shouldn't assume that other media will also adopt that form.
Indeed, in his famous media transformation theory, Ong (1977)
argues that historical introduction of writing technology made
linear thinking possible. The ability to turn back a few pages and
refresh both the writer's and the reader's memories enabled writers to produce long, systematic treatises like Aristotle's *Art of
Rhetoric* and Plato's *Republic* since "in a completely oral noetic
economy, thought which does not consist in memorable patterns
is in effect nonthought: you can normally never get it back
again" (Ong, 1977, p. 191). Thus, before the technology of writing was available to assist the writer's memory with the production of long, complex argumentative structures, Ong (1977)
argues that:

> Such a feat is impossible. The closest an oral culture can come to a
> systematic treatise is through stringing together a series of apho-
> risms: "The early bird gets the worm. All that glitters is not gold. He
> who hesitates is lost." (p. 87)

Based on Ong's observations about the structure of oral texts
and based on certain similarities between listening to oral discourse and reading electronic texts, Bolter (1991) and Brent
(1991) have observed a tendency toward the aphoristic and a
movement away from systematic, linear texts in the electronic
medium. Bolter points out that "each unit [of e-text] may be
approached from a different perspective with each reading" in the
electronic medium (p. ix), indicating that, like Iser's reader, each
individual constructs his or her own textual constellation. As a
consequence of this, Bolter concludes that "electronic writing will
probably be aphoristic rather than periodic" (p. ix).

This suggests that texts intended for electronic publication may differ significantly in form from texts intended for print publication. It also suggests that "the technological characteristics of the medium itself reshape our lives not just by giving us new tools to play with but by reshaping our consciousness on a fundamental and subliminal level" (Brent, 1991).[3]

And yet, although it may be the case that e-readers do have to depend on their memories for the construction of texts more than print readers do, Iser's (1980) theory doesn't allow us to simply conclude that memory is solely responsible for the meanings readers and e-readers construct. Iser adds two additional components that he calls the "repertoire" and oppositional "strategies" to the process of meaning construction. The addition of these factors are of particular importance because it is through the function of a reader's repertoire and strategies that community is introduced into the e-reading *and* e-writing processes in a way that challenges many of the expectations we might have about the shape of e-texts.

In the process of reading, Iser says we are constantly recreating meanings. As we read, we are constantly looking forward, forming expectations based on what has gone before. We constantly participate in a process of constructing meanings, and, to engage in this construction process, we need pre-existing forms to guide our best guesses about the way the text will take shape. According to Iser:

> This process is steered by two main structural components within the text: first, a repertoire of familiar literary patterns and recurrent literary themes, together with allusions to familiar social and historical contexts; second, techniques or strategies used to set the familiar against the unfamiliar. (1980, pp. 62–63)

However, assuming that Iser is correct in his assertion that readers and writers depend on a repertoire of pre-existing forms, conventions, or codes to give meaningful shapes to texts, researchers are still left with a problem since Iser doesn't answer

---

[3] Some will note the lack of page numbers in the parenthetical citation here and elsewhere. This is not an oversight on the part of the author, rather it is because the publication being cited is an electronic one. Such publications do not have pages since they are printed on display screens rather than paper. Also, because screen sizes vary dramatically from terminal type to terminal type, it is not possible to number the screens.

the next obvious question: Where does this repertoire come from? How do readers develop what Culler (1980) also called that "amazing *repertoire* of conscious and unconscious knowledge" that enables "literary competence" (p. 101, emphasis added)?

Fish (1980a) addressed himself to these questions in his famous "Interpreting the *Variorum*" essay, and it was there that he developed his concept of the interpretive community as an answer. For Fish, readers and writers learn their repertoire from the interpretive communities they inhabit because:

> Interpretive communities are made up of those who share interpretive strategies not for reading (in the conventional sense) but for writing texts, for constituting their properties and assigning their intentions. In other words, *these strategies exist prior to the act of reading and therefore determine the shape of what is read* rather than, as is usually assumed, the other way around. (p. 182, emphasis added)

Fish's introduction of community into the discussion is important because it once again problematizes the production/consumption binary implicit in the information-transfer model. As Fish states clearly in the preceding quote, the effects of interpretive communities obtain for the writer, not just the reader. Thus, like so many other communitarian theorists, Fish makes community part of the production process. He makes the reader a coproducer of meaning rather than a consumer.

When I say that Fish makes the reader into a "coproducer," I intend for that term to have two different meanings. In the first sense, coproducer suggests that it is the reader who, during the act of reading, determines or controls the meaning of the text. That is, *after* the text exists, it is the community of readers who assigns meaning(s) to it. Or to put this in Iser's terms, until the reader reads the text, it hasn't really been produced since "the text only takes on life when it is realized" or since the "convergence of text and reader brings the literary work into existence" (1980, p. 50).

In the second sense, the term coproducer suggests that the community plays a role in the invention process. Like Vitanza's (1990) "tyrannical" audience or like the traditional print publisher in Sullivan's (1991) analysis, a coproducer shapes meaning both before words appear on the screen and as the text is being written. In other words, communities of readers write the writer *prior* to the act of word production. Thus, to say coproducer has two senses is to suggest that: 1) readers write texts, and 2) readers write writers (Porter, 1992, p. 82).

It is through the second sense of the term coproducer that it becomes possible to develop a deeper understanding of why the editor of a journal like *Publish* would be pleased that her staff produced the journal electronically without making it look electronic. It also helps to explain why articles in e-journals like *PMC, EJournal*, and *EFFector Online* don't look like the repetitive, aphoristic prose an Ongian analysis might lead us to expect. In short, the reason that Rosenzweig (1991) wants her journal to look like a print journal and the reason PMC and other e-journals don't distribute repetitive, aphoristic prose is that the communities that read these journals expect traditional print forms, and the editors and writers know it.

Although the electronic publishing technology may allow for and may even encourage different conventions and discursive practices, a particular community's *a priori* expectations of the scholarly article seem to play a larger role in shaping articles submitted to publications like *PMC* than do the technological capabilities of electronic publishing. Indeed, the very fact that the texts distributed by *PMC* or *EJournal* are called articles suggests how important the print analog has been in determining attitudes about e-texts in these publications. Currently, virtually everything about *PMC* except for its method of distribution replicates traditional academic journals.[4] It has editors who solicit articles from scholars of postmodernist thought, a distinguished board of reviewers who help insure the quality of the articles distributed by the journal, and finally it has copyright registration that limits unauthorized copying of the articles to guarantee that the authors will get credit for their work. In this sort of electronic publication, even the most casual reader of "articles" in electronic journals will recognize that they don't exhibit the repetitive or aphoristic features we might expect of electronic publications. Instead, they exhibit all the features we expect of traditional academic articles—they are impersonal in tone, hierarchically arranged, resplendent with long, complex, argumentative structures, and full of critical references to other scholarly works. Indeed, they even use mechanisms of traditional scholarship such as endnotes and Works

---

[4] In fairness to the editors of *PMC*, it should be noted that there is an electronic discussion group called PMC-TALK that is associated with the *PMC* journal. PMC-TALK encourages a more open and interactive discussion of issues in the study of postmodern culture. However, PMC-TALK is a separate electronic publication and therefore needs to be distinguished from the *PMC* journal.

Cited sections, despite the obvious fact that these mechanisms are almost completely useless to e-readers who can't flip back and forth between pages of the text.[5] In short then, it could be said that these electronic publications are examples of poor electronic writing because they do not address the needs of e-readers.

Yet from a historical perspective, it's not surprising that electronic publishing on WANS would borrow many of the conventions of print media, including mechanisms that are clearly inappropriate for the medium. The histories of writing technologies and publishing media are full of examples where new technologies and new media borrowed analogs from their predecessors. Bolter (1991), for example, has observed how Gutenberg and other early printers "attempted to replicate manuscripts" that the scribes of Gutenberg's day produced by hand. He goes on to note that "it took several decades for printers to realize that there was no need to use abbreviation and ligatures that rendered the text easier to write (by hand) but harder to read" (p. 64; see also Connolly, et al., 1991a, pp. 37–39). Similarly, programs from television's golden years show the influence of print, theater, and radio on the (then) new medium. Rather than the dramatic visual images we've come to expect of modern television programs, early television often depended on techniques developed for the stage, the print, and the radio media for its effects.

Today's television programs depend on elaborate sets and dramatic, even extravagant visual action shots to suture the various components of the program together. Yet, during its infancy, television programs depended on dialog and character development to forward the plots. Visually speaking, early television programs would be considered boring by today's standards. Actors and actresses tended to stand, rooted to one spot, depending on rapid verbal exchanges of dialog developed earlier by popular radio dramas. Of course, the poor sensitivity of early microphones and the large size of the equipment used contributed to the limited use of visual action; it was simply too difficult to move the cameras and

---

[5] My comments here obtain for e-readers on mainframe computing systems where the examples I've used are going to be found. The texts distributed on WANS such as Internet, BITNET, or USENET usually require mediation by software found on mainframes, and these utilities often don't allow or make it extremely difficult for a user to jump back and forth between the middle and the end of long files. Obviously, however, a hypertext environment encourages readers to navigate through a text (with varying degrees of freedom) so that the linkage between the reference mark for an endnote and the endnote itself is actually easier for a user to follow in an electronic environment than it is in print.

recording equipment of the period much. However, it also seems likely that both producers and audiences built on the interpretive skills they had developed for the media that preceded television. Even though the visual element was there to be exploited by the new medium, the more familiar spoken word remained the primary focus of attention in these early dramas.

Nor is this sort of borrowing limited to some primitive practice without analog in the mature, modern television medium. Even today, vestiges of television's indebtedness to print on the evening news may be seen. Why is it, for example, that newscasters sit, occasionally glancing down at the sheets of paper before them as though they were reading from them, when every viewer knows they are actually reading from teleprompters? Why make this obviously artificial, almost ritualized gesture to the printed word if not to garner credibility from the well-established ethos of print journalism and to profit from the logocentrism of western culture? Clearly, even in an age where sound bites have become visual spectacles, the ritualized conventions of old media forms are maintained.

WHAT'S AT STAKE IN ELECTRONIC PUBLISHING?

Each of these examples of a new medium's indebtedness to the media that preceded it resurfaces the poststructuralist problem of accounting for change. The same dilemma found in contemporary literary theory re-emerges: that is, Moi's (1985) observation that "all forms of radical thought inevitably remain mortgaged to the very historical categories they seek to transcend" (p. 88). Post/structuralism may be different than structuralism, but, as its very name implies, it depends on structuralism for its existence. As Derrida (1990) pointed out, one can't "start with disorder;" one must "start with the tradition" (p. 11), and this is as true for new media as it is for schools of criticism. Intelligibility for an audience, the appeal to common sense, demands that producers invoke existing conventions and familiar forms.[6] Thus, audiences are coproducers or even "tyrants" because they dictate the forms producers may use (Vitanza, 1990, p. 1). Furthermore, because those forms must be *shared* knowledge (i.e., *sensus communis*), they cannot be completely new; they must have a communal history.

---

[6] For a more thorough explication of the demands of intelligibility and its relationship to common sense, see Kant's concept of communicability in Chapter Four.

Electronic publishing is no different; it too is mortgaged to the media that have come before. Its audiences are no less tyrannical than any other medium's. Consequently, like the printing press and television, it too is "often used only as a more efficient means to achieve traditional ends" (Connolly, et al., 1991a, p. 38). As the examples of the electronic journals demonstrate, there are those who simply use the medium to distribute what are essentially the same sort of texts we find in print journals. Thus, the forms of discourse available to producers of electronic texts seem predetermined by the reified conventions of extant, constitutive communities. In short, electronic publishing from this perspective becomes what Wilson (1988) calls a "technology of control"—that is, a force for social management and fascism.

And yet, there are those who view electronic publishing as a powerful democratizing force. de Sola Pool (1983) calls electronic publishing a "technology of freedom;" Tehranian (1988) calls it a "technology of power;" and Rheingold (1993) flatly asserts that:

> If a BBS (computer Bulletin Board System) isn't a democratizing technology, there is no such thing. For less than the cost of a shotgun, a BBS turns an ordinary person anywhere in the world into a publisher, an eyewitness reporter, an advocate, an organizer, a student or teacher, and potential participant in a worldwide citizen-to-citizen conversation. The technology of personal telecommunications and the rich, diverse BBS culture that is growing on every continent today were created by citizens, not doomsday weapon designers or corporate researchers. (p. 131)

Clearly, for proponents of this view, electronic publishing technologies represent a tremendous opportunity to encourage direct participatory democracy.

Old technologies and media forms placed severe restrictions on democratic systems. For example, the United States was forced to develop the electoral college system because of limited means of communication; it simply wasn't technologically feasible for voters to participate directly in elections when the fastest available means of communication depended on horses. Instead, a system of representation had to be worked out for voting and, for that matter, every other aspect of the day-to-day governing of the country as well.

Of course, representative democratic systems drive a wedge between individual citizens and government. The voices of individual citizens are necessarily mediated through numerous levels of representation, and, conversely, information regarding the government's activities is mediated as it travels back to the individual (see Tehranian, 1988, pp. 50–53). Furthermore, to understand the "technologies of freedom" perspective on electronic publishing, it is important to note that the terms mediation and representation suggest supplementation and/or loss. Putting aside for the moment the issue of whether a message can exist without a medium, mediation or the act of putting a message into a medium suggests that the content is altered. Put in terms of McLuhan's (1972) famous dictum, the medium massages the message. Thus, for critics of representative democratic systems, to mediate is to create an alternative or an Other reality.

Similarly, representation, suggests that the originary presence of the object being represented is either lost or supplemented. As the poststructuralist critique of presence makes clear, the representation of an object cannot be the thing itself; it is a simulacrum, a copy. Hence, the signifier (the simulacrum) floats free from the referent (the object) because the presence of the original is lost, and new meaning is supplemented. In terms of representative democracies therefore, citizens' objects float free of their representatives' simulacra. The will of the people is lost because the peoples' presence is lost to alternative simulacra.

As a consequence of all this message massaging and the loss of presence, critics of representative democracy argue for *direct* participatory democracy, and they see in electronic media a potential means of realizing this heretofore abstract and ideal form of democracy. As Tehranian (1988) puts it, "If democracy is considered government by dialog, the new technologies have turned the theoretical possibility of *direct* democracy and democratic will formation into a real opportunity" (p. 214, emphasis added). Electronic publishing (at least from this perspective) thus offers voice to people who have been silenced by oppressive, exclusionary social forces and political hegemonies. It gives expression to people for whom no appropriate simulacra can be found. It is a centrifugal force that works against centralization, conformity, and homogeneity.

It is worth noting that the argument that electronic publishing can somehow recover or even more closely approximate a direct presence lost through mediation stands in contradiction to Poster's (1990) analysis of the mediation resulting from NT. Poster uses the same idea of simulacra produced by mediation described in the previous paragraph, but he uses it to show how (rather than reducing the distance between a presence and a simulacrum) electronic mediation has the opposite effect (pp. 8–14). He argues that electronic texts represent a third stage of mediation that is more distant than either the first, oral stage (where the speaker is physically present) or the second, print stage (where the book is physically present and the author's presence is represented in it [p. 6]). For Poster then, presence in the electronic medium is "decentered, dispersed, and multiplied in continuous instability" because electronic texts exist in a virtual as opposed to actual space (p. 6). Thus, the idea of using electronic publishing to produce a more *direct* form of participatory democracy becomes extremely problematic.

However, in spite of Poster's insightful analysis of the problems of representation, there are at least three basic reasons why proponents of direct participatory democracy continue to find such promise in electronic publishing: 1) access to means of production, 2) access to privileged information, and 3) loss of repressive contexts.

Access to Means of Production

The increasing access to means of production that results from electronic publishing was partially explored in the preceding discussion of desktop publishing. Yet, new technology makes it possible for individuals not only to produce professional or authentic looking publications "from their basements" (Wahlstrom, 1989, p. 175), but it also allows them to become powerful distribution centers; it allows them to become what many are starting to call electronic citizens.

Today, with $200–$300 for a modem, communications software, a used PC, and a telephone line, an individual can set up his or her own electronic bulletin board system or BBS. Or with a $2,000–$3,000 investment in the electronic equivalent of the printing press, private citizens can produce and distribute World Wide Web publications on any topic or topics they consider important, and have the ability to reach a potential audience easily as large as their local newspaper or television station. To start a BBS, all you need to do is publish a telephone number other computer users can dial to access the BBS, store publications on your hard drives, and wait for people interested in the BBS's topics to start communicating. And the potential political effect of even such a small BBS can be startling. Consider, for example, the following anecdote from Deward's (1988) *Electronic Citizenship*:

> Dave Hughes is a pamphleteer and activist in the tradition of Tom Paine or the U.S. Revolution's Committees of Correspondence, but he uses a laptop computer instead of a quill pen, and a modem in place of a printing press. He set up his first grassroots computer bulletin board as a platform for complaints about a local condominium developer in his home town of Colorado Springs. Provided with the written transcripts of comments by more than thirty builders, gathered via the computer bulletin board, the building department ruled in favor of the homeowners. Hughes, a retired West Point instructor and veteran of Korea and Vietnam, now runs Chariot, a sophisticated bulletin board system in Colorado Springs. He uses his computer and modem to mobilize action in local political matters, such as the city councilman he helped elect and the proposed city ordinance he helped defeat. (pp. 2–3)

Hughes' experiences are not unique. In 1988, Rheingold reported that there were an estimated 7,000 to 10,000 BBSs in the United States (pp. 6–5), a surprisingly large number when we consider that the mass marketing of personal computers didn't begin until the 1980s. Furthermore, the numbers of BBSs seems likely to increase even more dramatically as more nonprofit organizations become aware of their potential. The Society for Technical Communication, for example, set up a BBS that STC members can access to get a nationwide listing of other public domain bulletin board systems, an online searchable bibliography of all articles printed in *Technical Communications* since 1978, bibliographical information about doctoral dissertations and masters' theses, a national listing of job openings in technical communications, a message system allowing callers to communicate with each other, and many other options ("STC's BBS," p. 8). Similarly, the Indiana Department of Education set up a BBS called "IDEAnet" which allows elementary, secondary, and college teachers and students from all over Indiana to share information and discuss their concerns. The Society for Critical Exchange has its "College of Electronic Theory" BBS on the Cleveland FreeNet, and the NCTE's Committee on Instructional Technology and the Association for Business Communication are also currently discussing ways of setting up BBSs for their members.

All of these examples are based on a select group of organizations interested in promoting writing; an individual interested in other areas such as religion, environment issues, politics, or pornography will find a similar explosion in the number of BBSs. Consequently, private individuals and nonprofit organizations all over the country are finding that WANS and BBS technologies allow more individuals to distribute information more easily about a more diverse number of topics than was ever possible when commercial printing houses held the only available means of publishing. And therefore, proponents of electronic citizenship argue that BBS technology encourages more people to become directly involved in the free exchange of ideas essential to participatory democracy—though, as the next chapter will show, this exchange of ideas may not be as free as some would have us believe. Nevertheless, proponents of electronic citizenship like Connolly, et al. (1991a) argue that "the new electronic technologies, including digital technologies, are powerful media that constitute an increasingly important institution for information dissemination for all citizens" (p. 37).

Access to Privileged Information

The second feature of electronic publishing that proponents of direct participatory democracy see as valuable is that the technology gives a wider range of social classes access to information. In one sense, this is the flip side of the access to means of production argument. Because more and more private individuals and small organizations can produce information, individual readers may consume a wider variety of facts, arguments, and interpretations than is possible when an elite few determine who can publish and who cannot. As Barlow (1992) put it:

> A clear demonstration of this principle was visible during the recent coup in the Soviet Union. Because of the decentralized and redundant nature of digital media, it was impossible for the geriatric plotters in the Kremlin to suppress the delivery of truth.

Other examples closer to home indicate how increased access to information seems to prevent an elite few from dominating the versions of reality represented for public consumption. For example, during the U.S. invasion of Panama, private American citizens whose sources of information were limited to traditional print and television news media received a very different picture of the conflict than did readers of USENET's MISC.HEADLINES discussion group. In the traditional media, much was made of the professionalism of American troops. Special analysts (usually retired military officers) were hired by the major television networks to explain how having an all volunteer force allowed the United States to put committed, superbly trained troops in the field, thereby avoiding the kinds of atrocities committed by the nervous, frightened, trigger-happy draftees of the Vietnam era.

In the MISC.HEADLINES group, certain individuals also deployed this same strategy to reassure readers that Panama would not become America's second Vietnam. However, because MISC.HEAD-LINES is an open forum where individuals from all over the world can publish, other views of the military conflict were also given voice. Readers of MISC.HEADLINES also read accounts of frightened, young American troops patrolling city streets, so terrified by the prospect of snipers that they mistakenly shot an innocent, unarmed Spanish journalist. The fact that this and other such incidents received virtually no coverage in the U.S. print and television media are examples of how the re/presentations and media/tions of an elite few leave individual consumers with an extremely limited number of simulacra upon which to base their versions of reality.

However, beyond simply offering consumers a greater variety of simulacra to choose from, there is another sense in which providing greater access to information can lead to a more direct form of participatory democracy. The argument here is that giving greater access to information helps break down the class structures inherent in representative democratic systems. In other words, electronic publishing can be used to give the lower and middle classes access to information that previously had been out of their reach because of its expense, information that they can then use to construct their own simulacra.

To put this in the same sort of terms Kuhn (1970) uses to describe paradigm shifts, greater access to facts and information means that there is more opportunity for the disenfranchised to point out phenomena that represent challenges to established paradigms. Indeed, this same line of argument could account for much of the recent interest in North's (1987) concept of the practitioner. Classroom teachers have traditionally been seen to have a subservient and almost parasitic relationship with theorists. However, North attempts to elevate teachers' status in the field by making the practice side of the Theory/practice binary into a source of information or a source of phenomena that may challenge entrenched theories. That is, North's view makes teachers into a valuable repository or database of information which, consequently, forces the theoretical elite at least to account for the views of teachers.[7] It gives those on the margins the opportunity to discover events, facts, or phenomena that can't adequately be explained by traditionally accepted theoretical models, thereby forcing changes and revisions in the old in order to accommodate the new. In this same way then, the greater access to information afforded by WANS allows more people to function as agents of change and forces entrenched and elitist systems to take the views of more individuals into account.

Consider, for example, the effect WANS might have on our educational system. Traditionally, only the very wealthy could afford to give their children access to the information services provided by top research institutions. The classrooms, libraries, and other resources of Harvard, Yale, Johns Hopkins, and other large research institutions traditionally have been beyond the reach of all but a select few. However, the use of WANS for distance education and the networking of students at different colleges and universities is breaking down institutional walls. In a writing course which I taught in the Spring of 1992, for example, my students participated in online classroom discussions with students at St. Catherine's College in St. Paul, Minnesota; Clarkson University in Potsdam, New York; Eastern Michigan State University in Ypsilanti, Michigan; and Ecole Superieure d'Electricite in Paris, France—all at the same time.

This use of WANS in educational settings challenges traditional notions of the classroom. "My" students were no longer walled up inside a room with the ideas, information, and perspectives of just one instructor; they had (at least) five instructors, each one pulling on a different pool of resources, offering different teaching strategies, and providing different interpretations of the subjects being

---

[7] Obviously, this position overlooks the fact that teachers cannot be seen either as a "valuable repository or 'database' of information" if the data contained within "them" are flawed due to methodological errors. However, it must also be pointed out that to make the methodological argument against the value of teachers' data is to resituate the issue on epistemological and theoretical grounds, thereby reasserting the primacy of Theory over practice. Phelps (1991) makes a similar point regarding the status of North's practitioner in her article, "Practical Wisdom and the Geography of Knowledge in Composition." She counters North's assertion that advocating teacher research and "lore" is "a means of re-empowering practitioners" by pointing out that "if, however, 'research' continues to mean only formal inquiry, and formal inquiry is the only legitimate source of knowledge, then these efforts do not really change anything except, perhaps, to give some practitioners a marginal role in research" (Phelps, 1991, p. 864). In other words, though some space for insights of practitioners may be created, the primacy of Theory over practice remains intact and unchallenged.

discussed in our virtual classroom. Through the use of WANS, physical presence is no longer required to gain access to what Bourdieu (1984) calls the "educational capital" provided by particular institutional sites. Thus, middle class students in Indiana can participate in some of the same educational experiences that, for example, only those wealthy enough to go to school abroad could afford.[8]

Proponents of direct participatory democracy see this sort of electronic publishing and wide-area networking activity as a means of breaking down or at least beginning to cut across traditional socioeconomic classes because it gives more egalitarian access to the information used in decision-making. Soon, they argue, it will no longer be necessary to travel to large research libraries to collect the information we need to construct arguments that will affect governmental and other decision-making processes. Through WANS, distant and underfunded researchers, educators, and students will have the same access to information that only the privileged elite once had. Indeed, once the U.S. Congress authorized the funding of NREN, the new, high-speed research and education network, "a one-room schoolhouse in rural South Dakota could download sizable chunks of the Library of Congress during lunch hour" (Rheingold, 1991a, p. 37). This kind of technological progress has led proponents of direct participatory democracy to argue that WANS and electronic publishing will eventually break the information access monopoly of the upper class—though, once again, this presupposes that WANS and electronic publishing will remain free of economic or governmental regulation. More importantly however, proponents of electronic publishing continually fail to recognize the tremendous regulatory power of consumers' *a priori* expectations or the ways readers write writers.

Loss of Repressive Contextual Cues

The third feature of electronic publishing and computer-mediated communication that holds out promise for direct participatory

---

[8] In the example here, I've described only individual courses that have moved online; however, entire degree granting programs and even universities are beginning to appear online. See, for example, the article "Happily Modeming to School" in the Spring 1992 issue of *Online Access* where Earnest catalogs eight institutions offering advanced degrees in business administration, general education, or other areas that have typically been pursued by nontraditional or continuing education students who cannot attend regular university classes because they work full-time and have children, spouses, mortgages, or other obligations that prevent them from having access to traditional educational environments (pp. 6–7).

democrats is the way electronic publications eliminate many con-
textual cues, and thereby authorize voices traditionally silenced in
other media. As Eldred (1991) has noted, "almost everyone who has
worked with the technology notes that networking's main advantage is the egalitarian quality of the participants' discourse, the
dissolving of certain inequities—produced by gender, class, eth-
nicity, and personality differences" (p. 53). Electronic messages in
open forums like MISC.HEADLINES or PURTOPOI lack many of the
social and cultural forces that operate in oral situations. Because
discussions occur in a virtual rather than a physical space, many
of the spatial cues participants use to determine their place in the
social hierarchy are missing. Students in a virtual classroom
aren't constantly reminded of how unimportant they are because
there are no neat little rows for them to sit in and because nobody
is at the front of the room to dominate and direct the discussion.
Similarly, in an on-line business meeting, there is no head or
chair to the conference table and no visual representation of the
distance of each person from that head.[9] Physical presence within
these spatial arrangements neither authorizes nor silences participants; instead, in online discussions each person "speaks" from
the same ill-defined virtual space.

Furthermore, as Eldred noted, gender, class, and racial considerations are more difficult to introduce into e-mail discussions because of the loss of physical presence. Outward
appearance, hand and facial gestures, the well-timed cough—all
are missing from e-mail exchanges. And this observation has led
many to argue that individuals who would normally remain
silent in oral exchanges to keep from drawing attention to their
physical appearances are, instead, authorized to speak in e-mail
discussions. Thus, the argument is: no longer oppressed by the
white, masculine, homophobic gaze of superiority, voices previously unre*present*ed in traditional discourses are now given a
forum where they may be heard. In other words, with the elimination of repressive contexts, people are thought to feel freer to
express their true inner selves via e-mail. There have even been
empirical studies that would seem to support this contention.
For example, Kiesler, et al. (1985) conducted a study comparing
the oral communication of two people meeting for the first time

[9] It is worth noting that the terms head and chair have, of course, become titles
of authority rather than merely descriptors of a spatial location, indicating how
much importance we have put on physical presence and spatial relationships in
our oral discursive practices.

with the computer-mediated communication of similar pairings. In their study, Kiesler, et al. found that the computer users were five times more likely to engage in emotionally revealing behaviors than were people in oral pairs (p. 97), suggesting, as Eldred (1991) also points out, that "on-line conversations are usually much more forthright than face-to-face encounters" (p. 49). In short then, e-mail is often touted as a liberating force that lets its users escape repressive social contexts, enabling them to speak with voices that are supposedly more sincere, honest, authentic, or true reflections of their individual selves. Freed from the corruption of social mediation (a freedom challenged in the subsequent chapters), e-mail voices are thus said to be more direct forms of representation.

These claims about the ways networking promotes more egalitarian discourse are perhaps the direct participatory democrats' most powerful arguments in support of their project. They give the impression that technologies of freedom or wide-area networks can be used to give voice to the true, inner thoughts of both the oppressed and the unoppressed. What's more, they suggest that fundamental, systemic changes in our political, educational, and social relationships are what's at stake in any debate about the future of electronic publishing. Indeed, Rheingold (1993) claims that "the political significance of CMC lies in its capacity to challenge the existing political hierarchy's monopoly on powerful communications media, and perhaps thus revitalize citizen-based democracy" (p. 14). Similarly, Barlow (1992), cofounder of the Electronic Frontier Foundation, argues that the "most profound consequence [of wide-area networking] should be the global liberation of everyone's speech. A truly open and accessible Net will become an environment of expression which no single government could stifle" (see footnote 3). Whether or not a "truly open and accessible Net" is possible (or even desirable) is a central issue taken up more directly in subsequent chapters. However, for the time being it is enough to point out that these are the three arguments that are commonly offered in support of electronic publishing as a democratizing force.

WHO CONTROLS OR OWNS ELECTRONIC TEXTS?

Clearly, the increased access to available means of production and consumption and the encouragement of more egalitarian forms of discourse are compelling arguments for the increased use of

WANS technology in our society. Certainly, these arguments make clear that important issues are at stake in the control of e-texts, for there are few in our society who would not oppose censorship and who would not support more pluralistic involvement in our government.

However, despite the laudability of the goals, arguments like Barlow's still assume the "presence" of an active agency. They presuppose a theory of subjectivity capable of resistance and an epistemological stance that still has its roots in the Kantian concept of common sense and the supersensible realm of Truth to which common sense gives us access (Kant, trans. 1988).

In Barlow's (1992) electronic essay "The Great Work," one can see how arguments for using WANS to promote direct participatory democracy (which is what Barlow means by "the Great Work") leads to this individualistic communitarian view of subjectivity. However, before I begin my examination of how Barlow's essay reveals his dependence on individualistic communitarian ideals, I should also note that Barlow's work is of particular interest here because Barlow is the cofounder of the EFF or Electronic Frontier Foundation[10] which, along with EDUCOM, is one of the most active and influential organizations in the development of WANS technology. For those unfamiliar with WANS politics, the EFF might be considered "the ACLU of wide-area networking." It has had and continues to play a significant role in the formation of WAN policies by providing legal assistance in court cases involving WANS, offering expert testimony at congressional hearings on the NREN, stimulating and supporting both academic and technological research on WANS, and serving as the public's watchdog for governmental activity. Because he is one of the leaders of this organization and because the EFF has played such an important role in WANS development, Barlow's comments are thus particularly interesting in the context of this discussion and need to be treated seriously.

At the beginning of his essay, Barlow invokes the work of Teilhard de Chardin in support of his project, pointing out that Teilhard saw the final goal of human evolution as that moment

---

[10] The EFF's other cofounder and current president is Mitch Kapor, the principle developer of the Lotus 1–2–3 spreadsheet program, CEO of the huge Lotus Development Corp., and Chairman of the Commercial Internet Exchange. In addition to cofounding the EFF and serving on its Board of Directors, John Perry Barlow is perhaps best known as the lyricist for the Grateful Dead. Other notable figures in the EFF hierarchy include Steve Wozniak, cofounder of Apple Corp., and Jerry Berman, former head of the ACLU Information Technology Project.

"when all consciousness would converge into unity, creating the collective organism of Mind" (Barlow, 1992). He then goes on to say of wide-area networking that:

> Whether or not it represents Teilhard's vision, it seems clear we are about some Great Work here ... the physical wiring of collective human consciousness. The idea of connecting every mind to every other mind in full-duplex broadband is one which, for a hippie mystic like me, has clear theological implications, despite the fact that most of the builders [of WANS] are bit wranglers and protocol priests, a proudly prosaic lot. What Thoughts will all this assembled neurology, silicon, and optical fiber Think? (Barlow, 1992)

Whether we're dealing with Teilhard's "Omega Point" or Emerson's "OverSoul" or Kant's "Realm of the Supersensible," Barlow's position clearly indicates that he is taking a transcendentalist epistemological stance and is promoting the development of a unified consciousness that exists outside, above, or beyond the constituted consciousness of a local, contingent, and particular community. Indeed, as Barlow suggests in his use of the term theological, he is dealing with a god-like form of consciousness, one that is general, absolute, and universal. Consequently, Barlow doesn't see the liberation of individual voices as a means of allowing competing ideologies to be heard; for him, all ideologies are forms of false consciousness. Political, economic, and social contexts mediate between the pure thoughts of one individual and another. Contexts and ideologies are corruptions of the commonsensical, self-evident Truths that will be made manifest when there is no longer any noise or filter to disrupt the signal being sent to receiver. When every individual brain is hardwired to every other brain, there will no longer be any need for violent and oppressive class systems, no need to adjudicate between competing versions of reality, no need for rhetorics. Instead, we will all be unified under the harsh light of one absolute, acontextual Truth.

Thus, for Barlow, those who argue that there must be commonly observed conventions in order for communication to occur are merely protocol priests who want to maintain their authority and dominance over others; they are "a proudly prosaic lot" who lack the imagination to see how the anarchy of free expression can (paradoxically) lead to the "collective organism of Mind." Barlow thus devalues the roles that tradition and the pre-existing expectations of audience play in the development of electronic media. Indeed, his attack on the protocol priests reveals this limitation in his position, for protocols, despite Barlow's antagonism toward them, are what make networks and networking possible.

A protocol, in the context of WANS technology, refers to the standards or conventions used to transfer data across a network. In effect, a protocol represents an agreement among system administrators on the common language that their computers will use to talk to each other. The fact that computers may be physically connected together doesn't mean that they form a network for the same reason that sharing geographical and spatial boundaries isn't a sufficient condition of community. The individual computer sites or network nodes only represent the physical makeup of a network; for *networking* to occur, there must also be the same sharing of values, expectations, or mutual knowledge discussed by communitarian theorists like Hillery (1955, 1959), Effra (1974), Taylor (1982), and Sandel (1982). In networking systems, protocols represent this same kind of sharing.

For example, individual computer sites on the Internet use the TCP/IP or Transmission Control Protocol/Internet Protocol, and this protocol, as its name implies, controls the transmission of data. To send data from a network user's host computer to some other remote computer on the network, the Internet uses packet-switched networking technology. This means that data from a user are broken down into small, easily transferred chunks that are then stuffed into packets or envelopes that are then stamped with the address of a remote computer. The packets are then sent through a chain of sites on the network until they reach the remote computer whose address was stamped on the packets. Once the packets arrive, they are unpacked, reassembled, and processed. However, without some kind of protocol to guide this process, the remote host computer wouldn't know how to reassemble the packets into a usable (we might even say meaningful) form. Indeed, without mutually observed conventions, first, by the host site that creates the packets; second, by the nodes between the sender and receiver that forward the packets along; and, third, by the remote site that interprets and reassembles the packets, *no communication would be possible*. The host computer wouldn't know how to create packets and address them; the sites between the host and remote computers wouldn't know how to interpret the addresses stamped on each packet or how to forward the packets along the chain to the remote site; and finally the remote site wouldn't know what to do with the packets once they got there.

Of course, when I say that without protocols, no communication on networks would be possible, I'm not saying that the

TCP/IP protocol previously described is a technological reality we must accept. The TCP/IP is only one of many protocols, each with its own brand of politics and ideological implications. My point here is not that protocols represent a technological determinism that is above critique. In fact, I do offer critiques of both the packet-switched and store-and-forward protocols used by Internet and BITNET (see Howard, 1992) elsewhere. My point is that *some* kind of protocol is required for communication to occur. Hence, Barlow's attempt to eliminate protocol priests is concomitantly an attempt to eliminate communication itself.

Barlow's (1992) acontextualized, information-transfer model of computer-mediated communication is idealistic and fails to take into account the necessary mediation and representation that occurs on WANS even at their most elementary level. Indeed, despite the fact that Shannon's information-transfer model has its analogical origins in electrical engineering technology, the processes used in packet-switched technology more closely resembles Iser's (1980) theory of textual gaps discussed at the beginning of this chapter. In other words, just as Iser's readers are confronted with a series of textual events that they must reassemble into meaningful wholes, networked computers are confronted with a series of packets that they also must reassemble. And just as readers depend on their community's repertoire of pre-existing conventions, networked computers depend on their community's protocols to both produce and consume information.

FOUR ANSWERS

Although Iser's theory more closely resembles the actual process of packet-switching, it would be a mistake to completely dispense with Barlow's information-transfer model, for it offers an answer to the question of who controls the e-text in ways that Iser's model cannot. In other words, Barlow's model is useful, if only as a heuristic, because of its difference from the other answers to the question of who controls the e-text discussed in this chapter. In fact, there are four different approaches to electronic publishing that show that, depending on the perspective taken, either the publisher, the reader, the interpretive community, or the author may control or own the meaning of electronic texts. Sullivan's (1991) and Wahlstrom's (1989) analyses were useful because they showed how publishers can control texts; Haas' (1989) and Ong's (1977) discussions of memory suggest how readers control texts; and, finally, Iser's repertoire and

Fish's (1980a, 1980b) interpretive community offer communal codes and traditions as other potential factors that may control texts. Rather than the publisher, the reader, or the interpretive community, Barlow's model is useful because it implies that the author controls an e-text since it is the author's original insight into the self-evident, acontextual realm of Truth that ultimately controls e-textual meaning for Barlow.

We need all these explanations of who controls e-texts if we are to evaluate the explanatory power of each individual theory. None of these approaches alone is able to completely suture the possibilities in electronic texts; each has blind spots. For that matter, even if it were possible to utilize all of these approaches simultaneously (an impossibility given the epistemological incompatibilities between them), then we still could not exhaust the range of factors that may contribute to the control of electronic texts. There is no alter/native framework that will encompass the whole of the electronic publishing medium; there is no frameless frame.

However, it is possible to play each approach in relation to an/Other to see what explanatory space is described. Consequently, armed with an understanding of what's at stake in electronic publishing and the question of who controls it, the next chapter turns to an examination of the play between individualistic and constitutive communitarian approaches to a particular community in the WANS medium.

chapter four

Theoretical
Conceptions of
Community

INTRODUCTION

I have suggested that electronic communities are analogous to traditional communities that communicate through the printed medium, and, furthermore, because the NT medium defamiliarizes assumptions researchers tend to make about print- or speech-based communities, it is possible to gain the critical distance necessary for a better understanding of theoretical models of discourse communities. The difference between electronic communities and print-based communities will enable the conditions necessary for knowledge production, and since difference requires that each side be given voice, we need to establish the print-based notions of community from which I will differ and often defer.

Unfortunately, there is a problem with simply positing the existence of electronic communities. Because of the spatial baggage it has traditionally carried, the term community cannot be so easily applied in electronic environments as we might think. Consider, for example, the problem of prosecuting California-based system operators for maintaining an adult BBS that allowed users in Tennessee to download X-rated electronic images (Rose, 1995, p. 102). The problem is that the Supreme

Court has consistently held that the obscenity of materials must be judged in the context of *local community* standards so that people have the right to choose whether or not they wish to live in morally restrictive or liberal communities. If someone in Tennessee (where X-rated images are considered illegal) connects to a BBS in California (where they are not), then the question is which community standards should obtain? Should the system operators in California be responsible for obscenity laws in someone else's community? Should the Tennessee users be held accountable for taking actions that violated the laws of their community? Or is there a third alternative? Are there one or more online, electronic communities here that exist independently of the spatially-based communities in Tennessee and California? And if there are legally recognizable online communities, as Rose (1995) suggests, then "shouldn't we allow them to function in their own right, and not hold them hostage to the rules of whatever land-based jurisdiction chooses to haul an online user into court on a given day" (p. 102)? More importantly, if there are online communities, then what theory of community can we use to articulate the borders between particular communities so that it is possible to examine and discuss the local standards of a specific online community? To begin developing such a theory of community, this chapter examines some previous definitions and uses of community.

VARYING SOME CONCEPTIONS OF COMMUNITY

As a theoretical concept, community has garnered considerable attention in the field of rhetoric, and, as a result, several rhetorical theorists have already traced the term discourse community back to the sociolinguistic term speech community as it was developed by Labov (1970), Hymes (1980), and Halliday (1973) (see for example Freed & Broadhead, 1987; Nystrand, 1982; Porter, 1992, 1986; Rafoth, 1990, 1988, and Romaine, 1982). Because the linkage between speech community and discourse community already seems well-established in our field, it is not necessary to rehearse the traditional introduction to the speech community. I want to deviate from the approach rhetoricians have traditionally taken in their discussions of discourse community in order to focus on the term community from a multidisciplinary perspective. I will only point out that rhetorical theorists, Freed and Broadhead for example, have generally focused on distinguishing the concept of a speech community from a discourse community, "in order to signal the focus on the written rather than just the spoken" (1987, p. 154).

There is explanatory power to be gained by examining the term community for its own sake since communitarian theorists who utilize concepts like speech community, discourse community, or interpretive community must presuppose some theory of community however tacit or unvoiced. Merely coupling community with some other term may not be enough and may even compound the problem since, as Stamm (1985) notes:

> The concept of community becomes a potential "spoiler" as it is all too casually coupled with a number of other concepts.... The deception is that community appears to narrow down the meaning of the term it's coupled with, to make reference to a particular kind of identification, attachment, involvement, and so on. (p. 13)

In actuality, community has a great deal of play in it; Hillery (1955), for example, found 16 different conceptions in his review of the term, and he was looking at the uses of community prior to 1955 (p. 112). Based on his survey of 94 definitions of the term, Hillery concluded that "when all of the definitions are viewed, beyond the concept that people are involved in community, there is no complete agreement as to the nature of community" (1955, p. 119). It therefore seems clear that, "if we want to be clear about the meanings of the various concepts of community tie, we'd better start with community" (Stamm, 1985, p. 13).

THE SPATIAL AS A CONDITION OF COMMUNITY

An examination of the term community (*sans* speech) shows that the early sociolinguistic use of the term was based, at least initially, on the pedestrian notion of community as a geographical or spatial unit: that is, a village, town, burgh, or neighborhood. Indeed, perhaps the most influential of those early sociolinguists, Labov (1970), basically was functioning as a dialectologist studying the correlation between geographical location and vernacular so that the term community essentially represented the geographical boundaries within which the ethnographer was situated. And, of course, this spatial view of community made sense because the oral behaviors studied by dialectologists generally presuppose face-to-face communication and close physical proximity. Yet, despite the fact that NT doesn't require close physical proximity, space and spatial metaphors are also extremely important in electronic environments. It is common-place for networkers to use the term cyberspace to describe the con-text in which NT communications exist. Indeed, networkers often talk about navigating through cyberspace and traveling to various electronic communities around the Net. Interface designers often draw maps of their programs to represent the virtual space through which users must travel, an activity that helps them write more usable software and that also allows Selfe and Selfe (1994) to point out that "the maps of computer interfaces order the virtual world according to a certain set of historical and social values that make up our culture" (p. 485). Thus, even though WANS have given us the technological ability to transcend the limitations of physical prox-imity, we nevertheless seem metaphorically mortgaged to the spa-tial in NT theory.

This same spatial view of community has dominated the com-munitarian literature. As Stamm (1985) notes, "most researchers agree that a community can be a place with bound-aries that distinguish it from other places" (p. 18). And Hillery (1955) argues that the spatial is the most significant and persis-tent factor in the 94 definitions of community he surveyed. He found that "a majority of the definitions include the following as important elements of the community: area, common ties, and social interaction (in increasing importance for each separate element, respectively)" (p. 118).

This emphasis on the spatial that Hillery found in 1955 has continued to serve as the basis for several definitions and typolo-gies of community. For example, in his 1959 essay "A Critique of Selected Community Concepts," Hillery himself offers the native village as a kind of Arnoldian touchstone for other types of com-munities. He proposes that the village serve as the ideal model against which all other types of communities should be compared, and defines the village as "a social group inhabiting a common ter-ritory and having one or more additional common ties" (p. 237). By emphasizing common territory over and above all other additional common ties, Hillery makes geographical boundaries a necessary condition of community.

To be fair, it should be noted that Hillery (1959) recognizes the limitations of the spatial when he observes that "possibly some day man can ignore these [geographical] barriers" (p. 240), open-ing the door for McLuhan's (1968) "global village," Hiltz and

Turoff's (1978) "network nation," and what I am calling electronic communities. However, Hillery (1959) dismisses this as speculative and argues that "large collectivities," like the world, nations and even major cities, lack "spatial integration" and therefore make poor communities (p. 240). Thus, Hillery, for all practical purposes, makes spatial boundaries into an essential component of community.

Another communitarian theorist who makes the spatial into a criterion of community is Marcia Effrat. In her 1974 book *The Community*, Effrat also proposes that geographical boundaries should serve as one of two criteria for determining whether or not a particular grouping represents a community. Her second criterion is the existence of institutions—political bodies for example. However, in Effrat's system, unlike Hillery's, the presence of geographical boundaries is a sufficient condition for bestowing the status of community on a group rather than just a necessary condition. The existence of spatial boundaries is enough for Effrat to bestow community status on a collectivity.

Even when communitarian theorists don't use the spatial as a sufficient or necessary condition of community, they often use it as a measure of the cohesiveness of a community. Taylor (1982), for example, argues that there are three core characteristics that communities share (p. 26). First, they share, to varying degrees, some set(s) of "beliefs and values" (p. 26). Second, a community's members must communicate in such a way that "relations between members should be *direct* and they should be *many-sided*" (p. 27). And third, communities have a characteristic that Taylor calls "reciprocity" (p. 28). Reciprocity is an extremely important concept in communitarian theory, one to which we will return in greater detail later. But for the moment, it is sufficient to say that reciprocity describes situations where individual members of a community engage in seemingly altruistic behaviors for the purpose of achieving their long-term goals (cf. Corlett, 1989, pp. 16–22; Taylor, 1982, p. 28). In other words, members of a community make short-term sacrifices in order to receive the long-term benefits of membership in the community.

However, in the present discussion, it is Taylor's (1982) second characteristic that I wish to emphasize, particularly his emphatic assertion that relations "should be *direct*" (p. 27). His use of "should" here betrays the fact that Taylor is not simply describing characteristics of community, though this is what he appears to want us to believe when he writes that:

there is not and there cannot be an exhaustive specification of the conditions for the correct use of the concept [of community], a set of criteria or tests which are both necessary and sufficient for something to be deemed a community. There are, however, three attributes or characteristics possessed in *some* degree by *all* communities. (p. 26)

However, by discussing attributes that a community should have, Taylor slips into a prescriptive mode of discourse and ends up arguing that relations between members of a community *need* to be "direct to the extent that they are unmediated—by representatives, leaders, bureaucrats, institutions such as those of the state, or by codes, abstractions and reifications" (p. 28). This emphasis on direct, unmediated communication between members of a community has the effect of reintroducing the spatial into his discussion, for he essentially rules out any nonspatial modes of communication when he eliminates institutional or other potential modes. He clearly prefers face-to-face forms of communication over others. Thus, when he comes to a community like the academic community (one which has his first and third attributes but has limited *direct* relations between its members), he is forced to conclude that it is "less of a community than, for example, primitive communities" (p. 28). For Taylor therefore, the spatial becomes a means of determining a particular group's degree of "communitiness." Furthermore, his use of primitive communities as the touchstone against which the academic community is compared suggests that, like Hillery (1959), Taylor also uses the village as the ideal form to which all other forms must measure up.

LIMITATIONS OF THE SPATIAL

Clearly then, the spatial has served an important role in communitarian literature, often defining what is and is not a community. It is most often used overtly—either by itself or in conjunction with concepts like shared beliefs and institutions—to determine whether a grouping may be called a community or not. Alternatively, as was illustrated by Taylor's three characteristics of community, the spatial covertly creeps into a theorist's discussion where it continues to serve as the basis for including some collectivities and excluding others. For students of electronic communities, however, this commonplace, geographical notion of community is inadequate for the following three reasons.

First, the spatial element of community does not account for what are otherwise commonly accepted as legitimate communities. It excludes important collectivities that most people would normally include—for example, environmentalists, bankers, or chemists. And yet, so compelling is the spatial, there are even communitarian theorists who continue to use it as an important component in their definitions of community in spite of its limitations. Stamm (1985), for example, continues to use place as one of his major features of community,[1] while admitting that "it's [sic] utility has been quite limited, as most communities are not spatially confined to strict territorial boundaries" (p. 16). The spatial has tremendous difficulty accounting for what Taylor (1982) calls "intentional communities," (e.g., "monastic" or "utopian" communities) or for "specialised [sic] communities" (e.g., the academic community or the economic community [p. 26]). These sorts of intentional or specialized communities are bounded by their members' goals and intentions rather than geographical location and are therefore excluded by the spatial use of the term; yet, intentional and specialized communities are precisely the type that can be found in electronic environments.

Second, the spatial notion of community is inadequate for NT researchers because it presupposes the kinds of media a community can use for its communicative ties. It has the effect in communitarian theory of privileging orality over NT. Communication on computer networks cut across spatial boundaries. In fact, it is extremely difficult to specify any physical location for NT. Network users use the metaphor of virtual space to describe the location where they communicate because they speak amidst the virtual memories of their computers' memory chips. For this reason, networkers frequently sign their e-mail messages "Virtually Yours" to signify the transient, ephemeral space they occupy in their computers' short-term memories. Hiltz and Turoff (1978) have also noted this difficulty with the traditional notion of community. They point out that a computer network "obviates the necessity to be co-located in a dense urban

---

[1] The other two elements of Stamm's (1985) community are structure and process. By structure, Stamm is referring to the same sorts of institutions seen in Effrat's (1974) system. By process, he is referring to shared goals and values and the social activities intended to achieve them (cf., pp. 17–19).

area in order to have sufficient cheap communication ties" (p. xxvii), ties that dialectologists like Labov (1970) presupposed in their research. Instead, Hiltz and Turoff (1978) argue that "in place of thinking of a nation or society as a collection of [geographical] communities, we need to think of it as a complex set of overlapping networks of actual or potential communication and exchange" (p. xxviii) and, thus, distance themselves from the spatial definition of community.

Finally, the spatial notion of community is problematic because it doesn't address the status of the individual within the community, nor does it address the role of epistemological and ideological forces within the community. In fact, a vulgar, geographical view of community may actually lend itself to the notion that communities are composed of individual, transcendent subjects who have been accidentally collected together within a fixed space.

DEFINITION AND PLAY

Clearly, NT researchers need a definition of community that is more inclusive than the traditional use of the term, both in terms of the types of communities it admits and the factors it takes into consideration. Unfortunately, however, as Taylor (1982) notes, "'community' is an *open-textured* concept" (p. 26) and resists attempts to "close" (Eco, 1979, p. 8) or "cerne" it (Smith, 1988, p. xxx). One of the reasons for the open-textured nature of the term is that a particular conception of community deeply imbricates a theorist in hegemonic processes, since to offer a definition of community, the communitarian theorist must address questions involving subjectivity, epistemology, and agency. To offer a definition of community is, therefore, to make the kind of totalizing gesture poststructuralists seek to avoid or, more accurately, to defer (since the articulatory moment makes complete avoidance impossible [cf. Laclau & Mouffee, 1985, pp. 86–88, 105]). Consequently, I shall not attempt an all-encompassing definition of the term community that will allow me to get outside all other definitions to show that my particular definition is better. As Hillery (1959) states so forcefully, "salvation is not to be achieved by redefining community. That approach has been attempted enough now to demonstrate its futility" (p. 241). Instead, we need to examine how the term plays between such binaries as privacy versus security, liberty versus justice, agency versus subjugation, and (particularly in the field of rhetoric) resistance versus accommodation.[2]

COMM/*UNIS* AND COM/*MUNUS*: PLAYING THE BINARY

Corlett (1989), in his book *Community Without Unity*, shows how tracing the etymological roots of community leads us into the kinds of binaries previously listed. As Corlett notes, the English word community originates from the Latin root *communis*, which is usually translated as "common." The issue for Corlett is where the prefix *com* ends. As he notes, "If the final syllables of *communis* are *unis*, one might combine them with *com* and say 'with oneness or unity'" (p. 18). This interpretation certainly has validity, for the same combination operates in the word communion, another derivative of *communis*. On the other hand, it is possible to combine *com* with *munus*, the Latin word for "gifts" or "services." Thus, the division com/munity yields "'with gifts or service' instead" (Corlett, 1988, p. 18), an interpretation Taylor (1982) also suggested when he made reciprocity a requisite of community.

On the surface, this distinction between "with unity" (comm/*unis*) and "with gifts" (com/*munus*) may seem tenuous, trivial, and far removed from the electronic networks; yet, it actually has significant implications for the status of the subject and the potential for agency which neither communitarian theorists nor NT researchers can ignore. When we examine electronic subjectivity in the community "with unity" (the comm/unity), we are confronted with a wholly situated subject; that is, a subject in communion with the other members of the electronic community, one who is unable to act outside the boundaries established by his or her subjugation to the unity of the community. On the other hand, when we examine the subject in the community "with gifts"

---

[2] I use the term play here in its poststructuralist sense. As was noted in the Introduction, the play of a boundary between binaries describes a space for critique. As Derrida (1987) notes in his essay "Parergon," the analytical boundaries or frames we use to describe the objects we wish to study are "essentially constructed and therefore fragile" (p. 73). Thus, there is always a space of overlap or excess where the boundaries vibrate or play like the string of a guitar. Hence, by constituting different descriptions of community as objects of study, I necessarily bring their boundaries into play. My task then is to show where this play occurs.

(the com/munity), then we are faced with a Kantian rational subject, one who is able to engage in "objective" critique and able to exercise the Will in order to act as an agency of change beyond the boundaries of community, a subject who is able to choose between electronic communities based on the most advantageous reciprocal relationships offered by those communities.

CONSTITUTIVE, INSTRUMENTAL, AND SENTIMENTAL CONCEPTIONS OF COMMUNITY

This division between the constituted and the rational subjects of community has also been noted by Sandel (1982), who uses it as the basis for his typology of communities. Sandel refers to what I've been calling the comm/unity view as "the constitutive conception" of community (p. 150). For subjects of Sandel's constitutive communities:

> Community describes not just what they *have* as fellow citizens but also what they *are*, not a relationship they choose (as in a voluntary association) but an attachment they discover, not merely an attribute but a constituent of their identity. (p. 150)

Thus, members of constitutive communities are situated subjects; their identities are "defined to some extent" by the subject positions they occupy in the community (Sandel, 1982, p. 150). It must be noted that, by making the qualification "to some extent," Sandel is indicating that he "would not replace the self with constitutive community" (Corlett, 1989, p. 21). Sandel still would leave space for aspects of an essentialist subject in his constitutive community. However, other communitarian theorists do not leave such a space, so unlike Sandel, when I use the term constitutive community, I am referring to a wholly situated subject.

On the com/*munity* or "with gifts" side of the binary, Sandel locates the individualistic conceptions of community. He then further subdivides individualistic conceptions into two types: instrumental and sentimental conceptions of community, borrowing from Rawls' (1971) discussion of "social union" in *A Theory of Justice* (Sandel, 1982, p. 148). In Sandel's individualistic conceptions of community, members of both instrumental and sentimental communities are bound together by the same reciprocity mechanism found in Taylor's (1982) theory. Members of individualistic communities are bound together by the desire for *munus*;

that is, by the desire for the gifts, services, or "remuneration (*re* + *munus*)" (Corlett, 1989, p. 18). In short, they are bound by the positive effects of membership in the community, they are bound "with gifts" (*com* + *munus*).

According to the instrumentalist view of individualistic communities, members of an academic electronic discussion group like Megabyte University, PURTOPOI, or HUMANIST join for personal gain. They join, for example, to acquire prepress publications distributed for comments among members of a group, to obtain calls for papers or conference proposals before these calls are sent out using traditional methods, or just generally to keep abreast of cutting edge developments in a field. We can see how strongly motivated individuals are to obtain the benefits of membership in such electronic communities in cases where individuals have been excluded from community. For example, *The Chronicle of Higher Education* reported that, on the "Society for Women in Philosophy List" or SWIP-L electronic discussion group, one SWIP-L member threatened to sue the group's manager and the university that supports the SWIP-L's operation because other members of the group called for his expulsion from the list (DeLoughry, 1994, p. A21). In this particular case, the individual in question allegedly violated the group's policies by sharing the SWIP-L's messages with an outsider and a "prominent critic of much feminist scholarship" (DeLoughry, 1994, p. A21). In effect, this individual was accused of giving an outsider and outspoken critic access to privileged insights about the feminist community, insights that might be *instrumental* in future published attacks against other members of SWIP-L. The position being expressed is that enemies of a community ought not be allowed to obtain the remuneration reserved for members of the group. The accused individual (who has not admitted to violating the group's policies) argues that, as a professor of philosophy who has an interest in feminism, he has every right to participate in SWIP-L and that denying him the remuneration due the group's members without just cause is a violation of his legal rights. Now putting aside the question of whether or not this individual ought to be excluded from SWIP-L, what is important here is that both sides are adopting an instrumentalist view of community in support of their arguments because they are both claiming that members are bound to the group because of its particular and distinct benefits.

The distinction between instrumental and sentimental individualistic communities is, for Sandel (1982), essentially a question of why members are motivated to actions that further community rather than self interests, and the difference between the two is based on the egoism/altruism binary. In the instrumental community, "individuals regard social arrangements as a necessary burden and cooperate only for the sake of pursuing their private ends" (Sandel, 1982, p. 148). Hence, they are motivated by egoism. Clearly then, the instrumental community model is based on simple economic metaphors, and reciprocity is its guiding principle. Members choose to enter into relationships, activities, and even those particular communities that reward them with the most remuneration (Corlett, 1989, p. 18). To decide what remuneration is best for them, members need to objectively perceive the world around them. Members need to perceive objects as they really are rather than the way they have been constructed by their communities.

In sentimental communities on the other hand, "the participants have certain 'shared final ends' and regard the scheme of co-operation as a good in itself" (Sandel, 1982, p. 148, quoting Rawls [1971]). Members here are motivated by altruism; they are "moved by affection and ties of sentiment" (Rawls, 1971, p. 178). And the rationale underlying the sentimental conception is more complex than the simple economic exchange behind the instrumental. The sentimental theory of community is certainly individualistic since it depends on the feelings and emotions of an particular, individual self in order to explain the motivation to act. But the assertion that members of sentimental communities "regard the scheme of co-operation as a good in itself" is more difficult to explain than the economic model, for it appeals to a higher goodness than simple self-interest. Instead, one engages in altruistic behaviors because one has particular faculties that are able to perceive a higher, eternal Truth, a Truth that transcends mere greed or the community's socially constructed truths.

This sentimental view of community seems to be the type that Rheingold (1993) describes in *The Virtual Community* when he explains why a commercial electronic conferencing system called "the WELL" seems to him to be a community. Rheingold argues that the strongest communities are those founded on appeals to their members' "barn raising" spirits rather than their mere "horse trading" avarice (p. 59). For him, the way people on the WELL willingly share their knowledge and expertise with others is what makes the WELL a sentimental community. He goes on to say that:

Reciprocity is a key element in any market-based culture, but the arrangement I'm describing feels to me more like a kind of gift economy in which people do things for one another out of a spirit of building something between them, rather than a spreadsheet-calculated quid pro quo. When that spirit exists, everybody gets a little extra something, a little sparkle, from their more practical transactions. (p. 59)

In other words, people in the WELL community share with each other because, according to Rheingold, they believe it is the right thing to do and not merely because they expect to profit.

Of course, for the NT researcher the obvious problem with the kind of sentimentalist view of community Rheingold privileges in his book is that he must impose his own ideologically saturated narrative on the behaviors of the other WELL users in order to make the claims he does. In other words, he gets caught in the old intentionalism problem because the distinction between instrumental and sentimental conceptions of community that he wishes to make depends on the ability of the researcher to ascertain the intentions of the members of the communities being described.

Though this distinction between the instrumental and the sentimental conceptions is an important one, the key point to be made is that both the instrumental and sentimental conceptions view communities as collections of transcendent subjects rather than as mechanisms of subjugation. Whether members of a community act to further their own self-interests or whether they act in accordance with some higher Truth, the main point is that they are subjects before they are subjected; their identities exist *a priori*. Consequently, members of individualistic communities (whether instrumental or sentimental) are said to be transcendental subjects since, as Kant (trans. 1988) points out in *The Critique of Judgment*, "a transcendental principle is one through which we represent *a priori* the universal condition under which alone things can become Objects of our cognition generally" (p. 20). To put this another way, in order for subjects to know what is in their best interests in the instrumental community or in order for subjects to know what is morally good in the sentimental community, they must be able to transcend a community's constituting forces, and, as will be explained when we discuss Kant's view of community, his concept of subjective necessity empowers them with that authority.

THE CONSTITUTIVE CONCEPTION OF COMMUNITY: ALTHUSSER'S "INTERPELLATION"

Turning now to some examples of theories that exhibit features of constitutive and individualistic conceptions of community, perhaps one of the best known theories that corresponds to the view of subjectivity in the constitutive community or the comm/unity comes from Althusser's (1971) discussion of the interpellation mechanism in his essay "Ideology and Ideological State Apparatuses." In this essay, Althusser argues against the vulgar Marxists' notion of ideology as false consciousness. For vulgar Marxists, ideology is a distortion of the Real. Like shadow-figures in Plato's cave allegory, ideology produces or re/presents a kind of secondary or pseudoreality without material existence. And a similar position will be elaborated in much greater detail when Kant's division between the sensible and supersensible realms is discussed later. However, the main point is that agency, from this perspective, comes when the subject escapes the distorting effects of ideology through historical critique. For Althusser, however, *all* societies create their own versions of reality, and these versions have positive ontological status. He writes, "ideology *always* exists in an apparatus" or one might say community (1971, p. 166, emphasis added). He then immediately goes on to state that, "this existence [of ideology] is *material*" (p. 166, emphasis added).

By giving ideologies material existence, Althusser seeks to change ideology from a negative concept into a positive one, and he uses the same line of argument Gadamer (1988) uses when he seeks to change the enlightenment's "prejudice against prejudice" (p. 240). Both Althusser and Gadamer argue against self-awareness and historical critique as sources of agency. For both:

> History does not belong to us, but we belong to it. Long before we understand ourselves through the process of self-examination, we understand ourselves in a self-evident way in the family, society and state in which we live. The focus of subjectivity is a distorting mirror. The self-awareness of the individual is only a flickering in the closed circuits of historical life. That is why the prejudices of the individual, far more than his judgments, constitute the historical reality of his being. (Gadamer, 1988, p. 245)

Thus, for Althusser and Gadamer, there is no act of pure perception on the part of the subject within the comm/unity, for the individual's own sense of self-awareness is itself constituted by ideologies and prejudices which pre-exist the individual. Or, to keep this in Althusser's terminology, because individuals are interpellated or hailed into particular subject positions, they cannot escape the ideologies of their communities. Their versions of reality are constituted by their ideologies, *including* those versions formed by radical historical critique. The very forms or categories a subject uses to think those radical thoughts are subject to a pre-existing ideology inscribed in language.

Althusser's interpellation mechanism works through the every-day language of a society or a community. As he notes, interpellation "can be imagined along the lines of the most commonplace everyday police (or other) hailing: 'Hey, you there!'" (1971, p. 174). Interpellation then is the singling out of the individual by means of the pre-existing social formations inscribed in linguistic codes or discursive structures. And as Laclau and Mouffee (1985) point out, "a discursive structure is not a merely 'cognitive' or 'contemplative' entity; it is an *articulatory practice* which constitutes and organizes social relations" (p. 96). Althusser's argument thus parallels Benveniste's (1971) arguments in "Subjectivity In Language" where Benveniste observes that:

> Consciousness of self is only possible if it is experienced by contrast. I use *I* only when I am speaking to someone who will be a *you* in my address. It is this condition of dialogue that is constitutive of *person*. (p. 729)

Thus, interpellation is the calling of the individual into a *socially predetermined* space through language. It is the unique placement of the individual in a contrastive relationship with other members of a society which, paradoxically, *unites* the individual to the community. I say paradoxically since it is through difference and distinction that this unification takes place. Interpellation thus becomes the communion of the particular part to the general whole.

For NT researchers, Althusser's concept of interpellation is particularly valuable because it provides us with a language for describing the different ways media work on subjectivities. Yet, although it offers tremendous explanatory power for NT researchers, it can be taken too far. In Althusser's (1971) own work, interpellation has another role beyond the mere subjugation of the individual, one that must certainly make him a constitutive communitarian theorist. For Althusser, interpellation (and the ideological formations that make it possible) are *necessary* conditions for *any* social unit or community, which is why he can assert that "ideology *always* exists in an apparatus" (p. 166, emphasis added). Interpellation is the glue that binds societies and communities together or, more accurately, unites individuals into communities. It is this move that makes Althusser's theory doubly restrictive for the subject. Not only is the subject's version of reality a function of ideological interpellation, but, as Smith (1988) also notes, "ideology is inescapable since it is the device which guarantees the cohesion of social formations of any sort" (p. 15). There is no escape for the Althusserian subject.

Althusser has simply replaced one kind of rational subject with just another kind of unified subjectivity. Rather than conceiving of a fragmented, indeterminate subject as a counter to the vulgar Marxists' enlightened subject, Althusser ends up "positing a 'subject' entirely cerned insofar as it seems to exist as a unity which is dependent upon a supposed unity of interpellative effects" (Smith, 1988, p. 18). Ideology simply replaces immanent law as the originary source that will determine an individual's subjectivity and therefore leads to ideological determinism.

Yet, despite these problems with Althusser's theory (problems which we will see in other constitutive communitarian theorists in the next chapter), Althusser clearly makes subjectivity contingent on the particular community. Community precedes identity, and for this reason he serves as a representative constitutive communitarian theorist. By way of contrast, Kant will serve as a representative individualistic communitarian theorist.

THE INDIVIDUALISTIC CONCEPTION OF COMMUNITY: KANT'S *SENSUS COMMUNIS* AND SUBJECTIVE NECESSITY

At first glance, it may seem odd to discuss Kant's (trans. 1988) *Critique of Judgment* as representative of any communitarian theory, for on the surface, Kant doesn't seem to be interested in developing a theory of community at all. Rather, in the Preface, he states that he is interested in demonstrating that the aesthetic judgments of individuals are based on "independent *a priori* principles" (p. 4), principles that transcend the merely fashionable and contingent values one typically associates with communities. However, it is precisely because Kant finds fashionable, transient tastes abhorrent that makes him so important to communitarian theory, for it is often to a Kantian version of subjectivity that individualistic communitarians turn when they are confronted by the kind of ideological determinism found in a constitutive theory of community like Althusser's (1971). In other words, Kant is worthy of attention if only because his theories are used as foils for many of the issues constitutive communitarians must address.

But there is another reason for examining Kant in this context, for Kant's theory of aesthetic judgment is more closely tied to society and communal life than is commonly thought. Because of Kant's importance to the liberal humanist tradition, it easy to overlook the fact that Kant actually makes communal life a *precondition* of aesthetic judgment. For Kant, "the impulse to society is natural to mankind," and furthermore, "*sociability* is a property essential to the requirements of man as a creature intended for society, and one, therefore, that belongs to *humanity*" (trans. 1988, p. 155). Thus, Kant makes communal life into one of the "independent *a priori* principles" he set out to discover in *The Critique*. And from this observation that sociability is a fundamental condition of humanity, he then goes on to make it an prerequisite of aesthetic judgment. He writes:

> With no one to take into account but himself a man abandoned on a desert island would not adorn either himself or his hut, nor would he look for flowers, and still less plant them, with the object of providing himself with personal adornments. *Only in society does it occur to him to be not merely a man, but a man refined in the manner of his kind* (the beginning of civilization)—for that is the estimate formed of one who has the bent and turn for communicating his pleasure to others, and who is not quite satisfied with an Object *unless his feeling of delight in it can be shared in communion with others.* (trans. 1988, p. 155, emphasis added)

From this, it should be easy to see why Kant can be and perhaps even should be considered a communitarian theorist. For him, human beings don't even search for the objects requisite for aesthetic judgments unless they first exist "in communion with others;" that is, in communities.[3]

---

[3] Indeed, Kant (trans. 1988) suggests that aesthetic judgment and community are equiprimordial when he links aesthetic judgment to "the beginning of civilization." He even goes so far as to offer a means of determining if an individual is a member of a community or is, to use his terms, "refined in the manner of his kind." He seems to recognize that the aesthetic judgments one offers become a mechanism for giving an estimate of one's location in a community. Or to put this in Bourdieu's (1984) terminology, the judgment of taste that an individual shares "in communion with others" becomes a kind of cultural capital, purchasing the individual a particular space in a community and, ultimately, serving as the basis for class distinctions throughout an entire community. Nor is Kant satisfied with using aesthetic judgment as a mechanism for locating individuals within communities; he even uses it as a means of classifying whole civilizations. Further on in the same paragraph from which the passage above was excerpted, Kant asserts that "civilization has reached its height" when "it makes this work of communication [i.e., the communication of aesthetic judgments] almost the main business of refined inclination" (trans. 1988, p. 156), suggesting that whole communities, like the individuals who inhabit them, can be classified according to their aesthetic judgments. An interesting aside here would be a discussion of how this utilitarian usage of aesthetic judgment conflicts with Kant's own, well-known attitudes toward objectivity (cf. Kant, trans. 1988, pp. 49–50, 69); however, in terms of the discussion here, it is only necessary to observe how much Kant depends on a concept of community for his theory of aesthetic judgment so that he may be qualified as a communitarian theorist.

Given then that Kant is a communitarian theorist and, further-more, given that he raises many of the issues that reoccur in com-munitarian theory, I now wish to turn to his discussion of *sensus communis* or common sense for three reasons. First, it is in the discussion of *sensus communis* that Kant struggles with the binary between comm/unity and com/munity. Second, Kant will make common sense a necessary condition of subjective neces-sity, a concept that is critical to an understanding of individualis-tic conceptions of community. And finally, the concept of common sense is important in its own right because it is a persistent and pervasive issue in communitarian theory.

We have already explored how Kant made communal life a pre-condition of aesthetic judgments, but because I want to offer a some-what radical reading of Kant here, I need to be more precise. More specifically then, Kant (trans. 1988) argued that it was the ability to "share" or to communicate the aesthetic judgments of taste that brings them from the realm of mere potentiality into realm of actu-ality (p. 155). For Kant, the communicability of aesthetic judgments is therefore a condition of their empirical existence (p. 84).

However, communicability brings its own set of conditions to bear on the judgment of taste. For communication to occur, there needs to be some common ground between participants. And Kant not only requires communicability of aesthetic judgments, he would also have them "admit of being universally communicated" (p. 83). In other words, because Kant wants to show that aesthetic judgments are based on "independent *a priori* principles" (p. 4), they cannot be accepted by some but not by others; rather, "the judgment of taste exacts agreement from every one" (p. 82). Consequently, Kant asserts that "the judgment of taste, therefore, depends on our pre-supposing the existence of a common sense" (p. 83).

Now, a less exacting theorist than Kant might claim that the existence of common sense was a sufficient condition for arguing that aesthetic judgments were indeed based on "independent *a priori* principles," for if judgments of taste were based on common sense, then every human being would assent to them on the grounds of our shared humanity.[4] However, Kant, to his credit,

---

[4] My logic here comes from Gorgias' famous three part attack on the possibil-ity of *a priori* knowledge—that is, "first, that nothing exists, secondly that even if anything existed it could not be known by men, and thirdly that even if anything could be known by anyone it could not be communicated to anyone else" (Gorgias, trans. 1988, p. 256). Kant addressed the third dictum in the universal communi-cability of common sense, and he presupposes the first when he describes the unity of nature. He must now address the second dictum in order to provide a liai-son between the first and third.

recognizes that "we assume a common sense as the *necessary* condition of the universal communicability of our knowledge" (p. 84, emphasis added); he does not, however, make *sensus communis* a *sufficient* condition of the universal validity of aesthetic judgments. Common sense allows one only to argue that a judgment *ought* to accepted, not that it *will* be (p. 84, see also pp. 21–22), and the reasons Kant can't make *sensus communis* into a sufficient condition lead to the very heart of the constitutive vs. individualistic binary.

In the beginning of the Third Critique, Kant makes a division between the what he calls the sensible and the supersensible realms. The sensible deals with the empirical world and the supersensible with the metaphysical, literally that which is "beyond the physical" (*meta + physis*). Between these two realms he maintains that "there is a great gulf fixed;" however, despite this split, "the latter [the supersensible] is *meant* to influence the former [the sensible]" (p. 14). That is, the supersensible determines what potentialities become actualized in the sensible realm. Now, common sense is situated in the sensible realm because it is based on inductive or what Kant calls reflective reasoning (p. 18). Reflective reasoning moves from the perception of particular empirical events to a description of general rules, laws, or principles, as opposed to deductive or determinant reasoning that moves from universal rules, laws, or principles to a description of particular events. Consequently, inferences based on common sense, like all other reflective judgments, are merely probable because they begin with particular and contingent phenomena from the sensible realm. Determinant conclusions, on the other hand, have their grounding in universal, *a priori* principles from the supersensible realm. Unlike determinant resolutions then, the judgments of *sensus communis* cannot claim to have articulated a universal principle from the supersensible realm unconditionally; they can only make a probable claim.

Kant therefore cannot use common sense to argue that aesthetic judgments are based on independent *a priori* principles located in the supersensible realm. If he tried to make this argument, it could easily be countered because of his division between the sensible and the supersensible. For example, one could argue that it is impossible to prove that an individual's sensation of the color red is the same as some other person's sensation of the same color. Both parties may agree that the color is a *fact*, but the *truth* of the color must remain indeterminate. We only believe that the truth of the color has been established because we tend to think "that the statement of a fact is a truth and that any truth enunciates a fact" (Perelman & Olbrechts-Tyteca, 1969, p. 69). However, because of the relationship between Kant's sensible and supersensible realms, he can only accept the latter proposition. The supersensible's absolute, universal truths are "*meant to influence*" the sensible's contingent, particular facts (Kant, trans. 1988, p. 14), not vice versa. Consequently, Kant's division between the sensible and the supersensible operates like a cosmic sausage grinder. It is an irreversible process that makes it impossible to reason backward from a particular sausage to the recovery of an originary pork steak.

Kant's problematic leads to the very crux of the individualistic vs. constitutive binary because it is how communitarian theorists resolve this problematic that determines their location on one or the other side of the binary. In Althusser's (1971) case, the problem is resolved by making common sense a function of ideological interpellation. We all agree that red is red because we have been interpellated into a system that makes it impossible for us to see anything else. We are inescapably bound together in the community by this consensus; that is, we are literally trapped "with our senses" (*con + sensus*). Because constitutive communitarians like Althusser make ideology the source of common sense, no higher authority than ideology can so bind us, nor can we appeal to any higher authority independent of ideology to support our judgments.

And Kant is certainly aware of the constitutive communitarian position, as can be seen when he asks:

> Does such a common sense in fact exist as a constitutive principle of the possibility of experience, or is it formed for us as a regulative principle by a still higher principle of reason, that for higher ends first seeks to beget in us a common sense? Is taste, in other words, a natural and original faculty, or is it only the idea of one that is artificial and to be acquired by us, so that a judgment of taste, with its demand for universal assent, is but a requirement of reason for generating such a con*sensus*? (trans. 1988, p. 85)

Kant's questions here are central to the division between constitutive and individualistic communitarian theorists. Do our judgments have their sources in the constituted and constitutive principles of an artificial sense that is acquired through some social mechanism like interpellation (the constitutive view)? Or do our judgments have their source in the higher principles of the supersensible? Are we motivated by judgments that have their basis in universal truths, judgments like the individualistic communitarians' assertion that "the scheme of co-operation" is "a good in itself" (Sandel, 1982, p. 148)? The way communitarian theorists answer Kant's questions determines whether they will be labeled constitutive or individualistic. These questions therefore point to a potential space of play between the constitutive and individualistic binary.

But how does Kant answer these questions? I have yet to examine the basis for classifying Kant as an individualistic communitarian theorist (in fact, so far in this discussion of common sense, all Kant has done is to admit that at least some judgments are based on socially constructed values). And perhaps more importantly, I have yet to examine how Kant turns his cosmic sausage grinder backwards by showing how reflective judgments of particular events can nevertheless be universals.

For Kant to argue that aesthetic judgments are necessarily valid for all human beings and not just for the particular community an individual inhabits, he must find what Perelman (1969) calls a liaison. He must find something "which allows for the transference to the conclusion of the adherence accorded the premises" (Perelman & Olbrechts-Tyteca, 1969, p. 49). That is, he must produce some mechanism that allows him to transfer the universality of the supersensible to particular reflective judgments. Kant needs to find a way to situate subjectivity above the particular community so that the validity of subjective judgments are not relative to one community but are valid for all communities. Thus, as Kant himself puts it, "the reflective judgment which is compelled to ascend from the particular in nature to the universal stands, therefore, in need of a principle" (p. 18). The liaison or principle that Kant uses is called subjective necessity and is "a necessary idea for everyone" (p. 84).

Kant's argument for subjective necessity is based on the presupposition that the universe is ultimately intelligible or knowable. Nature, for Kant, is not chaotic but acts in accordance with universal laws. There is a unity or a finality behind the manifold experiences we have when we observe natural events. In other words, there must be a natural order to things. Particular natural phenomena may seem contingent, indeterminate, and chaotic in the experiential moment, but ultimately natural objects operate in uniformity with this universal natural order or, to use Kant's terminology, with this unity of nature (p. 23). Now, if nature is systematic and regular, if there is a unity of nature, then it may be possible to know it. Kant calls this possibility of knowing the "principle of finality" since to know a thing, as Aristotle also argued, is to know the conditions or causalities of its final form (*forma finalis*)—hence the term finality (p. 23, see also pp. 61–63).

However, proving the *possibility* of knowing is not the same as proving the finality of nature. We still have to have *access* to the means of knowing before knowledge can actually come into being (see footnote 4; subjective necessity supplies those means. Kant writes:

> Particular empirical laws [produced by reflective judgments] must be regarded, in respect of that which is left undetermined in them by these universal laws, *according to a unity such as they would have if an understanding (though it be not ours) had supplied them for the benefit of our cognitive faculties*, so as to render possible a system of experience according to particular natural laws. (trans. 1988, p.19, emphasis added)

A little further on Kant adds, "nature is represented [by the faculties] as if an understanding contained the ground of the unity of the manifold of its empirical laws" (pp. 19–20). Thus, our cognitive faculties have been preconditioned to re-*present* the objects of perception in uniformity with natural laws by some higher, god-like force or what elsewhere Kant calls "a will that would have so ordained it" (p. 61). In other words, our senses have been hard-wired or customized to perceive according to the laws of nature. Nature's universal laws must have been inscribed in our human nature since, Kant argues, if this weren't the case, we wouldn't understand anything in nature (p. 25). He therefore concludes that "the finality of nature for our cognitive facilities and their employment...is a transcendental principle of judgments" (p. 22). Hence, an act of pure perception (one that has not been corrupted by dependence on normative social values [see Kant, trans. 1988, pp. 75–80]) is said to have subjective necessity and carries the same demand for "universal assent" as does an objective necessity (p. 84).

Under certain conditions (one of which, of course, is the assent of common sense), individuals are able to transcend the mediation of relative cultural values and *directly* apprehend the *forma finalis* of an object. One of these special moments of pure experience (such as the experience of the sublime where there is an excess of primal terror) gives the subject access to the finality of nature since "it is in human nature that its foundations are laid, and, in fact, in that which, at once with common understanding, we may expect everyone to possess and may require of him" (p. 116). In terms of communitarian theory, subjective necessity is extremely important because it allows the subject to stand outside the community and make judgments that are incontestable, self-evident, and inviolable.

Returning to Sandel's (1982) division between sentimental and instrumental conceptions of community, it finally is possible to see why both are subsumed under individualistic conception of community. Both require Kant's subjective necessity to make their claims about the subject. In the case of the sentimental conception, subjective necessity makes it possible for the subject to discern what is a higher good than the constructed morality of the community because the subject is in possession of eternal rather than contingent truths. And in the case of the instrumental conception, subjective necessity makes it possible to see how an individual's self-interest transcends mediation by cultural values so that the subject can truly know what is in his or her own best interests. That is, the individual can truly experience the empirical world without mediation by ideology.

It is on the basis of subjective necessity therefore that Kant may be classified as an individualistic communitarian theorist. Indeed, because he wants human beings to be motivated by the higher, eternal truths of the supersensible realm rather than by what they observe in the empirical world, he could be considered a sentimental theorist.

SUMMARY

In this chapter, I have examined some of the various ways theorists have tried to define or develop taxonomies of community. The most pervasive approach was to use spatial boundaries as a sufficient or necessary criterion for deciding what is and is not a community. However, these approaches were abandoned because the spatial:

1. excluded important types of communities,
2. privileged orality over all other communication media, and
3. did not address the epistemological and ideological implications of membership in a community.

Because of these limitations, I therefore turned to community typologies by Corlett (1989) and Sandel (1982) since their community types were based on the status of the subject within communities. Both of these theorists used the division between subjects whose identities were constituted by the community and subjects whose identities existed prior to the community as the basis for their distinction between conceptions of community. Sandel further divided his individualistic conceptions into sentimental and instrumental types based on whether the subjects had access to and were motivated by higher, supersensible truths (the sentimentalist view) or whether they had access to and were motivated by the empirical, sensible facts which they objectively perceived (the instrumentalist view).

Having established the binary between comm/unity and com/munity or between constitutive and individualistic conceptions of community, I then turned to Althusser (1971) and Kant (trans. 1988); first, because they exemplified these two conceptions of community, and second, because they framed issues that will be addressed in subsequent chapters. What role, for example, does common sense play in communitarian theory, and what are the effects of arguments grounded on common sense? What is the role of reciprocity in the cohesiveness of a community? How does subjective necessity enable agency, and what alternative sources of agency remain when subjective necessity is challenged by a theorist? How does a theorist's definition of ideology effect the role it plays in the formation of communities and the theorist's epistemological stance? And finally, what is the relationship between Kant's supersensible and sensible realms? Is the supersensible "*meant* to influence" the sensible, as Kant suggests (p. 14)?

This last question is of particular importance since it will be directly addressed in the next chapter when we examine the relationship between theory (supersensible truths) and practice (sensible facts). Because of this relationship, I will ultimately argue that neither individualistic nor constitutive conceptions of community are wholly adequate for use by NT researchers since both are imbricated in what Fish (1985) calls "theory hope." In other words, I will argue that both these conceptions of community encourage a determinism that is incompatible with rhetoric.

chapter five

Community as a Concept in Rhetorical Theory

INTRODUCTION

In the January/February 1990 issue of the *Journal of Advanced Composition*, Derrida, with surprising candor and forthrightness, tells us, "I don't start with disorder; I start with the tradition. If you're not trained in the tradition, then deconstruction means nothing. It's simply nothing" (p. 11). He goes on to say, "I'm in favor of tradition. I'm respectful of and a lover of the tradition" (p. 12).

Many, no doubt, will find these remarks surprising, perhaps even self-contradictory considering their source. They sound too much like something T.S. Eliot might have said to have come from the guru of deconstruction. And yet, Derrida has captured what has become a dominant problematic in the field of rhetoric: the opposition between the need for stable traditions and conventions of a community and the concomitant need for dynamic change and resistance within that same community.

Derrida's comments here, considered in light of his career-long quest to unearth the essentialism upon which traditions are based, points to the need that even the most radical critiques share, the need for well-established conventions. Indeed, as Crowley (1984) has remarked, "deconstruction cannot happen without a tradition to deconstruct" (p. 393). Critique simply cannot occur *sine qua non*; we are all, as the Heideggarians remind us, "born into a language" that precedes us. And yet, as Nystrand (1990) has pointed out, the need for "principled descriptions" (p. 10) raises a problem for those who wish to make a clean break from oppressive or exclusionary traditions, since it suggests that there will be at least a residue of the old in the new or, as Moi (1985) puts it, since "all forms of radical thought inevitably remain mortgaged to the very historical categories they seek to transcend" (p. 88).

For NT theorists, the residue of rhetorical theories based on print and oral discourse is the mortgage we must carry. Like Faigley (1992) in his excellent book *Fragments of Rationality*, most of us view networked text through the lenses provided by rhetorical theories of community. And like Faigley, we hope that this new medium will transform our traditional composition classrooms into the "Achieved Utopia of the Network Classroom" (Faigley, 1992, p. 163); that is, a classroom where authority does not reside solely in the teacher's voice, but is distributed across the individual members of the classroom community in ways that encourage multiculturalism and polyphony. Because of our dependence on rhetorical theories about print and oral discourse communities, the questions NT theorist ask are:

> What might happen if we were to disrupt standard classroom practice and introduce new forms of written discourse? Would it be more difficult to preserve the rational, autonomous subject? (Faigley, 1992, p. 165)

In the recent works of such diverse rhetorical theorists as Bartholomae (1985), Bazerman (1990), Bizzell (1986, 1990), Brodkey (1989), Chase (1990), Frey (1990), Fulwiler (1990), Harris (1991), Lassner (1990), Mailloux (1989), Myers (1986), Nystrand (1990), Porter (1990, 1992), Tompkins (1987, 1988), and Vitanza (1990, 1987), this problem of tradition manifests itself as an ever-increasing concern with the problem of entering, building, and maintaining communities on the one hand, while concomitantly searching for ways of helping writers resist the ideological determinism of those same communities on the other. Unfortunately, because of the diversity of these theorists and the complex ways they tie their projects to some version of social constructionism, it is difficult to characterize what Connors (1990) has referred to as the "parlorsocialverationdialogiclectic-constructionist" movement (p. ix).

Therefore, in this chapter I focus on some of the basic convictions or tenets of social constructionist thought in rhetorical theory, for I wish to situate or "cerne" (Smith, 1988, p. 5) my project in the ongoing discussion surrounding discourse communities and the roles consensus (*con* + *sensus*) and dissensus (*dis* + *sensus*) play within them. More specifically, I review the social constructionist theorists, as well as others who utilize some aspect of the social constructionist perspective, to show how the binary between accommodating the traditions of the community and changing or resisting them is implied or addressed by these theorists. In other words, I examine how the constitutive and individualistic binary developed in the previous chapter has been articulated by rhetorical theorists.

In terms of the discussion of NT, this review is particularly important for three reasons. First, as we have already seen, one of the major arguments for the increased use of NT to bring about social, political, economic and pedagogical change has been that the NT medium enables the formation of resisting subject positions. To test this claim, it is necessary to develop a more thorough understanding of how individuals may resist or be compelled to accommodate interpellative forces. Second, because the next chapter offers a rhetorical analysis of texts produced within a particular electronic discussion group, I need to develop further the critical framework that I will use to analyze those electronic texts. And third, to understand the ways that NT both challenges existing theories of community and is explained by those theories, it is necessary to review what those theories are.

To begin the review of the binary between accommodation (the constitutive view of community represented by Althusser) and resistance (the individualistic view of community represented by Kant), we should go back two decades and come to terms with the broad-based, interdisciplinary social constructionist movement since this movement has provided much of the context for contemporary discussions of community within the field of rhetoric. Social construction developed out of the work of theorists in a number of different fields: Thomas Kuhn's work in the history of science (1970, 1977), Rorty's in philosophy (1979, 1985), Geertz's in anthropology (1983), Latour and Woolgar's in sociology (1979), and Fish's in literary theory (1980a, 1980b, 1980c, 1985). However, in the field of rhetoric and composition, Bruffee (1972, 1984, 1986) generally is acknowledged as the first major proponent of social construction,[1] and it is largely through Bruffee's polemical bibliographic essays that many composition specialists were introduced to the theories of Kuhn, Geertz, Rorty, and Fish. Beginning with his 1972 *College English* article "The Way Out" and more recently in his 1984 and 1986 articles "Collaborative Learning and the 'Conversation of Mankind'" and "Social Construction, Language, and the Authority of Knowledge," Bruffee's work has set the tone for current discussions of the term community, and the related terms collaboration and conversation. These in turn have provided the backdrop for discussions about building communities of writers in the composition classroom and the ways NT enhances community development.

The next section identifies four tenets of social construction that emerge from Bruffee's review essays. Subsequent sections demonstrate that a fifth tenet of social construction that Bruffee does not address emerges from the critique of theory hope worked out by Fish (1985) and applied to composition theory by Bizzell (1986, 1990). On the basis of these five tenets, I argue that two types of determinism become apparent: what I call utopian and pragmatic determinism. Finally, I show that these two types of determinism are inadequate for any NT researcher who views rhetoric as a process of adjudicating between competing knowledge claims or discursive practices.

THE FIRST FOUR TENETS OF SOCIAL CONSTRUCTION

Essentially, Bruffee (1986) offers the following overarching definition of the social constructionist position:

A social constructionist position in any discipline assumes that entities we normally call reality, knowledge, thought, facts, texts,

---

[1] Any attempt to trace influence is always a perilous undertaking, and certainly there are other theorists who have strongly influenced the shape of the social construction movement in rhetoric and composition; Bizzell, Farrell, or Kneupper for example. However, since Bizzell (1986) often cites Bruffee as her authority, and since Farrell's (1976) and Kneupper's (1980, 1981) impact seems mostly to have been in the speech and communication journals, Bruffee's work appears to have had the most significant impact on English departments.

selves, and so on are constructs generated by communities of like-minded peers. Social construction understands reality, knowledge, thought, facts, texts, selves, and so on as community-generated and community-maintained linguistic entities—or, more broadly speaking, symbolic entities—that define or "constitute" the communities that generate them. (p. 774)

Clearly, in this definition, Bruffee attempts to align his project with Rorty's philosophical critique of foundationalism. Indeed, in his 1986 essay "Social Construction, Language, and the Authority of Knowledge," Bruffee expends a great deal of antifoundationalist ink attempting to distance his theoretical and pedagogical positions from those of the process or cognitivist movement in composition. Although Bruffee is engaged in the process of distinguishing social construction from the four "important assumptions of cognitive thought" (p. 776), he concomitantly articulates four basic tenets of social constructionism:

1. Knowledge is particular and contingent
2. Cognition is social in its forms, functions, and origins
3. An individual's subjectivity is determined by the community
4. Judgments can never be justified by appeals to general Theory

First Tenet: Knowledge

In articulating the first tenet, Bruffee (1986) begins by attacking the foundationalism of cognitivist epistemology and ends up offering a social constructionist's definition of knowledge. He argues that the cognitivist seeks knowledge of universal laws of nature or what Kant called finality in the previous chapter. On the other hand, the social constructionist does not seek this underlying structure of reality; the social constructionist "assumes that there is no such thing as a universal foundation, ground, framework, or structure of knowledge. There is only an agreement, a consensus arrived at for the time being by communities of knowledgeable peers" (p. 777). Clearly then, Bruffee is following and expanding on Kuhn's (1970, 1977) observations about the contingent nature of knowledge as it is constructed by scientific communities, and he attempts to distance his epistemology from such metaphysical foundations as laws of nature. Knowledge for Bruffee is particular and contingent rather than timeless and universal; it depends on the consensual validation of a particular community at a particular moment.

Second Tenet: Thought

In developing his second tenet of social constructionist thought, Bruffee (1986) seeks to drive a wedge between the Cartesian subject and thought and, thereby, offers his own social constructionist version of thought. In the place of the cognitivists' concern for discovering the structures and processes that occur inside the "black box" of cognition, Bruffee urges us to view thought as "internalized conversation" (p. 777; see also Bruffee, 1984, p. 639). Borrowing from Oakeshott's (1962) metaphorical observation that "civilized" people "are the inheritors, neither of an inquiry about ourselves and the world, nor of an accumulating body of information, but of a conversation" (Oakeshott, 1962, p. 199; qt. in Bruffee, 1984, p. 638), Bruffee (1984) observes that many of the "social forms and conventions" of conversations simultaneously serve as the structures of "reflective thought" (p. 639). Unfortunately, Bruffee is unnecessarily confusing in his definition of what constitutes or enables thought, and his particular approach to thought has serious implications for his ideas about what and how we should teach composition. However, at this point it is sufficient to observe that the second tenet of social construction that Bruffee (1986) addresses is that there is no act of pure perception, that the ability to think is enabled by the existence of rules or forms that are provided by our particular social situation.

Bruffee's (1984) discussion of cognition can be supplemented with Bizzell's (1982) narrative of how these rules or forms we think with become internalized. She argues that "the infant doesn't learn to conceptualize in a social vacuum..., but is constantly being advised by more mature community members whether her inferences are correct, whether her groupings of experimental data into evidence are significant, and so on" (p. 217). The consequences of this observation about the social origins of thought have been hotly contested, for as Fish (1985) has remarked, an individual "agent cannot distance himself from these rules [of the community], because it is only within them that he can think about alternative courses of action or, indeed, think at all" (p. 113). The issue of agency that Fish raises here will be central to any attempt to examine the nature of change in the conventions of electronic discourse communities; however, for the purposes of this section it is enough to note that the second tenet of social construction is that the beginnings, categories, forms, and purposes of thought are all social.

Third Tenet: Subjectivity

The third tenet of social construction Bruffee (1986) addresses is a logical consequence of the two previous tenets, for it follows that if a theorist wishes to avoid the foundationalism of a unified, rational subject and if an individual's very thoughts are determined by adherence to the rules or forms of the community, then subjectivity itself must also be a construct of the community. And indeed, in differentiating social construction from the cognitivists' essentialist foundations, Bruffee observes that, for the social constructionist, an individual's subjectivity "is a construct largely community generated and community maintained" (p. 777). However, Bruffee acknowledges that only some social constructionists support the poststructuralist critique of the transcendent self and, in fact, as subsequent sections show, the retrogress into essentialism continues to plague many self-proclaimed social constructionists. I would argue, however, that (because such essentialism violates both of the first two tenets) the third tenet of an adequate version of social constructionism is that subjectivity is a social construct.

Fourth Tenet: Theory/theory

The fourth tenet of social construction Bruffee (1986) addresses once again is complicated by problems that are explored in the next section; however, the concept generally can be understood as Bruffee's version of the critique of the traditional relationship between Theory[2] and practice precipitated by Fish's famous "no consequences" claim in his 1980 *Is There A Text in This Class* and by Knapp and Michaels' 1982 article "Against Theory." Although Bruffee attempts to outline the traditional view of the Theory/practice relationship as it applies to cognitivism (p. 778), he ends up confusing the issue by introducing the claim that social construction eliminates questions posed by the subject/object binary because it does not recognize what Kant (trans. 1988) called the "great gulf" between "the realm of the natural concept, as the sensible, and the realm of the concept of freedom, as the supersensible" (p. 14). Bruffee is too busy sniffing out the cognitivists' dependence on a unified self and ends up leaving

---

[2] In capitalizing Theory, I am attempting to distinguish between Theory based on metaphysical foundations and theory as a form of practice. See Fish's (1985) essay "Consequences," p. 125, for further discussion. See also Bourdieu's (1982) *Outline of a Theory of Practice* pp. 16–30, and de Certeau's (1984) *The Practice of Everyday Life.*

his own backdoor open to antifoundationalist critique. Still, the basic point to be made here is that "big-T" Theory traditionally has been seen to hold the universal high ground, which thereby provided justification for contingent practices. Traditionally, Theory has been able to inform practice because it is able to get outside, above, or beyond the particular and contingent context in which practices occur. However, given the antifoundationalist epistemology of social constructionism, it becomes impossible for theorists to occupy any space outside their particular communities. As was explained in tenets one and two, all thought and knowledge is mediated by the "rules of thumb" provided by the community (Fish, 1985, p. 108). Thus, the project of discovering a Theory capable of justifying particular practices is doomed to failure before it is even begun. Instead, theory itself becomes a kind of local, historically situated practice (Fish, 1985 p. 125; see also Bizzell, 1986, p. 52; Rorty, 1985, p. 136). Consequently, the fourth tenet of social constructionism is that the traditional appeal to a Theory based on self-evident premises in order to support pedagogical practices is no longer a sufficient condition for choosing one set of practices over another.

To summarize then, the four tenets of the social constructionist project worked out, or at least alluded to, in Bruffee's 1986 bibliographic essay "Social Construction, Language, and the Authority of Knowledge" are as follows. First, knowledge is particular and contingent; it depends on community for its existence. Second, thought is social in its forms, functions, and origins; it is qualitatively different from community to community. Third, an individual's subjectivity is determined by the community. And fourth, neither the choice between competing practices nor the individual practices themselves can be justified by appeals to general Theory.

Thus, Bruffee's bibliographic essay serves as a useful guidepost to any examination of social construction because it articulates many of the basic assumptions behind the movement's thought. However, any serious examination of social construction that goes through Bruffee must also come to terms with problematic self-contradictions in Bruffee's work.

AN ANTIFOUNDATIONALIST'S FOUNDATIONALISM

Although Bruffee aligns himself with the antifoundationalists' project, his theory ultimately slides back into a kind of foundationalism, and I should point out here that I am adopting Bizzell's (1986) definition of the term:

When I refer to "foundationalism," I wish to focus precisely on the beliefs that an absolute standard for the judgment of truth can be found, and that employment of this standard in evaluating knowledge enables the individual mind to transcend personal emotions, social circumstances, and larger historical conditions, and to reflect critically on them. (p. 39)

Initially, comparing Bizzell's definition with Bruffee's (1986) assertion that "there is no such thing as a universal foundation, ground, framework, or structure of knowledge" (pp. 776–77), there does not appear to be any conflict; Bruffee seems to situate himself firmly in the antifoundationalist camp. And yet, when we examine Bruffee's argument that our field should look to social construction as an alternative to cognitivism, it could be argued that Bruffee gets caught in a self-contradiction. Bruffee (1986) argues that "the first reason" our field should embrace social construction "is the *disinterested* desire we all share to improve our understanding and expertise as scholars and teachers" (emphasis added, p. 776). In this gesture toward a disinterested space where we as a field can reflect critically on our scholarship and pedagogy, Bruffee reinscribes the very foundationalism he found so abhorrent in the critique of cognitivists. By privileging social constructionist methods of analysis above cognitivist methods on the grounds that the antifoundationalist critique leads to disinterested (and therefore superior) forms of scholarly knowledge and teaching practices, Bruffee ends up with an untenable self-contradiction; he ends up promoting a foundationalist project under the guise of antifoundationalism. In short, he is forced to argue that antifoundationalist methods of critique lead to higher forms of thought which *cannot* be subjected to or disciplined by local and contingent disciplinary formations because they are disinterested. And yet, at the same time that he is making this argument for the disinterested value of antifoundationalist method, he has already argued that thought is an internalized conversation that *is* subject to the constraints of the community. Indeed, in the 1984 essay "Collaborative Learning," he writes that:

To the extent that thought is internalized conversation, then, any effort to understand how we think requires us to understand the nature of conversation; and any effort to understand conversation requires us to understand the nature of community life that generates and maintains conversation. (p. 640)

Clearly then, Bruffee gets caught in serious self-contradiction. This self-contradiction becomes even more problematic when we consider Bruffee's attitude toward the relationship between thought and pedagogy. Bruffee (1984) argues that, since students' thought is also internalized conversation, "the way they talk with each other determines the way they will think and the way they will write" (p. 642). Consequently, "We [as teachers] should contrive to ensure that students' conversation about what they read and write is similar in as many ways as possible to the way we would like them eventually to read and write" (p. 642). Such a perspective toward the purposes behind our pedagogies (particularly when it is coupled with the assertion that only antifoundationalist methods of analysis can lead to disinterested forms of thought) comes perilously close to brainwashing.

Given the self-contradictory stance that Bruffee adopts in his review of social constructionist thought, any NT researcher who wishes to employ the basic premises or tenets of social construction will need to qualify Bruffee's articulation of social construction to avoid the dilemma of his position. Thus, a fifth tenet of social construction must be added to the four I've already reviewed, one that forces antifoundationalists to adopt a self-critical examination of their own theoretical practices.

THEORY HOPE: A FIFTH TENET

The fifth tenet of social construction that has emerged is Fish's (1985) critique of what he calls "theory hope" (p. 112)—that is, the hope that a general theory of interpretation can be found that will allow us to sort out the contingent problems of particular situations without regard for their historical situatedness. The critique of theory hope is the contemporary social constructionists' articulation of the same individualistic/constitutive communitarian binary that I described in the previous chapter and the Derridean (1990) binary with which I began this chapter. Furthermore, a critique of theory hope is critical to any adequate formulation of the social constructionist project, first, because it firmly locates the social constructionist project within the realm of rhetoric (see Bitzer, 1978, pp. 68–69; Bizzell, 1986, p. 38; Farrell, 1976, pp. 7–9; Fish, 1985, p. 119, 125; Rorty, 1985, pp. 134–136). Second, a critique of theory hope is necessary because, as Bizzell has argued forcefully in a number of articles (1982a, p. 238; 1982b, p. 206; 1986, p. 54; 1990, pp. 672–674), it forces theorists to consider what Bruffee does not—that is, the sociopolitical consequences of their Theoretical practice(s). This latter is a particularly important observation for NT researchers. Since we are currently facing critical choices about the directions our networks will take, we *must* consider the socioeconomic impacts of those choices, and we need analytical tools that will enable us to determine whether or not we are encouraging electronic participatory democracies or big cyber-brothers.

It is possible to explain the critique of theory hope as an extension of the fourth tenet since it can be characterized as the hope that an adequate epistemological foundation can be discovered that will allow us to choose objectively between alternative discursive practices. In this traditional version of theory hope, theorists seek "to form a general theory of interpretation" based on universal principles (Rorty, 1985, p. 134), principles such as Chomsky's "innate language apparatus" (Habermas, 1970, p. 361), natural cognitive processes, or Kantian categories, which (because they are believed to have been derived from some supersensible realm outside or above the contingent) can then be applied to any situation, regardless of its sociohistorical context. From the social constructionists' perspective, "this substitution of the general for the local has never been and will never be achieved" (Fish, 1985, p. 110). The erection of a disinterested Theory is doomed to fail, as Fish goes on to explain:

> Simply because the primary data and formal laws necessary to its success will always be spied or picked out from the contextual circumstances of which they are supposedly independent. The objective facts and rules of calculation that are to ground interpretation and render it principled are themselves interpretive products: they are, therefore, always and already contaminated by the interested judgments they claim to transcend. (p. 110)

Thus conceived, theory is always subsumed by the realm of the particular and contingent; it is, therefore, a form of practice itself rather than a means of escaping practice (hence, the need for distinguishing between Theory and theory).

However, if the previous critical articulation of theory hope merely results from an extension of what I have been calling the fourth tenet of social construction because it has been applied to traditional foundationalist approaches to Theory-building, then it is in its self-conscious application to antifoundationalist methods of analysis—as, for example, in the previous critique of Bruffee—that it perhaps emerges as a fifth tenet. By locating theory in the realm of practice, the critique of theory hope becomes a double-edged sword because it forces scholars to consider *any methods* of analysis that "promise to screen out of consideration the personal, social, and historical interests" which inform practice[3] (Bizzell, 1986, p. 41), and, of course, this must include antifoundationalist methods themselves.

Turning then to the assumptions that have been used to authorize antifoundationalists critiques, "there is a tendency for the method of analysis itself to fill the authoritative role previously occupied by a foundationalist theory" (Bizzell, 1986, p. 40). That is, there is the threat that the antifoundationalist method will offer a means of escape—a "Way Out," to borrow a term from one of Bruffee's (1972) article titles. There is the threat that the rigid application of the method will empower the user by giving him/her self-conscious distance from the oppressive systems of thought and, furthermore, that this disinterested distance either will enable him/her to choose less oppressive systems or authorize him/her as an agent capable of changing the discursive practices of his/her community. Indeed, the pervasive use in our field of the terms empowered, enabled, and authorized serves as a powerful indicator of just how serious this threat of theory hope has become. Several computers and composition theorists have also located this threat in the early work on NT in the classroom. Faigley's (1993) use of the term "Achieved Utopia" to describe networked classrooms forces us to question the empowering effects of NT (p. 163). Similarly, Stuckey's (1991) examination of the exclusionary effects of technology on rural students in her work *The Violence of Literacy*, and and Selfe's 1994 article on "The Politics of the Interface" seriously problematize the view that technology will provide us with a way out of exclusionary pedagogical practices. We are beginning to realize that the danger terms like empowerment pose lies not so much in the need for methods of resisting the pressures of exclusionary or oppressive practices; rather, the danger is that antifoundationalist methods simply will replace foundationalist Theories, reinscribing the same patterns of violence, exclusion, and oppression as they become reified into a sort of antifoundationalist foundationalism. In short, the danger of theory hope is that the antifoundationalist method will become a new form of naive determinism, for, as Lentricchia (1985) points out, "determinism will permit no rhetoric" (p. 162).

---

[3] Bizzell's use of the term personal could be construed as the reintroduction of a unified subject into the equation; however, if one holds to the third tenet previously outlined and to the feminist concept of positionality that Bizzell employs in her 1990 article "Beyond Anti-Foundationalism," then subjectivity remains local.

UTOPIAN AND PRAGMATIC DETERMINISM

Two types of determinism emerge from this critique of theory hope. In the first type of determinism, theorists appeal directly to axiomatic principles that they believe to be *outside* the community.[4] I call this type utopian determinism. In the second type of determinism, the conventions *within* the community itself are reified into axiomatic principles. I call this type pragmatic determinism.

Utopian Determinism

How antifoundationalist method becomes utopian determinism already has been partially covered in the discussion of the ways the method itself can be seen as providing its user with critical distance. For theorists such as Bruffee (1986), Farrell (1976), and Spellmeyer (1989),[5] the method of critique becomes a means to get *outside* of the situatedness of a historical moment, outside the normal, orderly discourse of a community, thus allowing an individual to engage in revolutionary discourse or to choose between competing practices (Bruffee, 1986; Doheny-Farina, 1989; Kuhn, 1970; Rorty, 1985).

The problem for utopian theorists is not that choices between competing practices occur; obviously, people do make such choices. Nor is it that some kind of critical distance can be gained by employing antifoundationalist critiques. As I have already argued and will argue at greater length in the last chapter, some distance can be gained by occupying a space in another, separate community where differences become apparent.[6] The problem for these theorists is that they wish to claim that the employment of

---

[4] I do not intend to suggest that *there are* axiomatic principles outside or above the community; indeed, much of my argument heretofore has tried to show that what have been considered universal truths are, in fact, social constructs or the reified conventions I describe in my discussion of pragmatic determinism below. Nevertheless, there are theorists who continue to believe in and to seek absolutes that will validate their theories, and it is this belief that differentiates between the two types of determinism.

[5] I have already critiqued Bruffee on this point. For a similar critique of Farrell, see Bizzell (1986) pp. 41–44. For a critique of Spellmeyer, see Miller's (1990) "Comments" pp. 330–334.

[6] For perspectives other than those offered by the feminist standpoint theorists on the critical distance achieved by difference or *divisio*, see Bartholomae (1985) p. 138; Doheny-Farina (1989) p. 18; Fish (1985) pp. 120–121; Porter (1990) p. 194; Ronald (1988) pp. 134–136; Rorty (1985) p. 136.

the method leads to higher forms of reasoning or to the "assumption of a wider consciousness" (Farrell, 1976, p. 15). Such claims are a retrogress into foundationalism because they attempt to offer a disinterested space above interested practices. In other words, the scientists' claim that the strict application of, for example, the Agassi method of performing biological observations is supposed to enable the unmediated "gaze" of the biologist is foundationalist because it assumes that the biologist has been purged of ideologies and has achieved pure vision. This claim is analogous to the pseudosocial constructionist's argument that antifoundationalist method leads to higher forms of cognition because, ultimately, both claims would have us "assume that a complete self confronts a solid world, perceiving it directly and accurately, always capable of capturing it perfectly in a transparent language" (Scholes, 1984, p. 655).

However, this does not yet explain how this view leads to determinism. In the final analysis, such a claim becomes deterministic because individuals are thought to appeal to this disinterested space in order to determine which choices should be made in any particular situation in the same way that the Chomskian linguist might appeal to the "linguistic universals which predetermine the form of all potential languages" (Habermas, 1970, p. 361). It becomes deterministic because, as Fish (1985) points out:

> The practitioner gives himself over to the theoretical machine, surrenders his judgment to it, in order to reach conclusions that in no way depend on his education, or point of view, or cultural situation, conclusions that can then be checked by anyone who similarly binds himself to those rules and carries out their instructions. (p. 110)

Thus, just as Campbell (1968) critiqued deductive methods of inquiry for *predetermining* the discoveries a scientist or rhetor could make (pp. 197–205), the pseudosocial constructionist can be accused of determinism because the choices made by a user of the antifoundationalist method will be predetermined by the interpretive framework of some privileged community that sees its Theory grounded on universal truths.

Pragmatic Determinism

The second type of determinism, pragmatic determinism, accepts the view that we can't get outside a "disciplinary matrix" (Kuhn, 1977, p. 297). Instead, this view, like the constitutive conception of community, emerges from the argument that we are all caught in the "prison-house" of our respective interpretive communities. We are all socialized into a particular language that precedes us, a language which, as Benveniste has argued so forcefully, determines the subject positions we can occupy.[7] Viewed from this perspective, our community's "paradigms" or "discursive practices" (to borrow terms from Kuhn, 1970, and Foucault, 1972, respectively) provide us with the very forms or categories with which we think and through which we perceive or, more accurately, interpret the world around us. In short, this view argues that communities predetermine what Berlin (1982) has called "an epistemic field—the basic conditions that determine what knowledge will be knowable, what not knowable, and how the knowable will be communicated" (p. 767). Thus, we seem totally isolated within the boundaries of the particular community, cut off from all appeals to either an empirical reality or a transcendent self because, as Bizzell (1986) notes, "any reference incorporated into [the language of the community] will inevitably be transformed into terms acceptable to the discourse" (p. 50).

It is important to note at this point, however, that the position I have reviewed so far *does not necessarily lead to determinism.* This view leads only to the second type of determinism when the conventions of the community simply replace the axiomatic principles from which decisions between competing practices had been logically deduced. In other words, pragmatic determinism emerges when the conventions of the dominant discourse community become reified or when the discursive practices of the community are seen to have the same ontological status as axiomatic principles had in the first type of determinism. An obvious and well-documented example of an academic community where local conventions become reified is the scientific community.

Numerous studies have shown that scientists tend to operate as though the discursive practices of the scientific community had the status of self-evident truths (Bazerman, 1981, 1985; Kuhn, 1977; Latour, 1987; Latour & Woolgar, 1979; Mulkay, 1977; Myers, 1985a, 1985b, 1986a, 1988; Overington, 1977; Winsor, 1989; Ziman, 1968). Latour, in his 1987 book *Science in Action,* argues that scientists often view data produced by their instruments and methodological procedures as if they were direct, unmediated perceptions of reality (pp. 64–70). And in their often cited ethnographic study *The Social Construction of Scientific*

---

[7] See also Silverman's (1983) *The Subject of Semiotics,* pp. 3–53, for a useful review of the literature describing the linguistic construction of subjectivities.

Facts, Latour and Woolgar (1979) demonstrate how scientists may reify the processes of scientific inquiry, turning them into black boxes or (and here Latour & Woolgar borrow their terms from Derrida) "inscription devices." The point is that scientists often allow themselves to believe that an inscription device—a thermometer for example—is a transparent reflector of the empirical world. The mediation of the inscription device is lost or forgotten during the reification process so that data comes to have the same idealized status that axiomatic principles held previously. This leads to determinism because, when the conventions and discursive practices of a community become reified to this degree, as Young (1981) points out in his introduction to Foucault's "Order of Discourse," "their effect is to make it virtually impossible to think outside them. To think outside them is, by definition, to be mad, to be beyond comprehension and therefore reason" (p. 48). Thus, the reified conventions predetermine what is thinkable.

The pragmatic determinism resulting from reified conventions has also been addressed by Farrell in his 1976 essay "Knowledge, Consensus, and Rhetorical Theory." Farrell applies Bitzer's famous definition of the rhetorical situation (see Bitzer, 1968, 1978) to show why reified conventions, or what Farrell (1976) calls "fully realized consensus" (p. 8), locate us outside the realm of rhetoric. As he notes, central to Bitzer's definition of the rhetorical situation is the criterion that "the outcome of the situation must be indeterminate" (1976, p. 8); that is, there must be an issue where adjudication cannot be predetermined by appeal to *a priori* and self-evident premises. He then goes on to argue that, within a community, fully realized consensus, reified conventions, or, for that matter, axiomatic principles "would undermine the first constituent of rhetorical situations by rendering them determinate" (p. 8), thereby locating us outside the realm of rhetoric.

Thus, two types of determinism are revealed by the critique of theory hope. The first sort, utopian determinism, explicitly seeks to locate axiomatic principles *outside* the community in some universal or metaphysical realm. The second type, pragmatic determinism, uses discursive formations from *within* the community itself, but it reifies them, imbuing them with the same universalizing or totalizing power that was previously given to axiomatic principles. In both cases, however, as I have attempted to show in my review of Farrell, theorists are confronted with determinisms that are antithetical to rhetoric—or at least any rhetoric defined as a process of adjudicating between competing knowledge claims.

RHETORICS OF RESISTANCE AND ACCOMMODATION

At this point I can return to the arguments that I began in the discussion of Kant and Althusser's theories of community, for the critique of theory hope and the two types of determinism it reveals lead back full circle to the individualistic/constitutive binary. Once again, there is the opposition between the utopian project of locating a space that enables us to resist and make choices between competing paradigms without regard for their situatedness on the one hand, and the pragmatic recognition that all choice is located within a particular community on the other. Neither of the poles in this binary is acceptable to rhetoricians or to NT researchers since both lead to one or the other type of determinism. Composition studies has thus been split between rhetorics of accommodation and rhetorics of resistance.

Rhetorics of Accommodation

As Howard and Dedo (1989) have argued, "rhetorics of accommodation recognize that discourse communities have their own epistemologies, methods of argumentation, theories of what constitutes valid forms of evidence, and methods for discovering that evidence" (p. 6). Theorists who adopt this position stress the need for students to be socialized into the language of the academic discourse community since "the failure to demonstrate one's adherence to the values of the discourse community is to be silenced or, in Perelman's terms, to be disqualified as 'recalcitrant'" (Howard & Dedo, 1989, p. 6). The student who wishes to gain access to the privileges that accompany membership in a community "has to learn to speak our language, to speak as we do, to try on the peculiar ways of knowing, selecting, evaluating, reporting, concluding, and arguing that define the discourse of our community" (Bartholomae, 1985, p. 134). For the student to do otherwise, as Foucault's (1981) "procedures of exclusion" make clear, is to be excluded from the community of those who speak rational discourse; it is to be silenced because he speaks the language of the madman whose "word may be considered null and void, having neither truth nor importance" (pp. 52–53).

Given then the need to learn the language of the community in order to speak and be heard, proponents of this view argue that they are empowering students' voices by giving them access to a language through which they can be heard. Theorists such as Bartholomae (1985), Bazerman (1979, 1980, 1981, 1988), Bizzel

(1982a, 1982b), Bruffee (1984, 1986, 1990), Culler (1980, 1988), Fish (1980a, 1980b, 1980c), McLeod (1990), Reither (1985), Ronald (1988), and have all argued for the practical importance of socializing students into the conventions of the community. As Bruffee has put it in a 1990 issue of *College English*, our job is to teach students to "read texts in ways that really do make some kind of sense to members of some community, [to] write texts that really can get something across to the members of some community or other, and [to] organize governments that really do promote the general welfare" (p. 694).

It is difficult to argue against the sober pragmatism of this position. If one of our goals as educators is to produce autonomous, self-governing members of a participatory democracy who are able to get jobs, able to pay taxes, and able to understand what they read well enough to place informed votes on complex socioeconomic issues, then surely we need to teach them the conventions they will need to employ to achieve these ends. However, as Chase (1988) has pointed out, "just teaching the conventions of a particular discourse community is not enough" (p. 21). Invoking the work of Freire (1985) and Giroux (1983) in support of his project, Chase goes on to argue that:

> When we focus on teaching students discourse conventions [...], we need to do so in a way that allows them to problematize their existence and to place themselves in a social and historical context through which they can come to better understand themselves and the world around them. (p. 21)

Thus, Chase critiques rhetorics of accommodation for their failure to teach students that the conventions of a discourse community are local, that they are socially constructed practices rather than revealed truths—that is, he critiques accommodationist rhetorics for allowing students to reify the conventions of the constitutive community in ways that lead to the pragmatic determinism described above.

Nor is Chase alone in this criticism of rhetorics of accommodation. Many theorists, including some who initially supported accommodationist rhetorics,[8] now argue that we must consider the corrupt and oppressive discursive practices we may promote when we attempt to socialize students into discourse communities, espe-

---

[8] See Fontaine (1988) or Paine (1989) for reviews of this change in attitude. See also Bazerman (1990) and Bizzell (1986, 1990) for examples of this change, or compare Culler's (1980) "Literary Competence" essay with his more recent work in *Framing the Sign* (1988).

cially the academic discourse community. As Fontaine (1988) points out, "before we champion the language of the academy over students' own, we must consider how the origins and effects of academic discourse are complicated by the political and psychological forces which motivate language behavior and by the way interpretive communities are constituted" (p. 92).

Critics of accommodationist rhetorics argue that to merely socialize students into a discourse community is to trap them in a vicious hermeneutic circle. Students cannot change the community without being socialized into it since in order to speak and be heard students must first learn the language of the discipline. And yet, once they have learned this language, once they have become authorized members of the community,[9] change is still impossible for two reasons. First, resistance is eliminated because, as was explained in the discussion of Althusser's (1971) constitutive community, the community's language interpellates or hails students into a particular subject position "in a manner that determines what is real and what is illusory, and, most important, what is experienced and what remains outside the field of phenomenological experience" (Berlin, 1988, p. 479). Second, resistance is eliminated because an attack on a community's oppressive discursive practices requires that you "use the same forms of argument and evidence you sought to change in the first place" (Howard & Dedo, 1989, p. 7), thereby eliminating any effective means of support. Thus, so strong is the ideological pull of a community's language on students that Lassner (1990) has observed that students using Rogerian forms of argumentation are involuntarily imbricated in the very ideologies they seek to oppose. Summarizing her students' attempts to use the Rogerian method of empathizing with and "fairly" representing their opponent's point of view, Lassner writes:

> Although the writers admitted it was a worthwhile effort to try to understand the values of their opposition, they also felt that "fair" was a judgment already biased in its suppositions. It impelled them to present the other side as equally valid in its need for recognition and protection as their own, and in a sincere voice. They said they felt out of sync with their adopted voice. (p. 224)

---

[9] See Kirsch (1987, 1989) for a discussion of how writers use the interpretive frameworks provided by their communities to interpret/construct rhetorical situations that will authorize their texts. For a review of the literature discussing this problem of authority, see also Mortensen (1989).

The observation Lassner's students make about the bias that fairness imposes on them does not represent an isolated point of view here. Vitanza made a similar observation concerning the bias of clarity in his presentation at the 1990 Conference on College Composition and Communication where he described what he has called "the tyranny of audience." He explains that:

> I *Just*-Think, however, that Audiences are highly over-rated. And why? Because they suffer from "trained incapacities." Because they often act like mendicants! Often they are far too dear! Too Lazy! And too Conscious! Their demand for clarity/charity, their demand: "*Make Everything Fit into What I Already Know; Make Everything Conscious!*," often *silences* what, in-language, "Desires" to be *Un*consciously heard. Quite Consciously, they lop off "the ear of the Other." They are betrayers of "the(ir) Other." (pp. 1–2)

Given Vitanza's attitude toward clarity, I cannot resist noting the ironic clarity of his position.[10] He is able to pack a dizzying number of observations into a tiny paragraph. However, I only wish to call attention to the two main points of both Lassner's and Vitanza's critiques of accommodation: first, their illustrations of how writers must accommodate the community's demand for fairness or the community's demand for recognizable forms of discourse that merit clarity and, second, their recognition that accommodation forces writers to employ discursive practices that *predetermine* what writers can say. Thus, they critique accommodationist rhetorics for forcing them into pragmatic determinism.

Among virtual communities and designers of computer interfaces, we can also find electronic audiences imposing similar demands on authors, except that, in addition to the demand for fairness and clarity, authors of software interfaces and hypermedia documents are required to adhere to communal standards of usability. For example, in 1992 I created an electronic discussion group called UTEST where usability testing researchers like myself, human factors engineers, and interface designers could have discussions about ways to develop and study more usable technologies.

---

[10] Porter (1990) has also observed the irony of Vitanza's position. It is perhaps also worth noting that, despite Vitanza's attempt to reclaim the silenced voice of the Other by developing new forms of discourse, he and other theorists who are involved in this poststructuralist project have been accused of simply producing another exclusionary language. For examples of this position see Hairston (1990) and Stewart (1990).

In addition to academic researchers interested in studying human-computer interaction, the UTEST list has attracted a large number of industry professionals from corporations such as Apple, AT&T, Compaq, IBM, Microsoft, Novell, WordPerfect, and many other companies that design, develop, and test computer products for public markets. Despite the intense competition between their respective companies, these individuals share an interest in making technology so accessible that they are willing to collaborate with each other in order to benefit the entire computer industry (like the VCR industry, the computer industry as a whole has suffered from consumers' sense that computers are hard to use). Two of the most pervasive and consistent themes that have emerged in our UTEST discussions have focused on established standards for software interfaces and the ways these standards limit the development of new metaphors for navigating through interfaces.

Imagine for a moment that you are a software engineer and that your company has tasked you with the development of a new word-processing package that will be WINDOWS 3.1 compatible. Obviously, if your product is going to be successful in today's marketplace, it's going to have to be usable, and as it's been clearly established that most users don't read manuals and documentation (Mirel, 1988), you're going to have to design an interface that makes it extremely easy for users to find, comprehend, and execute the functions your software will perform. What you need, in effect, is a *metaphor* for your interface that will help users bridge the textual gaps between the task they want to complete and the commands your software requires to perform that task. In other words, just as earlier we saw Iser (1980) theorizing that readers of literature must bring some repertoire of pre-existing conventions or gestalt to bear on the textual gaps in a piece of fiction in order for it to be meaningful, interface designers discuss the use of metaphors that will allow users to bridge the conceptual gap between human tasks and computer commands. As I develop an interface for a multimedia presentation, I have to find socially shared metaphors that will give my users/readers *predictive* power over the cyberspace I have created. I have to find ways that will allow them to predict that clicking on a particular button or icon will produce a desired result; I have to provide them with a metaphorical map of the electronic terrain to keep them from becoming lost in cyberspace. Using WINDOWS as an example, the bridge between the human task of storing and logically arranging files and the computer commands required is based on the business office metaphor of a file cabinet full of manila folders.

Of course, the problem with this particular office metaphor is that it is "constructing virtual reality, by association, in terms of corporate culture and the values of professionalism. This reality is constituted by and for white middle- and upper-class users" (Selfe & Selfe, 1994, p. 486). More importantly, however, all interface metaphors are ideologically saturated in some similar way. But even if you in your role as a software designer wanted to eschew the particular metaphors and ideologies of corporate culture to embrace some other metaphors and ideologies, the tyranny of usability would pull you back. Just as Vitanza (1990) in the midst of a critique of clarity was forced to adhere to the standards of clarity he shared with his audience at CCCC's, interface designers are also compelled to accommodate the standards of the operating systems for which they write. As a software engineer, you must assume that, since your word processor will run under WINDOWS, your users will already have some understanding of that system and other software packages that your competitors have designed to be compliant with Microsoft's published standards. You can assume, for example, that your users will already recognize an open manila folder icon as indicating that they have opened a subdirectory on their system or that some of your users are going to try entering <Ctrl>-X when they want to cut text from their documents since these are standards you and your colleagues share. Thus, to shorten your users' learning curve and to make your package more usable, you will be forced to accommodate the institutionalized metaphors of the operating system. The demand for usability (and clarity) compels you to deploy an accommodationist rhetoric and pragmatically predetermines the design directions your interface will take.

Rhetorics of Resistance

This type of critique of accommodationist rhetorics and the pragmatic determinism they enforce has led to the development of rhetorics of resistance. Proponents of resistance rhetorics seek to rupture the status quo and the stagnation it maintains by developing new forms or radical conventions. They seek radical forms of discourse that are capable of giving voice to those agencies of change that have been silenced by traditional, hegemonic forms.

Perhaps the best example of this desire to resist the oppression of entrenched discursive practices has come from particular versions of feminist literary criticism. Certain feminist theorists like Cixous (1986), Frey (1990), Jarratt & Reynolds (1990), Moi (1985), and Tompkins (1987, 1988) have all argued for the need to find radical forms of discourse capable of revealing a feminine voice freed from the constraints of the phallocentric tradition, a tradition that, as Tompkins (1987) points out, is as uncomfortable trying to adopt a feminine posture as is the posture Tompkins must assume when she tries to "wear men's jeans" (p. 170). Frey (1990), who is more specific about the phallocentric conventions that oppress the feminine voice, supplements Tompkins' graphic analogy when she writes that:

> I would not describe the conventions of mainstream literary critical writing as feminist. These conventions include the use of argument as the preferred mode for discussion, the importance of the objective and impersonal, the importance of the finished product without direct reference to the process by which it was accomplished, and the necessity of being thorough in order to establish proof and reach a definitive (read "objective") conclusion. (p. 509)

The exclusionary effect of the conventions that Frey enumerates, in particular the agonistic "use of argument," has led many feminists to experiment with alternative forms of argumentation such as the first person narratives Tompkins (1987) uses in her "Me and My Shadow" essay or the Rogerian modes of argumentation Lassner (1990) attempted to teach her students. Many of these experiments with alternative modes of argumentation and different authoring positions or voices are extremely promising. Indeed, in the last chapter, I will rely heavily on feminist standpoint theories in order to deal with the problem of theorizing resisting subjects in a way that avoids essentialism. Unfortunately, however, some of these experiments may still lead to utopian determinism because they tend to reintroduce a unified subject (however unintentionally). Tompkins' (1987) "Me and My Shadow" essay, despite the author's recognition of the constructed nature of subjectivities and despite the value of her insights into the conventions of academic discourse, seeks to legitimate those insights by appealing to the unique perceptions of an individual subject through the use of personal narratives. Similarly, Lassner's (1990) observation that her students "felt out of sync with their adopted voice" (p. 224) suggests that her students have sincere voices that they do not need to adopt, voices that are unencumbered and unmediated by the demands of external communities. Thus, there is a tendency for those who seek to empower a voice capable of resisting the oppression of traditional discursive practices to retrogress into essentialism and to reintroduce a transcendent subject that will be able to change those practices by getting outside them.

Nor is this tendency limited to particular feminist literary critics.[11] There are a number of theorists in composition such as Elbow (1987, 1982), Fulwiler (1990), Ritchie (1989), and Stewart (1990, 1988) who argue for pedagogies that help students develop a personal voice that allows them "to stretch beyond the limits of traditional thought" (Ritchie, 1989, p. 172). These writers actively encourage students to "ignore" their audiences' demands and the conventions of the community in order to hear the truth of their own "inner voices" (Elbow, 1987). They argue that the discovery or, more accurately, the revelation of a personal voice "is a liberating and self-actualizing experience for students, free at last to examine that which had been hitherto inaccessible and [to] say what had always been repressed" (Stewart, 1990, p. 691).

Among UTEST subscribers, a number of interface designers argue that the way to avoid culturally informed and repressive interface metaphors is to study the biological foundations of human thought and language. Calling themselves cognitive engineers, they argue that one of the effects of studying the biological foundations of cognition would be the development of natural language processors. We could then construct interfaces that would allow anyone who speaks a natural language to efficiently operate a computer because they would eliminate the exclusionary effects of metaphors based on, for example, corporate culture. Of course, the problem with this utopian vision of interface design is that it ignores the question of who gets to decide between what will be called a natural and an unnatural language.

Certainly, these theorists have the admirable goal of changing repressive social orders and institutions; yet, their dependence on the individual perceiving subject as the agency of change in their systems leaves them vulnerable to appropriation by a dominant elite and to the erection of universal theories of interpretation that lead to utopian determinism. As Berlin (1988) has pointed out, these theorists are ultimately led to the position that:

---

[11] As should be clear from my use of the word particular, I do not intend to suggest that *all* feminist literary critics are essentialists. Indeed, as a group, feminist literary critics have been one of the most successful in their attacks on essentialism. My point is that the temptation to locate the agency for radical change in a unified subject represents a danger for any rhetoric of resistance. It is a particularly pervasive and vexing problem from which no contemporary theorist is exempt.

when individuals are spared the distorting effects of a repressive social order, their privately determined truths will correspond to the privately determined truths of all others: my best and deepest vision supports the same universal and external laws as everyone else's best and deepest vision. (p. 486)

In other words, since to speak in a totally idiosyncratic voice is to speak a language that others can never understand because they lack the communal or "mutual knowledge" necessary for effective communication (Thomas, 1986, p. 580), proponents of a personal voice are thus forced to legitimate that voice in terms of shared experience, nature, or *sensus communis*. This leads to determinism since, as Perelman and Olbrechts-Tyteca (1969) note:

Common sense admits the existence of unquestioned and unquestionable truths; it admits that certain rules are "beyond discussion," and that certain suggestions "do not deserve discussion." An established fact, a self-evident truth, an absolute rule, carry in themselves the affirmation of their unquestionable character, excluding the possibility of pro and con argumentation. (p. 57)

Thus, theories that seek to legitimate a personal voice capable of resisting the repression of the dominant community's discursive practices often fall into the trap of utopian determinism because they appeal to common sense or to universal truths that we all share by virtue of our common humanity.[12]

In sum, rhetorics of accommodation have value because they help students gain access to the privileges of membership in dominant communities. However, rhetorics of accommodation may also lead to pragmatic determinism because once students have achieved membership in a community, they are unable to realize adequate grounds for changing it. Rhetorics of resistance, on the other hand, have value because they theorize agents of resistance able to resist interpellation into discourse communities, agents that can change the oppressive practices of the community. However, rhetorics of resistance may also fall prey to determinism because, in order to legitimate agency, they are often forced to appeal to a privileged space outside the community. Thus, theorizing resistance and accommodation while avoiding either pragmatic or utopian determinism has become one of the major problematics that any communitarian theorist in the field of rhetoric must confront.

---

[12] Again, I must point out that social constructionists do not accept the self-evident nature of common sense or universal human truths. Such truths are, from the social constructionists' point of view, social constructs.

SUMMARY

The previous two chapters showed that communitarian theories representing a number of different fields (sociology, political science, linguistics, philosophy, literary theory, and of course, rhetoric) have tended to locate their discussions of community in an individualistic/constitutive binary, a foundationalist/antifoundationalist binary, or a resistance/accommodationalist binary. Having established this oppositional framework for the discussion of communitarian theories from various fields and having exemplified its use by locating selected theorists within it, I then argued that neither of the poles represented in these binaries lead to an adequate theory of community for NT researchers because the discussion of community within such an agonistic framework has tended to maneuver theorists into either a utopian or pragmatic determinism, both of which were antithetical to rhetoric as a means of adjudicating between competing knowledge claims.

Some may attempt to construe the foregoing discussion as an enthymeme, particularly since the next chapter turns to a close examination of these binaries in a specific electronic discourse community. It may be possible for some to conclude that, because these binaries ultimately promote types of determinism that are hostile to rhetoric, rhetoricians should disabuse themselves of this oppositional framework in the transition from traditional media forms to the networked text medium; that is, we should turn from these agonistic relationships to some "Other," third term, capable of resolving the conflict either by validating the claims of one side over the other or by re-cerning or resituating the binaries in an alter*native* framework that will suture all the possible manifestations of community within some all-encompassing whole. However, I wish to discourage such an extrapolation, for it would be inconsistent with the Janusian methodology and goals of this study. As the Janusian metaphor suggests, I prefer to celebrate the play in the space between binary oppositions or even multifaceted poles. As was stated in the Introduction, I do not seek to eliminate existing theories by locating them within some natural or frameless frame; my purpose is not to destroy or even deconstruct (in the pejorative sense that word is sometimes used). Rather, in the next chapter I wish to explore the explanatory power of these familiar tools when they are applied to a new medium that has the effect of defamiliarizing many of the discursive practices taken for granted in traditional media.

chapter six

Electronic
Discussion
Groups or
Electronic
Communities?

COMMUNITY AS A METAPHOR FOR ELECTRONIC
DISCUSSION GROUPS

The ideal of direct participatory democracy has played a significant role in discussions of the electronic publishing medium.
House Speaker Newt Gingrich, for example, instructed the Library
of Congress to use Thomas Jefferson's theories of democratic government as the dominant metaphor for distributing documents
from 104th Congress as possible on its World Wide Web server "so
that ANY interested citizen could electronically access it at the
SAME time as the more traditional moneyed lobbyists and jour-
nalists" (Richard, 1995, p. 40). One result of this kind of activity
is that, when theorists describe the electronic discussion groups
that utilize the medium, they commonly use political communities
as their dominant metaphor. For example, Hiltz and Turoff (1978)
refer to electronic discussion groups and computer conferences as
though they were cities or neighborhoods existing within the virtual rather than geographical space of the "network nation."

Deward (1988) and Connolly, et al. (1991a, 1991b) also use this metaphor and talk about electronic citizenship within electronic communities. Indeed, Connolly, et al. are so imbricated in this metaphor of the political community that they claim that the need to construct a Bill of Rights for Electronic Citizens is mandated by the same communal needs that brought about the U.S. Constitution and Bill of Rights. They assert that:

> Just as the First Amendment establishes freedom of the press in the print media, an essential task of our generation is to create a "Bill of Rights for Electronic Citizens" that will define the kinds of freedoms and responsibilities appropriate to an information society. (1991a, p. 37)

Similarly, in the introduction to his book, *Electronic Citizenship*, Deward (1988) argues that:

> With the power of telecomputing, it is possible to expand dialogue, to show people that individuals can be effective, *and to organize groups of strangers into communities.* There are few more important tasks at every level *from the neighborhood to the planet* in the days ahead. (emphasis added, pp. 2–8)

These two quotes seem to suggest that the use of the political community as a metaphor may be motivated partly by the writers' rhetorical need to find a common ground between the uninitiated audience and themselves that will give a sense of urgency and importance to the writers' projects. As I pointed out in the Introduction, in order to authorize the study of NT to an apathetic or even hostile audience, theorists may tend toward aggrandizement and hyperbole.

However, this does not mean that the metaphor of community is without basis or effect when it is applied to electronic discussion groups. Indeed, I have also sought to authorize this project by pointing to the potential social, political, educational, and economic implications of NT. Yet, we also must recognize the danger of the community metaphor becoming reified in discussions of electronic discussion groups. In fact, this seems to be exactly what is happening. Recent works tend to treat electronic communities as though they were ontological givens rather than metaphorical constructions. For example, consider how, in his 1990 book *The Matrix*, Quarterman introduces his readers to the uses of networks:

> Network users group together in a variety of ways related to the underlying technology or to mutual interest. The networks and

> conferencing systems themselves produce communities of conve-
> nience of people with access to the same services or interfaces....
> Networks may be not only communities of convenience, but also
> communities of interest. Many of them form around people who are
> involved in the same sorts of activities. (p. 21)

For Quarterman, both the concept and existence of communities are unproblematic. The mechanisms of inclusion and exclusion that exist for Quarterman are basically technological; all you
need is access to a convenient interface to become a member of
communities that the networks themselves produce. Quarterman
seems to assume that, simply because it is possible to communicate on networks, everyone with access automatically will do so.
In other words, Quarterman equates the existence of technology
with usage.

This unproblematized view is certainly not limited to technolo-
gists like Quarterman; it also seems to inform some of the claims
composition instructors have made about the advantages of teaching with computer conferences on networks. Flores (1990), for
example, states that "the computer conference has the power to
enfranchise *everyone* in the classroom" (emphasis added, p. 111).
She argues that:

> The computer conference can allow for division and difference in
> ways that are more difficult to achieve in the traditional classroom.
> The conference gives each individual voice equal access at the same
> time that it prompts the individual to consider other voices and to
> acknowledge alternative perspectives. (p. 110)

Similarly, Selfe (1990) has argued that computer conferencing
improves discussions in the composition classroom by "encouraging more active and more egalitarian participation within academic conversations based on reading and writing" (p. 124).

The problem with these claims is *not* that they argue that networking and computer conferencing allow some voices silenced in
traditional classroom formats to be heard. Nor is the problem
that Flores (1990) and Selfe (1990) have claimed that computer
conferencing leads to more equitable participation in the classroom community. Indeed, I tend to agree with these claims based
on my own teaching experiences in both traditional and computer
classroom formats and could provide anecdotal evidence of students who (like Flores' example of the student with a severe stut-
tering problem [p. 111]) were better able to participate in
discussions. However, I take issue with the basis for these claims.
Even though Flores and Selfe make clear that they are aware of

the ways individuals are empowered and/or excluded by communities in print and oral media, these discursive practices don't seem to obtain in the NT medium. Instead, like Quarterman above, both seem to assume that simply because the technology exists, students and networkers will necessarily employ it. In other words, they seem to be equating freedom from the discursive practices in print and oral communities with freedom from *all* discursive practices.

In a more recent paper delivered at the 1992 CCCCs in Cincinnati, Selfe called attention to the problems with this view. In a study of computer conferences between Gail Hawisher's students and her own, Selfe found that the conference participants' discussions were dominated by the conference architect; that is, the teacher. Rather than escaping the discursive practices of their institutional sites by relocating the classroom community in a virtual space, Selfe found that students continued to privilege the teacher's voice, making more references to Selfe and her ideas in their discussions than to each other's. Similarly, in her examination of the same computer conference, Hawisher (1992) observed that students tended to use the virtual space as a place where they could please the teacher. Hawisher characterized the conference as a place where students can persuade the teacher that they are thinking individuals.

Clearly, Selfe's (1992) and Hawisher's (1992) findings suggest that the discursive practices of other media do, in fact, obtain in computer discussion groups. Far from being sites that enable free and open discussions, classroom computer conferences continue to exist within larger social and institutional frameworks and, thus, are at least partially influenced by them. Nor does this observation appear limited to electronic discussion groups created for academic purposes. In a study comparing e-mail usage at Southwestern Bell Corp. and Convex Corp., Sims (1992) found that corporate culture seems to play a large role in shaping individuals' use of NT at their institutional sites as well. Sims argued that the top-down, hierarchical organizational structure at Southwestern Bell produced more formal sounding messages. By comparison, the project-driven organizational structure at Convex and an environment where employees don't have to punch a clock tended to produce less formal e-mail messages. Although Sims' observations are based on her preliminary findings and although the degree of formality she found was based largely on her own intuitive reading of the messages she collected, Sims' study nevertheless calls into question the view that relocating discourse in new electronic spaces will automatically lead to free and open discourse. Like Selfe (1992) and Hawisher's (1992) observations, Sims' study indicates that we may need to locate our examinations of electronic discussion groups within larger cultural contexts rather than assuming that media differences alone can account for discursive practices in NT.

DO ELECTRONIC COMMUNITIES EXIST?

Returning to the previous discussion of community as a metaphor for electronic discussion groups, it can be seen that Selfe (1992), Hawisher (1992), and Sims' (1992) findings represent a serious challenge to those who take the factual existence of electronic communities for granted. Given the ways electronic discussion groups seem to be imbricated not only in print and oral media forms, but also in social, political, and economic institutions, we need to ask if distinct electronic communities are even possible. Or to put this another way, it seems clear that electronic groups exist, but is it possible to call these collectivities communities?

No doubt some will find this an odd question to ask in a project where the book's title seems to presuppose the existence of electronic communities. However, the question is far reaching in its implications and extremely difficult to answer. If it could be shown that electronic communities do exist and that they represent radical new sites that enable the formation of resisting subjects, of agencies capable of critiquing old, corrupt, and exclusionary discursive practices found in other media, then those activists and theorists who have called for the increased use of NT to bring about social, political, economic, and educational reforms will have a strong foundation on which to base their arguments. On the other hand, if it could be shown that distinct electronic communities don't exist, if it turns out that community was merely a convenient analytical metaphor that unfortunately has been extended far beyond the bounds of acceptable analogical reasoning, then many of the claims regarding the potential impact of the medium will be seriously diminished and will need to be reexamined.

Clearly then, the question of whether or not we can call electronic discussion groups communities is an important one; yet, it is an extremely difficult question to answer since the answer depends on how we define community. And of course, an NT researcher can take an individualistic or constitutive approach to the term. Consequently, for the remainder of this chapter, I wish to focus on one particular electronic discussion group, examining it from both the individualistic and constitutive communitarian perspectives. I propose to examine an electronic discussion group known as PURTOPOI (The Rhetoric, Language, and Professional Writing Discussion Group) to discover the ways it operates, first, as an individualistic community, and second, as a constitutive community. However, before I begin to examine PURTOPOI from an individualistic communitarian perspective, it is useful to explain what PURTOPOI is and why I have chosen to focus on it particularly.

WHAT IS PURTOPOI?

From a purely technical point of view, PURTOPOI is merely a list or a computer file that I created on February 28, 1990. PURTOPOI is called a list because it is composed of two parts: 1) a list of keywords that control PURTOPOI's day-to-day operations, and 2) a list of the e-mail addresses and names of people who subscribe to the list. A software package, known as LISTSERV, uses this file and the lists it contains to determine how messages sent to PURTOPOI will be manipulated. In other words, a user sends an e-mail message to the address where the list is stored (i.e., PURTOPOI@PURCCVM for BITNET users or PURTOPOI@VM.CC.PURDUE.EDU for Internet users). Then the LISTSERV program looks at PURTOPOI's list of keywords, determines what should be done with the message, and, finally, redistributes the message to every subscriber listed in the PURTOPOI file. Thus, LISTSERV lists like PURTOPOI allow an individual user to send an e-mail message to a large number of others without having to manually address the message to each individual recipient. Instead, users can send the message to one address and have it automatically redistributed for them.

It is useful to bear in mind that a LISTSERV list has at least two components because, although the primary function of a list like PURTOPOI may be the efficient redistribution of messages to large numbers of networkers, a list is more than just a collection of e-mail addresses. By convention, networkers use the term list in the singular form; however, the singular is misleading because it encourages some to overlook the fact that there is a list of keywords as well as a list of subscribers in a LISTSERV list. This keyword list tells the LISTSERV software how PURTOPOI should operate. The keywords affect such things as whether or not messages sent to the list are stored, who can join the list and who cannot, and who can send messages to the list and who cannot.

Generally speaking, the people who receive mail from a list or the subscribers have little or no control over the keywords used on a list, and, indeed, they are often unaware of why certain keywords are used and others are not. Decisions regarding keywords and other list operations ultimately belong to the listowners, the person or persons responsible for maintaining the list. Though listowners sometimes consult the subscribers on changes to a list's keyword configuration or on other aspects of a list's operations, most of these decisions (and, more importantly, the factors that influenced those decisions) are never known to subscribers; indeed, they often occur before there are any subscribers on the list because many of the keywords have to be chosen before a subscriber list can even be created. Furthermore, designing the architectural configuration of a list requires an understanding of the technology and of the LISTSERV software that is beyond the experience of most subscribers. In fact, many of the documents that explain keywords and list architecture are accessible only to listowners to prevent casual hackers from learning too much about keyword operations. Thus, listowners are in a unique position to offer special insights into a list or discussion group due to their privileged access to information.

PURTOPOI was chosen for this study because I was, along with Patricia Sullivan, one of its listowners and creators. Since I was one of PURTOPOI's original architects and have been an active participant in every subsequent change to the list, I can address factors that shaped the formation of PURTOPOI, factors that I could only guess at had I chosen a list on which I was only a subscriber. For example, as listowner, I receive immediate notification whenever a subscriber joins or leaves the list, information most subscribers seldom see. Also, as listowner, any complaints regarding the list's operations or discussions typically come to me personally so that I have been able to collect information on factors such as attitudes subscribers had toward the list's character, questions about what were appropriate topics for discussion on the list, and reasons that particular subscribers gave for leaving the list. And since these discussions are what networkers call "whispers," or private conversations take place outside the "earshot" of the group, they represent another kind of inside information to which subscribers do not have access. In short then, the decision to focus on PURTOPOI is the result of my ability to bring the special evidence that only a listowner can provide into the discussion of whether PURTOPOI is merely an electronic discussion group or an electronic community.

Of course, certain qualifications and caveats must be made here since my unique position as a listowner means that my interpretations of PURTOPOI's activities are also unique. My perspective on PURTOPOI is neither neutral nor value-free (but, of course, I have consistently argued that there is no such thing as a frameless frame that would let us adopt a neutral or value-free perspective). Nevertheless, while my understanding of the original goals I had for PURTOPOI allows me to describe why I chose the particular list configuration I did, it also colors my perspective on what happened. My sense of what PURTOPOI has become has been shaped in large part by what I thought PURTOPOI should have been. Thus, although it is important to note that my position as a listowner imposes certain limitations on my interpretations of PURTOPOI, it also must be noted (however paradoxically) that it is this same position that empowers me to speak. It is precisely because I had a sense of what PURTOPOI should have been and because I took actions that tried to move it in that direction that I am able to offer insights into the differences between my expectations and what I actually observed happening on the list. Were I an objective outsider, I would not have a knowledge of the situational contexts surrounding PURTOPOI and, thus, I would not be able to speak to the kinds of social, institutional, and technological frameworks that Hawisher (1992), Selfe (1992), and Sim's (1992) studies suggested was necessary for an examination of electronic communities.

PURTOPOI AS INDIVIDUALISTIC COMMUNITY

Chapter Four presented three major characteristics for individualistic communities. First, there is the need for shared purposes and common goals. Without the desire to achieve common goals, there is no reason for individuals to come together in the first place; there is no reason to participate. Second, individuals are indentured to the community by the mechanism of reciprocity. They are bound by the positive effects of membership in the community; that is, they remain members of the community (the *com + munus*) as long as their desire for gifts, services, or remuneration (*re + munus*) is met (Corlett, 1989, p. 18). Third, individuals must be able to resist and change the purposes of the community. Consequently, if PURTOPOI is to be considered a community in the individualistic sense, it should be possible to find evidence of these three factors.

A body of evidence indicates that, over all, the members of PUR-TOPOI share a common purpose; however, at the minute level of particular messages, the purposes for PURTOPOI appear to be in a constant state of negotiation and flux. On a day-to-day basis, the group's goals may seem to vary radically because new topics are introduced for discussion and because each new topic brings with it a new set of goals and new purposes. For example, individuals might ask pointed questions of the group, hoping to receive widely differing and diverse responses that will give them a sense of the range of possible approaches to a topic; that is, "I'm writing an article on X and am looking for books on the subject," or, "I'm curious about how other people teach their students to proofread for comma splices." On the other hand, individuals might seek consensus from the group on a particular problem; they may seek to unify the group by persuading them that their particular perspective on or solution to the problem is the soundest. At other times, someone might post a message that seeks neither a diversity of opinions nor a consensus. Messages such as announcements about recent publications, upcoming conferences, job openings, calls for papers, and so on seem to have the transmittal of information as their only purpose. Thus, the purposes of day-to-day messages in the group can vary widely.

Nevertheless, despite the variety of purposes that individual messages may have, the group as a whole and even the subgoals of the individual messages do appear to be governed by one general, overarching purpose: the informal discussion of issues and topics of interest to researchers in rhetoric and to writing teachers. This general goal was present when the list was originally begun and has been maintained throughout the list's history.

Originally, PURTOPOI began as a solution to a very specific problem within the Department of English at Purdue University. At the time, the problem was how to distribute information about the Professional Writing program at Purdue to students and teachers in the program. As is the case with many large departments, undergraduates, graduate student teaching assistants, and faculty in the department had radically different class, research, and teaching schedules, making it difficult for program administrators to distribute information to the staff and, more importantly, making it impossible for the staff to share ideas with each other. Indeed, in this particular case, it was possible for graduate students teaching the same classes never to meet.

Sullivan and I felt that this lack of communication seriously diminished the positive impact of the collegial experience. We felt that both the Professional Writing program and the people who taught in it would benefit from the opportunity to share their problems, teaching strategies, and research ideas with others in the English department since we knew from personal experiences that it is often the casual hallway conversation between colleagues that leads to some of the most profound insights. In fact, we decided to call the list "PUR" "TOPOI" because we wanted to indicate that the list was open to various programs in Purdue's English department for the discussion of a wide range of topics (and also because we were limited to an eight-character name). We consulted people in linguistics, rhetoric and composition, literature, and literary theory about the name and finally chose the "PUR" because the group was located at Purdue. We chose "TOPOI" because the term suggested a wide range of topics that could be discussed and because *topoi* also can mean that we can approach a topic from different places or perspectives. PURTOPOI, therefore, was originally intended to be a "place" where graduate student teaching assistants and faculty in the English department could gripe about students, share papers they were working on, and just generally carry on the sort of hallway conversations teachers always have, except that, through the electronic medium, we could talk to people we wouldn't normally meet in the halls because of schedule conflicts.

Although PURTOPOI's original purpose (the informal sharing of ideas and problems with other writing teachers and researchers) resulted from a very specific problem in one program within one department at one particular institution, it seems to have stayed with the list. Even though the list grew from approximately 30 members of Purdue's English department in February 1990 to 208 subscribers representing 124 different institutions from 9 different countries by April 1992, this concept of informally sharing ideas has been retained. Indeed, almost two years after the list was begun, subscribers continued to cite the informal, spontaneous character of the list's discussions as the reason they did not wish to have messages on the list quoted in published research.

Many subscribers argued that the purpose of PURTOPOI was to serve as a kind of testing ground for inchoate, unfinished ideas, and that citing them outside the context of the list was inappropriate. Some excerpts from this discussion about quoting follow; however, before presenting these excerpts, it is important to understand the conventions I will be using when I quote messages from PURTOPOI. First, when excerpting messages from PURTOPOI, I will offer some context or quote extensively from a discussion because of the dialogic nature of e-mail exchanges. E-mail exchanges on PURTOPOI are dramatic; the group is like a virtual theater where actors and actresses exchange lines on an electronic stage. Hence, as with any other drama, it's important to understand the scene in which the dialog takes place. Note also that I have retained the typographical conventions for e-mail, that I have not altered the spelling and punctuation of the originals, and that I have made no attempt to call attention to unconventional spelling or punctuation. Note too that ellipses within brackets indicate text has been deleted (ellipses without brackets were part of the original message). Also, double rules across the page indicate the beginning and end of a message. Finally (for reasons that will be made clear both in the excerpts themselves and in the discussion that follows), the actual names of the writers have been changed.

```
================================================================
Date: Thu, 5 Dec 1991 17:44:17 CST
From: Ellen C.
Subject: Re: fyi


[. . .] can e-mail be a "publication"? how about a
"presentation"? Does it count as a workshop?

================================================================
Date: Thu, 5 Dec 1991 19:39:21 EST
From: Tom H.
Subject: Re: fyi


I suspect, as with print texts, it depends on who is
distributing your text. I certainly consider the "e-
mail" I get from  PMC ,  EJournal ,  _CCNEWS_, and _EFFector
Online_ to be publications.

================================================================
Date: Sat, 7 Dec 1991 09:01:34 EST
From: Jerry P.
Subject: Re: fyi


[. . .] I have been wondering about this issue:
should we treat e-mail postings in the same way we
treat journal articles? And is all e-mail equal?

[. . .] I am wondering whether we can ethically use
electronic postings in paper publications without
securing the permission of the writer. (Of course
legally we can—the Fair Use principle applies--
```

but the question is more an ethical one having to do with how
we as members of a community treat one another).

```
================================================================
```

Date: Sat, 7 Dec 1991 17:15:14 -0500
From: Mary G.
Subject: Re: fyi

[. . .] individual postings should not be treated as
publications. [. . .] Treating individual posts as
"publications" would effectively destroy the special
status of those texts that had been published in
journals or presented at conferences.

[. . .] We might think of Purtopoi as a shared
brainstorming effort on issues in our field; if you
were writing an article, and you were citing someone
to back up your own arguments, would you want their brainstorming notes or some kind of finished
statement?

```
================================================================
```

Date: Mon, 9 Dec 1991 09:28:26 PST
From: Carl M.
Subject: Re: fyi

[. . .] I see mailings as more of a discussion,
and would hope that people would be as discreet as I'd expect
my friends to be with what I told them in a
private conversation.

```
================================================================
```

Date: Mon, 9 Dec 1991 12:31:17 EDT
From: Laura T.
Subject: don't quote me

I agree that e-mail posting is much more spontaneous
and context bound (responding to previous messages)
than journal articles. I would hate to see my e-mail
texts used as if they were journal entries. But on the other
hand, we use/abuse journal texts out of
context also.

```
================================================================
```

Date: Mon, 9 Dec 1991 13:02:11 EDT
From: Laura T.
Subject: quoting

Jerry P.—

To answer your question, I'd like to be able to say
something stupid and not be held to it, whatever that means.
The fun of these postings is that we can be
spontaneous, not have to worry about documenting,
proving, editing, etc.

==
Date: Mon, 9 Dec 1991 11:38:23 -0800
From: Mark D.
Subject: Re: fyi

I wouldn't care if anyone quoted me (not that anyone
would want to) as long as the citation made it clear
that this was "informal discussion," ie not always
based in solid research. In that respect, I think I
would call attention to the fact that for many of us
this is a forum or testing ground for "ideas in
progress," not cut-and-dried "findings" (the "nuggets
of truth" V. Woolf hears her library neighbor grunting over).

==
Date: Mon, 16 Dec 91 10:16:55 EST
From: Gil B.
Subject: Quoting

What makes quoting email messages complicated seems to stem
from the nature of the discussions: as noted
often on the groups I read, email tends to be more
informal, perhaps promoting exploratory messages. I
sometimes find it tempting to want to play devil's
advocate, just as I would in face-to-face discussions, mainly
because I know that the setting allows me not
to [be] wholly accountable for the arguments I give.
[. . .]
==

These excerpts reveal that many subscribers view
PURTOPOI's purpose as an informal discussion of issues in
rhetoric, a collaborative brainstorming effort, or as a private conversation among professional friends and colleagues.
PURTOPOI's purpose is to give them a testing ground for new
ideas or a space where they may play devil's advocate without
fear of damaging themselves professionally. This is essentially
the same purpose that people gave in March 1990 when the list
was only three weeks old and primarily composed of members of

Purdue's English department. More than 20 months prior the discussion above, subscribers produced the following when asked to describe PURTOPOI's purpose:

```
================================================================
Date: Mon, 12 Mar 90 23:51:16 -0500
From: Perry B.
Subject: purpose(s)


I would like to see this group become a permanent
(through a great volume of use) free forum of
expression. I hope this will become a resource for
the exchange of information about each of our fields
and projects/work in progress etc.


================================================================
Date: Tue, 13 Mar 90 02:29:49 -0500
From: Terry C.
Subject: purposes


I see this as an opportunity to develop and become a
part of an intellectual community--something I have enjoyed at
other universities, but have had a harder
time finding here (perhaps due to the size of our
dept.). I often need to "bounce" ideas off others to
clarify my own ideas and to become aware of my own
perspective and biases.


If only there were beer.
================================================================
```

Clearly, despite the time differential, the same ideas of informality and spontaneity are being expressed. The list is seen as a free forum of expression where ideas about work in progress can be bounced off others in much the same way that colleagues share ideas over beers at the local pub. Thus, if one of the criteria for an individualistic community is that a collectivity have a common purpose, PURTOPOI seems to have met it. Although the purposes of individual messages may vary and although it's conceivable that members who joined the list after these discussions or subscribers who do not post messages might have a different sense of the list's purpose, the fact that the purposes expressed in the preceding excerpts have remained constant, and the fact that no one challenged the purposes expressed by so many different subscribers provides strong evidence that PURTOPOI's more active members do have a common understanding of the group's purpose.

What's more, several of the excerpts suggest that many members have an active sense of group identity. Seven of the ten messages previously quoted used the first person plural, made reference to some shared possession such as our field, or even referred to the group as a community. Indeed, particularly in the messages on the quoting issue, there is a strong sense that individuals have responsibilities to others in the group. Members make clear that they see the quoting issue as one of trust in each other. They trust others in the group to treat their messages as discreetly as they would a private conversation among friends; they trust others to allow them to say something stupid without being held professionally accountable; they trust others to take context into account when interpreting their messages. As a member of PURTOPOI, I am obligated to uphold that trust since, as was noted in Chapter Four, "individuals regard social arrangements as a necessary burden" of membership in individualistic communities (Sandel, 1982, p. 148). In other words, if I choose to associate myself with the PURTOPOI group, I enter into a relationship with it. Consequently, despite the fact that, as a researcher working within an academic discipline, I am expected to give credit to other writers' ideas, my membership in PURTOPOI means that I am obliged not to hold other members of the group accountable for the sometimes foolish (as well as for the sometimes brilliant) comments that they made while they were testing out ideas on PURTOPOI's electronic stage. It is for this reason that throughout this document I have changed the writers' names on messages excerpted from a PURTOPOI discussion (cf. Howard, 1993). To do otherwise would, in the jargon of the Net, amount to a kind of cyber-rape, which is what networkers call the practice of reposting private, privileged electronic conversations in professional, public contexts where they will embarrass and humiliate the author. Thus, to cite PURTOPOI's members by name would violate their trust and destroy our reciprocal arrangements.

This, of course, brings up the second condition of individualistic communities that PURTOPOI must meet: there must be evidence that members of PURTOPOI remain members of the list because the reciprocity mechanism is operating; that is, there must be evidence that members make sacrifices or provide services for the group as long as they receive remuneration. And, of course, some evidence of reciprocity can be seen operating in the self-reflective concessions to quoting that I previously made. Ironically, however, perhaps the best evidence that the reciprocity mechanism does indeed operate on PURTOPOI can be seen when subscribers complain about not receiving remuneration for the sacrifices they make.

Because PURTOPOI's members are largely academics who need to keep up with professional journals and new books, to attend professional conferences, to research and write their own books and articles, and (of course) to grade student papers, subscribers already have tremendous demands on their time. For many of them, simply reading PURTOPOI's messages attentively seems to represent both a personal and a professional sacrifice. Thus, when they feel that the list is not providing them with the kind of information or interaction they desire, they leave or unsubscribe from the list. Often they are quite vocal as they leave, posting very explicit messages to the list that explain why they are leaving. For example, below are messages from individuals who unsubscribed from the list shortly after posting the following complaints about the unprofessional nature of the group's discussions:

```
==============================================================
Date: Wed. 15 Jan 1992 04:16:25 -0500
From: John B.
Subject: Re: signature files

I don't know about the rest of you, but I did NOT sign
on simply to engage in chit-chat. I tend to expect
this list to function as an electronic equivalent of a profes-
sional convention with some formal sessions and
some hallway conversations.

==============================================================
Date: Tue, 5 Feb 91 18:03:22 -0500
From: Mike R.
Subject: Re: Social and Linguistic Goals

[. . .] all I've seen on this list is sophmoric
chatter about whether this is a community or audience
and self-congratulation on how nice we're all being to each
other.
==============================================================
```

Although individuals occasionally post this sort of message to the whole group and then wait a few days to see if their messages have any effect before they unsubscribe, it's more common for dissatisfied subscribers to send a private message to the listowner that the group never sees. It's difficult to receive the authors' permission to quote these private messages (either because the authors have such negative feelings about the group that they wish to have no further association with its listowner or because they say they would be embarrassed to have such emotional messages quoted). However, at least in the following case, the author of one of these messages was kind enough to give me permission to quote her and requested that I use her real name.

```
================================================================
Date: Tue, 28 Jan 92 09:18:18 -0500
From: Donna Randall
Subject: Purtopoi


Tharon, I'd appreciate it if you could remove me from
the Purtopoi bulletin board. Although I really
enjoyed my participation in the summer, I'm finding it
too time consuming during the regular school year.
Also worth mentioning is that I'd be happy to wade
through the messages if I found many of them to be
worthwhile, but, alas, such is not the case. What I'm
seeing is that certain people get off on tirades on
the system when they should, instead, be communicating between
two or three of them, quite independently of
the bulletin board.
================================================================
```

What is particularly interesting about these messages for my purposes is the way that they indicate the economics of participation in the group. The time invested in reading the messages has to be worthwhile if individuals are to remain subscribers. Indeed, the expectation of remuneration for time spent on the group's communication is so strong that individuals seem to regard trivial discussions or chit-chat on the list as a virtual breach of contract and become quite angry about paying for something they feel they didn't get.

Unfortunately, however, it's not possible to say with any degree of certainty how much or what sort of remuneration subscribers expect to receive from PURTOPOI. Although one or more subscribers may unsubscribe from the list because they regard a particular discussion as too personal, "sophmoric [sic] chatter," or mere "chit-chat," others apparently do receive something of value from these personal discussions, despite the fact that they seem to have little or nothing to do with the purpose of the list—that is, sharing ideas about issues in the field of rhetoric and composition. Personal messages (e.g., such things as the birth of a new baby or the recent marriage of two list members to one another) do seem to have value to some subscribers since they do not unsubscribe from the list and may even actively participate in them. Indeed, individuals have offered interesting defenses of personal messages on PURTOPOI after those messages had been criticized as unprofessional. In defense of the personal, the excerpts below argue that such personal messages have value as "counters" or as a means of resisting the disembodied and ideologically-saturated voice of the authority or the professional:

```
================================================================

Date: Mon, 4 Feb 91 10:44:10 EST
From: Eric R.
Subject: [none]


[. . .] My guess is that with so much "disinformation" coming
through the electronic media (radio, tv,
beamed-down versions of national and international
newspapers), the rhetorical shift in *this* community [i.e.,
PURTOPOI] will in a sense counter the
disembodied authority of such media. In other words,
we will come to prize details that *reveal* the
subjectivity of the writer, that locate him/her
precisely in a place and time so as to flesh out
the otherwise disembodied voice.


================================================================

Date: Mon, 4 Feb 91 12:28:52 EST
From: Loni V.
Subject: Details that reveal


Eric R.'s comments on electronic communities prizing
communication which "fleshes out" disembodied email "voices"
seems to be confirmed by the occasional
batches of messages about personal concerns, events,
and the occasional gifts of poetry or well-crafted
essays which appear on the Megabyte network. I look
forward to them and squirrel them away in my hardcopy files. [.
. .]


I also prize the way that the personal messages give
me a glimpse of the rhythm of lives different from the all-con-
suming graduate-studentness I currently
inhabit. PURTOPOI started off this semester for me
with celebratory messages concerning a birth
announcement. And I confess to still have the
description of a deconstructive wedding posting ages
ago.

================================================================
```

The point I wish to make about these messages is that they suggest that reciprocity is not entirely dependent on a shared sense of the group's purpose or sense of identity, which brings me to the third standard an individualistic community must meet. The value or remuneration an individual receives from the community may have little to do with the perceived purpose or goals of the group. Indeed, the benefits of membership may even result from ideas or experiences that are opposed to the goals of either the individual participant or the group. For example, Loni V.'s message states that it's "the rhythm of lives" that are different from her own that makes the messages valuable to her. In other words, it's because she feels a sense of belonging that makes the messages prized. Similarly, for Eric R. it's the professionalism that provides him with remuneration. Thus, it would be a mistake to equate the simple achievement of a group's purpose with evidence of reciprocity. An individual may not identify with the group's stated purposes and yet will enjoy remuneration from it (e.g., pro-lifers may attend a pro-choice rally to learn more about both groups' positions). This observation is one of the reasons constitutive communitarians have difficulty with the individualistic communitarian view since it suggests that an individual can be a member of a group without sharing the group's values and purposes. And yet, as was explained in Chapters Four and Five, having independent, *a priori* values is critical to an individual's ability to resist and change a group's purpose. Nevertheless, if one can assume that PURTOPOI's subscribers remain so because they perceive some value in the list's discussions, then the preceding examples should make it clear that reciprocity is operating on PURTOPOI.

Returning then to the original question of whether electronic groups may be called communities, it appears that PURTOPOI at least can be considered an individualistic community based on the available evidence. Because I do not have statements of the group's purpose from every single PURTOPOI subscriber, it is not possible to say with certainty that every individual on the list shares an understanding of the list's purpose. Furthermore, at the level of individual messages, it seems clear that the day-to-day purposes of PURTOPOI discussions are constantly shifting and are renegotiated with each subsequent post. However, based on what individuals have said regarding the list's purpose, taking into consideration the fact that there was no dissent regarding these opinions when they were expressed, and given that this same purpose was expressed over a two-year period, it seems probable that PURTOPOI subscribers do have an overall understanding of the list's goals and purposes. Second, reciprocity does appear to be operating on the list as evidenced by the fact that absence of remuneration leads members to complain and/or to resign from membership in the group. PURTOPOI could thus be called an individualistic community whose members come together to informally discuss topics of interest to people who teach or do research on composition and rhetoric. However, because subscribers have an independent set of expectations regarding what they consider adequate remuneration for the sacrifices of membership, they are able to resist the group. Thus, despite the fact the group purports to be a site for the informal exchange of ideas, individuals can, as for example in the John B. and Mike R. postings above, seek to change the group by complaining about too much chit-chat since these trivial discussions did not meet their individual needs. Thus, PURTOPOI appears to meet all three conditions of the individualistic communitarian view of community: a shared sense of purpose, reciprocity, and the ability to resist the will of the group.

PURTOPOI AS CONSTITUTIVE COMMUNITY

Having examined PURTOPOI from the individualistic communitarian perspective, I turn now to the constitutive. Unlike the members of individualistic communities, members of constitutive communities are, of course, situated; the subject positions they inhabit are constituted by the particular community. As the discussion of Althusser made clear, the primary mechanism for subject constitution is interpellation, the calling of the individual into socially predetermined spaces through the use of discursive practices or conventions. Hence, to consider PURTOPOI a constitutive community, there must be evidence of discursive practices, conventions, or codes that enable subscribers to inhabit certain endemic subject positions and exclude others.

One of the ways to get a glimpse of the subject positions members of PURTOPOI inhabit when they post messages to the group is by examining the authorizing strategies they deploy. As Kirsch (1989) has shown in her research on audience awareness, writers construct "audiences and rhetorical situations in quite different ways by bringing unique 'interpretive frameworks' to writing tasks" (p. 58). In other words, writers must authorize their texts for a particular audience; they must empower and sanction their voices within the specific social context of the group they will address. Kirsch uses "the term 'interpretive framework' in order to indicate that writers' of tasks and contexts for writing can determine the they bring to composing" (1990, p. 324).

Taking Kirsch's conclusions one step further, it could be argued that writers inhabit particular subject positions that enable them to speak to a particular audience and that these subject positions are in part determined by the writers' interpretations of the particular audience. Thus, as noted in Chapter Two, audiences become coproducers. Just as audiences are invoked or hailed into particular subject positions by texts (see Ede & Lunsford, 1984, p. 155), writers are interpellated into particular subject positions by what Vitanza (1990) called the "tyranny of audience." Furthermore, it should be possible to see evidence of the subject positions writers occupy through the authorizing strategies they deploy; that is, the ways that they sanction their texts to the PURTOPOI membership.

As I mentioned in the previous section, PURTOPOI's discussions often take the form of dramatic conversations. In fact, several subscribers have called PURTOPOI an electronic parlor, drawing on Burke's (1973) famous parlor analogy to describe the ways members listen to an ongoing discussion, pick up a thread in the discussion, make a comment, and then watch as others attack or defend that comment (pp. 110-111). Given that this analogy does, for the most part, closely resemble the interaction of PURTOPOI's subscribers, it's not surprising to find that the most common authorizing strategies used on PURTOPOI are addressing the writer of a previous message by name, quoting a passage from a previous message, and/or stating disagreement with or support for a previous speaker. Some examples of these follow. Note again that pseudonyms have been substituted for actual names. Also, note that experienced e-mail users indicate that they are quoting from a previous message by preceding each line of the quoted passage with a ">" symbol.

```
================================================
Date: Thu, 28 Feb 91 20:41:01 -500
From: Marty G.
Subject: Re: free speech Q

I'll use Kate's post as a springboard for my own.
While I agree with her in principle, I think she is
clouding the issue. [. . .]

================================================
Date: Fri, 15 Feb 91 11:55:14 -0500
From: Gary C.
Subject: Re: a new lurker speaks, with an anecdote

In response to Jerry P.'s comment about writing block
and community:
```

```
> One of the largest problems I have with my
> students is that they are like the students in
> F's finishing school: they cannot write unless
> they have something breathing down their neck.
> That something is usually a deadline and a
> grade. [. . .]
```

```
With regard to writer's block, Mike Rose has found
that many blockers suffer from something like an
excess of community: they imagine that their work has
to meet standards that are more rigorous and more
specific than they can handle. [. . .]
```

```
================================================================
Date: Sun, 3 Feb 91 13:51:07 -0500
From: Perry B.
Subject: "local" communities
```

```
Pam's insight on this medium's seeming ability to
transcend geographic community boundaries is
interesting. Our communities have always been limited
by geographical features: rivers, mountains, oceans,
and the like. [. . .] What I am interested in is the
sociolinguistic implications for such a discourse
community. Geographic location is an important
influence in the performative competence of any
speaker of a language. Now that we are in part
eliminating such boundaries, what will the effects on world
language and world culture be?
================================================================
```

These authorizing strategies make it easy to see why so many subscribers find Burke's (1973) parlor analogy a useful means of describing PURTOPOI's discussions, since making references to points others have previously made is a common tactic utilized in ordinary oral conversations. Additionally, as Chapter Two argued, the ability to utilize established conventions from a pre-existing medium is a useful technique when dealing with a technologically immature audience in a new medium. What's more, as an authorizing strategy, this device has the advantage of almost automatically qualifying the writer's topic by virtue of having already introduced the theme to the group. Consequently, much of the burden of justifying the topic to the group has often already been accomplished for the writer by previous writers.

However, the subject positions enabled by this authorizing strategy are severely limited because even writers who wish to disagree with prior postings must enter into easily identifiable relationships with previous writers. As a result, the kinds of new topics that may be introduced through this strategy are limited by the oppositional, hierarchical, causal, or other conventional sorts of associations that can be made between two ideas. For example, in the first two excerpts above, Marty G. and Gary C. are quickly able to establish their positions through the use of oppositional relationships. Marty G. claims that Kate has "clouded the issue" and then is able to move on to his counterpoint. Gary C. also is able to make his point quickly by observing that previous research on writer's block means that Jerry P.'s use of grades and deadlines to motivate his students may actually cause writer's block rather than cure it. Because linkage through opposition is the sort of connection that readers recognize easily, the writers have little difficulty introducing their subjects for the group.

In the third excerpt, however, Perry B. occupies a much less obvious position in relation to the previous writer, and thus his posting begins to stretch the relational links that can be made with this type of authorizing strategy. Rather than depending on the close correlation that exists between opposites, Perry B.'s message depends on a relatively loose connection between someone else's observation that e-mail crosses geographical boundaries to his own interest in sociolinguistic change within speech communities. Ultimately, Perry B. is able to make the linkages between these ideas clear enough for him to introduce a new, though still-related topic for discussion. Nevertheless, it also should be clear from the problems associated with his posting that the introduction of new topics isn't going to take place in a group where writers are expected to use references to previous messages in order to authorize their own messages. Instead, writers are going to be limited to topics that are chained to discussions that have come before.

The strategy of referring to other people's points not only excludes radically new topics; it also introduces a personal element to the authorization issue that impedes many subscribers' participation. Obviously, choosing a topic that the group recognizes as a legitimate theme for discussion does not automatically imbue an individual with the authority to speak and be heard. Writers must also demonstrate that they are qualified to speak on the topic; they must show that they share "the peculiar ways of knowing, selecting, evaluating, reporting, concluding, and arguing that define the discourse of our community" (Bartholomae, 1985, p. 134). As an authorizing strategy, informally referring to other members of the group by their first names is one means of expressing membership in the group and thereby qualifying yourself to speak. In effect, it says, "I know other established members of this group well enough to address them on a first-name basis; consequently, I must also know their methods of discoursing well enough to speak authoritatively on this topic."

Taken at face value, this strategy of calling attention to personal relationships with other members of the group isn't, in and of itself, necessarily an exclusionary discursive practice. However, if this technique is the dominant authorizing strategy used by a group, then it is possible that new members of the group will come to see having personal relationships with other established members as a necessary condition of the authorization process. Unfortunately, if it were the case that people who lacked personal relationships with other members were in fact being excluded, it would be difficult to show evidence of this exclusion since these people would be silenced. Indeed, one can really only speculate about the actual reasons individuals "lurk" or fail to participate in PURTOPOI's discussions since they leave no textual evidence of their existence for consideration. Nevertheless, there is some evidence that new subscribers do indeed feel this pressure to demonstrate their personal relationships with other members of PURTOPOI before they may speak. Below, for example, is a new member's first attempt to break into the group's discussion:

```
===============================================================
Date: Sat, 2 Feb 91 12:27:42 EST
From: Mary M.
Subject: Re: audience/community and e-mail groups

I joined the purtopoi network last week and am trying
to plug in or catch up or whatever. I like Jerry P.'s
comment about the difficulty of erasing what you have written
on this [discussion group] and the spontaneity
of it especially since the publications that we write often
preclude the use of our real voices and any
spontaneity at all. This is a nice change. I thank
Stan D., Nora A., and Beth D. for introducing me.
===============================================================
```

This excerpt shows that it has taken this new subscriber less than a week to discover the strategy of referring to previous writers by name, indicating just how frequently this authorizing strategy is deployed by members of the list. Yet, unlike the other writers using this authorizing strategy, Mary M. doesn't appear to use the technique to contribute a new topic to the discussion. Indeed, beyond her agreement with Jerry P.'s previous comment, she adds little of substance to the discussion and merely reiterates what has already been said. Instead, it would seem that her main purpose here is to demonstrate her relationships with other members in the group. The fact that she chose to list the subscribers who had invited her to the join the list in a public message rather than thanking them privately suggests that establishing her qualifications for membership in the group is at least as important to Mary M. as is contributing substantively to the ongoing discussion. Clearly, Mary M. sees her personal relationships with other members as her qualification for membership in PURTOPOI. In other words, it is her ability to adopt the subject position of a personal friend that enables her to speak.

There is also evidence that individuals feel compelled to authorize their voices by proving that they have existing personal relationships because those who lack such relationships occasionally complain that they are being forced to lurk. For example, in a discussion that explicitly addressed the issue of why more people didn't participate in discussions, the following posting appeared:

```
===================================================
Date: Fri, 1 Feb 91 18:34:20 EST
From: Jack D.
Subject: Re: audience/community and email

If we are going to come to a full understanding of
this email phenomenon, we'll need to hear (ironically enough)
from more "lurkers." [. . .] Why do they lurk? I'll add some-
thing for analysis; it was a misgiving I
felt when I realized that several people on this net
know each other quite well professionally and/or
personally. I've been lurking more often since I
realized that, watching others talk to each other but
more reluctant than I used to be to press the "Reply"
key. [. . . ] Obviously, I haven't been silenced
however. :) [. . .]
===================================================
```

Jack D.'s posting is only one example of a number of similar postings that make clear that subscribers feel compelled to publicly display their personal relationships with other members of PURTOPOI. However, what's particularly interesting about Jack

D.'s posting is that he is able to joke about not having been silenced.[1] And this, of course, raises the question of why he hasn't been silenced and suggests that there may be other authorizing strategies that subscribers can deploy in order to give themselves voice.

Later in the same message, Jack D. explains that, before he realized that many people on PURTOPOI knew each other personally, he believed "that the community was held together *only* by a common interest in 'things rhetorical'" and that his own interest in rhetorical issues "provided me with a kind of 'equal status' that made it easier for me to get actively involved." In other words, despite the fact that Jack D. later learned that his lack of personal relationships prevented him from having equal status as a member of the group, he had been and still was able to participate in the group because of his interest in things rhetorical. Thus, it seems that it is possible to give oneself a voice on PURTOPOI by demonstrating a professional commitment to the field of rhetoric.

Ironically, however, this really only replaces one exclusionary discursive practice with another, for although it may be possible for subscribers to authorize their voices without having to demonstrate that they have personal friends in the group, those who are qualified to speak are still limited to established professionals in the field of rhetoric—for example, people with faculty or administrative responsibilities, teachers with a long history of classroom experience, and researchers with a discernible publication record. Thus, instead of calling attention to their personal relationships with other members, new subscribers have to call attention to their professional status in the field, and one strategy new subscribers use is describing some current professional project they're working on. For example:

---

[1] It's clear that Jack D. is making a joke here because he uses what networkers call a "smiley face" or an "emoticon." A smiley face is made by typing a colon, followed by an open parentheses, and is usually followed by a space to make it easier to read. This combination of characters produces what looks like a smiling face tipped on it side—e.g., :) . By convention, networkers place smiley faces after texts which they intend to be interpreted as humorous or facetious, as is the case with Jack D.'s message. In addition to humor, networkers can use similar techniques to express other emotions. Irony uses a "winky face"—e.g., ;-) —and sadness uses a "frownie face"—e.g., :-(. In fact, this sort of code can even be used to express physical characteristics of an individual. For example, 8-<) would be interpreted to mean that the author wears glasses and has a mustache. David Sanderson (1993) has compiled a dictionary entitled *Smileys* that lists over 650 different variations on the smiley.

```
================================================================
```

Date: Wed, 15 Jan 1992 10:12:00 CST
From: Barb F.
Subject: Libraries and Composition

I am new to the list and hope this sort of inquiry is appropriate. I am a librarian with the clumsy title
of "bibliographic instruction librarian," and teach
library/research skills across the curriculum. I find
composition/rhetoric a nicely related field and try to keep up
with what's happening. [. . .] I am coming to
the conclusion that librarians and writing teachers
have (probably all teachers, really) have different
attitudes toward of even definitions of research and
am planning to study those differences, once I figure
out what questions to ask [. . .]

```
================================================================
```

Date: Fri, 5 Jul 91 08:39:23 -0400
From: Carl M.
Subject: Hello, I'm . . .

Thanks for inviting me into the purtopoi "electronic
parlor." But what are the conventions for entering an electronic conversation? Do you have badges for new
people? Or hazing ceremonies? Lacking guidance on
this matter, I'll begin by asking for help. I'm doing
a review of "books" in the field of *computers and
writing* For *College English.* What books should I
look at? [. . .] I'm committed to the new NCTE
anthology edited by Gail Hawisher and Cindy Selfe, and
I'm thinking the I should include the Boynton-Cook
anthology edited by Carolyn Handa. What about
Marjorie Montague's "Computers, Cognition, and Writing
Instruction"? [. . .]

```
================================================================
```

Obviously, these new subscribers are struggling to understand
the particular discursive practices of PURTOPOI. Unsure of conventions that might be exclusive to PURTOPOI, both choose to
adopt the position of academic researchers. Both demonstrate they
are professionals: Barb F. by giving her actual title, and Carl M. by
explaining that he's already committed to writing for a major journal in the field of English. Barb F.'s post is particularly interesting
because her professional position is outside the field of rhetoric

and composition; thus, she attempts to build a bridge between the two professions when she says that she finds composition nicely related to her own work. It's also worth noting that she later directly contradicts this assertion when she claims that librarians and writing teachers have different attitudes and definitions of research, suggesting that her original attempt to bridge the gap between the two field may have been more a function of strategic necessity than actual belief. Carl M. has a less difficult time since the professional position he adopts is more closely associated to the field of rhetoric and composition. Nevertheless, Carl M. still goes so far as to offer a literature review that demonstrates that he's on top of the current work in the area. In short, he seeks to authorize his voice to the PURTOPOI group by demonstrating that he's already of member of a larger, professional community.

These two examples, however, deal with new subscribers trying to break into the discourse of the group for the first time. Once a member has initially broken the ice, it would be too inconvenient and awkward to authorize his/her voice by calling so much attention to his/her professional status in every subsequent posting. Yet, until individuals have firmly established themselves as a members of the group through a number of postings over a period of time, the need to authorize his/her voice remains. And this has led some PURTOPOI members to adopt yet another convention that networkers refer to as a signature file.

Because different networks and different computer systems treat e-mail messages differently, PURTOPOI subscribers do not always receive the "From:" line in an e-mail message's header. Consequently, it's not always possible to tell who wrote a message unless writers actually put their names at the end of their messages. Since subscribers frequently try to refer to previous messages by citing the author's first name, PURTOPOI members need to know who wrote a particular message in order to talk about it. Furthermore, as one subscriber put it, PURTOPOI readers need to know the name of a writer since "MUCH of our interpretation of a message is dependent upon our knowledge of who wrote it. What they've said before is a big and I think helpful part of that, so some form of identification is useful" (see Nora A.'s message later). As a result, PURTOPOI members agreed to sign their messages.

Now, many subscribers simply sign their messages by typing their names at the end of the message; however, others choose to use long signature files. Signature files or ".sig files" allow users to sign their messages automatically because several e-mail packages automatically append these files to the end of all outgoing messages. These files (which the users themselves create) always include the user's name. Typically, they also provide one or more e-mail addresses that others can use should they need to reply to the author of the message directly. Additionally, several PUR-TOPOI members include some and a few individuals even include all of the following: the name of their institution, the department in which they work, their job title, office telephone numbers, fax telephone numbers, U.S. Mail addresses, zip codes, and even famous quotations or epigrams that reveal something about the personality of the author (see Appendix A).

There appear to be two immediate effects of the longer, often ornate signature files. Both are exclusionary (indeed, as one subscriber put it, "if your signature requires more than 4 lines, you're too important"). The first effect is that the technological knowledge required to sct up a .sig file distinguishes the individual from other, more novice users. It indicates an understanding of the electronic medium that has come from long exposure and participation in electronic discussion groups, and, although this doesn't establish the individual's professional subjectivity, it does identify that person as an experienced member of the network.

The second effect depends more on the text included in the signature file and is the way members establish their professional status in the field. Because many individuals include institutional affiliations and official titles such as "Director of Freshman Composition" or "Professor of English and Linguistics," they call attention to their location in the hierarchy of the profession. In fact, one member even goes so far as to list three separate titles for himself, indicating that he is a Full Professor, Chair of a program, and Coordinator of a special research project at his large research institution. Obviously, it is not necessary to sign a message with these formal titles if the purpose of signature files is merely to provide others with the information they might need should they desire to contact the writer directly. Hence, they must serve some other purposes as well.

One of the ways to explore the purposes behind this convention and, more importantly, how it has been reified by many subscribers is through an examination of a dispute that resulted when I suggested to the PURTOPOI membership that we dispense with the practice of appending long signature files to messages in January of 1992.

As the listowner for PURTOPOI, one of the services I was able to provide when I designed the list's architecture was an archive of all the group's messages. Basically, I configured the list so that any message sent to the group was automatically saved into a database that subscribers could then later search should they need to retrieve an old message or want to review the group's discussion for a topic that they were researching. The problem was that storing this database on the mainframe computer at Purdue took up valuable disk space that other students and faculty needed to use; consequently, the space allocated to PURTOPOI was limited, and I was being forced to delete the older files from the database to make room for the new ones.

Since long signature files used up this limited space, I sent out a message asking that subscribers limit their signature files to not more than three lines because of the aforementioned space limitations. This first request met immediate resistance from subscribers who complained, for example, that three lines were not enough. Thus, I sent out another, longer message to explain the problem in more detail. An excerpt from this message appears below:

```
=============================================================
Date: Mon, 13 Jan 1992 22:54:47 EST
From: Tharon Howard
Subject: Re: signature files


[. . .] I don't think people realize how big a problem this
is. I'm really not trying to be "nitpicky."
We're talking about HUGE amounts of space when you
look at the long term.

Since P[UR]T[OPOI] began, it has received 1,397
messages and over 2 million lines of text. Now, if
everybody who posts has a signature file 6 lines long
(and many of the ones that have been used lately are
even longer), then we're looking at 8382 lines of
text. When you consider that all the messages for the ENTIRE
MONTH of December (which was our most active
month ever) only has 6248 lines of text in it, then
maybe you can get a sense of why I'm so concerned
about this. We're talking about having to give up
over a month's worth of messages over a two year
period just so people can "toot their horns" and toss around
titles. I just can't see that it's worth it.
[. . .] I still believe that long signature files are wasteful,
exclusionary, and arrogant.
=============================================================
```

This message sparked off a rather heated and unfortunate discussion regarding whether or not one individual's signature file was arrogant; however, what was particularly interesting about

this discussion in terms of the examination were the number of
messages that defended the practice of using long signature files
in spite of the fact that they excluded certain individuals and certain kinds of discussions. For example:

```
===============================================================
Date: Tue, 14 Jan 1992 14:47:42 EDT
From: Laura T.
Subject: signature files


John, I think your signature file performs a very
useful function. After making a casual study, I note
a direct correlation between signature files (or lack)
and the scale of rigid-to-loose in terms of philosophy
and style.

===============================================================
Date: Tue, 14 Jan 1992 16:59:05 -0500
From: Nora A.
Subject: signature blocks


When I first arrived at [my] University and tried to
catch up on the bb mail from the two lists I read
often, I found that few people included their names.
Since [the university's] system didn't give me return addresses,
I was reading many messages with no idea at
all as to who had written them. It was a very strange experi-
ence. I hate to admit that it made me uneasy
and frustrated. However, it made the point very
clearly that MUCH of our interpretation of a message
is dependent upon our knowledge of who wrote it. What they've
said before is a big and I think helpful part
of that, so some form of identification is useful. [.
. .]


They [signature files] do, however, create a persona
as well as an atmosphere. Their effect reminds me of
the difference between discussions in which we all
wear suits and carefully balance our tea cups as
opposed to sitting around in sweaters (or sweats) with
our feet up on the coffee table. [. . .]

===============================================================
Date: Wed, 15 Jan 1992 04:16:25 -0500
From: John B.
Subject: Re: signature files
```

[. . .] I also must admit that I like to see where
others are from, so I appreciate having affiliations appended
and consider it a courtesy. Nora A. is right about the way in
which appending names and
affiliations changes the character of the discussion.
It seems to me that it does encourage people to be
more professional with their postings.

In my opinion, the least professional discussions take place on
conferences where the participants all use
psuedonums or "handles." It seems to me that the
"name only" concept also reduces the sense of personal responsibility people have for the content of their
postings. [. . .]

Yes, Nora A., most people (the men at least) wear
coats and ties at the professional conventions I
typically attend.

==

The authors of these excerpts clearly recognize that the practice of using signature files does indeed affect the nature of the group's discussion, forcing them to take on the more formal characteristics of the larger professional community. They also make clear that the purpose for using signature files has at least as much to do with establishing one's professional subjectivity as it does with making it easy for others to reply to a writer's message.

Perhaps what is more interesting is the fact that the kind of discussions that signature files encourage and the kind of subjects who could participate in them are, in many ways, opposed to the kinds of discussions and subject positions that were authorized in the debate over quoting that was previously discussed. In the quoting debate, subscribers argued that making individuals professionally responsible for their postings would destroy the informal, spontaneous character of the list's discussions. In fact, two of the writers, Laura T. and John B., agreed that the practice of quoting messages from the group's discussions should be discouraged. And yet, in this discussion, the practice of using signature files is encouraged for precisely the same reasons that quoting was discouraged—because it would make subscribers "more professional with their postings" and because it would increase "the sense of personal responsibility people have for the content of their postings."

There is considerable evidence that signature files have indeed made subscribers feel that they have a personal responsibility for their postings and that they must be professional. A number of subscribers, particularly graduate students, complain in private messages to me that they feel too intimidated by the number of established professionals on PURTOPOI to post to the list, despite the fact that it is a place where graduate student teaching assistants could talk about their research and teaching. Once again, I must point out that because these students are silenced, they lurk on PURTOPOI and leave no textual evidence of their exclusion there. However, a few graduate students at Purdue have discussed their inability to participate on PURTOPOI in other forums. These people subscribe both to PURTOPOI and to a second list, called PURWCLAS, which was created as a purely pedagogical space where undergraduate and graduate students could discuss their readings for courses or continue unfinished in-class discussions. It is on this other list or in personal e-mail messages where they know they can't be heard by the PURTOPOI group that they reveal their fears about PURTOPOI. Note that, as with PURTOPOI excerpts, I am protecting the writers' identity:

```
================================================================
Date: Thu, 2 Apr 1992 11:06:03 EST
From: Tammy H.
Subject: grammar and psychology


I know I should've posted this to purtopoi, but
frankly I was too chicken, and I needed to post
something to purwclas -- so delete away if you
don't want to hear a personal account of grammar
and one of my students. [. . .]


================================================================
Date: Sun, 5 Apr 1992 19:29:38 EST
From: Tammy H.
Subject: Fear of PURTOPOI
Tharon--


You wanted to know why I was too chicken to post to
PURTOPOI; I'm not sure I can give you a coherent
answer, but I'll try my best. Maybe part of my fear
comes about because I perceive PURTOPOI as a group for recog-
nized professionals in our field. Even though
this is my third year here (my first in the PhD
program), I don't feel I know enough to participate
in this group.


================================================================
Date: Thu, 2 Apr 1992 23:43:36 EST
From: Sam J.
```

Subject: Re: grammar and psychology

```
I'll explain why I'm intimidated by PURTOPOI. [. . .]
To be brief, I feel that many people on the list know
a lot more than I do about the topics of discussion,
and that most of the people have more experience. I
do not want to mail something out that makes me look
like an idiot and have it be received by this group of people.
[. . .]
```

===

Two important points must be made here. First, in spite of the fact that PURTOPOI was originally designed to be a safe space where graduate students and people from areas other than rhetoric could come together and talk about their research and teaching interests, these excerpts make clear that many graduate students don't feel PURTOPOI is safe for them. Graduate students can't afford to "look like an idiot" on PURTOPOI's electronic stage because they know that they are likely to encounter the people sitting in the audience in other professional contexts. They know, for example, that the same person who thought their PURTOPOI postings were written by an idiot also may end up sitting across the table from them at a job interview. As a matter of fact, during one of my own job interviews, one of the interviewers announced to me and his colleagues that he had unsubscribed from PURTOPOI because of messages that I had sent to the list (and of course I couldn't help noticing that I wasn't offered that particular position). Obviously, with so much at stake outside the boundaries of PURTOPOI's discussion, it should come as no surprise that graduate students are reluctant to risk looking foolish or unprofessional on PURTOPOI.

The second point has to do with the seeming self-contradiction of those who first argued against the practice of quoting from PURTOPOI because it discouraged the testing out of new, inchoate ideas, but who then argued for the use of signature files because it promoted a more professional level of discourse. It could be argued that these really are not self-contradictory positions if we take into consideration the fact that professionalism is a question of degrees, not absolutes. The terms professional and unprofessional are not unequivocal categories where both a topic of discussion and a style or method for discussing it must be considered either entirely professional or completely unprofessional. Instead, we are dealing with a continuum, so that it is not necessarily inconsistent to say that one practice demands more formality than is desired while maintaining that another convention introduces a level of informality that is undesirable.

What is important about these two observations is that they both show how much the subject positions that individuals inhabit are determined, not by conventions and discursive practices endemic and indigenous to PURTOPOI, but by the conventions and discursive practices of academics in the field of rhetoric.

And this leads back to the question of whether or not PURTOPOI is a constitutive community. Definitions of professionalism and the ability to establish an individual's status in the professional hierarchy don't come from PURTOPOI; they come from a larger community that surrounds and cuts across PURTOPOI. In other words, if the subject positions that, for example, graduate students occupy are constituted well, they become members of the PURTOPOI group. Indeed, even the model of the collegial hallway conversation, which allowed PURTOPOI members to use strategies like informally addressing previous writers by their first names as means of authorizing their messages, comes from PURTOPOI's original situatedness in the academic institution. It is the members' familiarity with hallway conversations at professional conferences and other academic institutional settings that allows these sorts of authorizing strategies to work on PURTOPOI. Without having subjects who had first been constituted in the larger community of professional scholars, PURTOPOI's discursive strategies could not function, for there would be no pre-existing subject formations into which members could be interpellated.

Thus, it does not appear possible to call PURTOPOI a constitutive community. It is not a site where the formation of radical, new subject positions is enabled. This should not, however, be taken to mean that PURTOPOI is without discursive practices that interpellate individuals into pre-existing subject positions. As the examination of authorizing strategies deployed on PURTOPOI demonstrates, conventions like the use of signature files do indeed affect what may be said, how it can be spoken, and who may say it. Consequently, though PURTOPOI may not be a constitutive community in and of itself, it may be considered a "local manifestation" of a constitutive community or what Porter (1992) has called a "forum." As Porter points out:

> A forum is a concrete, local manifestation of the operation of the discourse community. It is a physical location for discursive activity—such as a journal, a conference, a corporation, or a department within a corporation. Forums provide well-defined speaking and writing roles for its members, who are, in turn, defined by those roles. A forum shares assumptions about what objects are appropriate for examination and discussion, what operating functions are

performed on those objects, what constitutes "evidence" and "validity," and what formal conventions are followed. (p. 107)

PURTOPOI certainly accomplishes all these functions and thus has all the characteristics of a forum. Conventions like making informal, conversational references to others in the group do indeed provide "well-defined writing roles for members." The limited number of associations or linkages that can be made between old, existing topics and the new topics a writer wishes to introduce does shape "assumptions about what objects are appropriate for discussion." Discussions about the discursive effects of formal conventions such as whether it's acceptable to quote messages from the list or whether to use long signature files do shape assumptions about "what operating functions are performed" on the topics introduced. And finally, in the quoting discussion for example, members argued that it was acceptable to present findings and arguments on PURTOPOI that were "not always based in solid research," clearly indicating that PURTOPOI does have a set of standards regarding "what constitutes 'evidence' and 'validity'" for the group.

Thus, though PURTOPOI cannot be called a constitutive community and should instead be considered a forum, the effects of constitutive communities can nevertheless be seen on it. As Porter (1992) points out, "the forum is a *trace* of a discourse community" (p. 108), or "the forum is a sign" of the discourse community (p. 109). Consequently, forums like PURTOPOI are the particular and contingent representations of a complex and dynamic system of intertextual relationships. In other words, PURTOPOI is a collection of dramatic textual *events* occurring in time that reflect the particular working out or instantiation of a complex web or network of differential relations. So, although PURTOPOI is not a constitutive community, it is at least a *sign* of them.

SUMMARY

In terms of their explanatory power as heuristics or as analytical frameworks that have given guidance to this examination of electronic discussion groups, both the individualistic and constitutive approaches to community reveal a great deal about electronic discussion groups. Each enables us to ask different questions of such groups, allowing us to explore different aspects of their composition. The individualistic offers insights into the purposes of such groups, what motivates their members, what must be sacrificed in order to benefit from membership in the groups, and how individuals can attempt to change the groups' discussions. The constitutive enables an understanding of electronic discussion groups' internal power relations, the mechanisms that allow texts to be produced, and the devices that prevent individuals from changing the groups' discussions.

However, in response to the question "is it possible to call PUR-TOPOI an electronic community," the answer is, once again, yes and no. It is possible to call PURTOPOI and similar groups communities if we are willing to adopt an individualistic communitarian's perspective, since such groups do seem to be collections of individual subjectivities bound together by their reciprocal relationships and their willingness to make sacrifices for the good of the group's common purposes. However, from the constitutive communitarian perspective, groups like PURTOPOI are not communities but are, instead, forums or local manifestations of constitutive communities that nonetheless determine what may be said, the manner through which it can be spoken, and who may say it.

Given these competing findings, what can be said to those activists and theorists whose arguments supporting the use of NT in order to bring about socioeconomic, political and educational change depend on the existence of electronic communities? Does the use of these two analytical frameworks shed any light on the claim that electronic communities eventually may become sites where radical, new subjectivities that are able to resist and ultimately change the corrupt and exclusionary practices of traditional media are formed?

Obviously, electronic discussion groups when viewed from the individualistic communitarian perspective do allow for the emergence of resisting subjects and agents of change. However, this finding depends on the existence of a transcendental subject, a subjectivity empowered with a knowledge of what is Right, Good, and True regardless of the medium in which it is operating. Such a finding neither advances nor denies the revisionary possibilities of NT since its operation is independent of media contexts. Furthermore, the constitutive communitarian finding that electronic discussion groups like PURTOPOI are not communities certainly cannot advance claims that depend on the existence of electronic communities. However, although groups like PUR-TOPOI are not communities, the observation that they are forums does seem to confirm findings discussed in Hawisher (1992), Selfe (1992), and Sim's (1992) studies at the beginning of this chapter.

As all three of those researchers observed, electronic discussion groups do not escape the discursive practices of their institutional sites by relocating their discussions in a virtual space. Instead, such discussion groups continue to exist within the larger social and institutional frameworks. And it would be a mistake to think of these larger social and institutional frameworks as singular and monolithic, for they are neither. As was observed in the previous section, they are complex and dynamic systems of intertextual relationships, changing and evolving in and across time. Furthermore, a forum like PURTOPOI should not be considered the product of one single system or community. Although a single system may be dominant in a particular forum, other competing systems may be present. As Porter (1992) notes, "forums represent conventional, sociological boundaries, where several discourse communities may intersect. We may, in investigating a forum, discover that several competing ideologies, methodologies, principles, and stances intersect" (pp. 95–96).

The finding that electronic discussion groups like PURTOPOI are forums where competing communities intersect leaves some hope for those who wish to argue that such groups can become sites where resistance and change is made possible. In the next chapter, I will examine an approach to forums and subject formation that explains why this is the case. However, for the purposes of this chapter, the revisionary promise of NT held out by many early theorists and activists cannot be supported by findings about PURTOPOI. The examination of PURTOPOI suggests that electronic discussion groups cannot become sites where radical, new subjectivities able to resist and ultimately change the corrupt and exclusionary practices of traditional media are formed. Instead, such groups seem to remain mortgaged to forms and practices that have come before.

chapter seven

Play, Positionality, and the Articulatory Moment

INTRODUCTION

We have examined the explanatory power the individualistic and constitutive communitarian perspectives offer the NT researcher. This final chapter explores how the view of electronic discussion groups as forums where competing communities intersect makes it possible to argue that groups like PURTOPOI may be able to serve as sites where resistance and change are possible, and thereby achieve one of the major goals of this project. To do this, I will: 1) briefly review how locating the act of critique in an inside/outside binary has contributed to the problem of theorizing resistance; 2) introduce the concept of "positionality," which several other rhetorical theorists have also borrowed from feminist standpoint theory; and 3) introduce the concept of the "articulatory moment," which comes from the work of Laclau and Mouffe (1985). Ultimately, the goal will be to re-envision the binary between individualistic and constitutive communitarian theories in a way that will allow researchers to utilize the individualist communitarians' concept of reciprocity, while maintaining the constitutive communitarians' cognizance of interpellation and subject formation. In other words, the goal is to describe "a praxis of resistance" that, as Smith (1988) has noted, "demands a theory of the 'subject' which allows for gaps and fissures in the agent's experience of interpellative messages" (p. 39). A revision of the individualistic and constitutive binary will allow me to show where these "gaps and fissures" exist and hopefully will enable me to lay the foundations for an approach to ethical membership and resistance in both electronic and print forums.

INSIDE/OUTSIDE

It is not necessary to view the revisionary process as necessitating the destruction of either the individualistic or constitutive approaches to communities. Rather, throughout this project I have consistently sought to demonstrate the explanatory power of each of these familiar tools; in fact, the previous chapter illustrates the usefulness of these approaches as analytical frameworks that enable researchers to constitute different objects as phenomena suitable for examination, frameworks that allow us to ask different questions of those objects. The individualistic framework made it possible to probe members' motivation to post messages and to remain part of a group, a question that's difficult to formulate within the constitutive framework. On the other hand, the constitutive framework made it possible to explore the writing positions members must adopt in order to be authorized by the group, thereby calling attention to another aspect of membership that is difficult to foreground within the individualistic framework.

To destroy one of these frameworks in favor of the other or to destroy both in favor of a third, alter*native* framework would be like building a house without doors to other rooms; it would, in effect, allow an observer to see only "the party in the parlor." Or to put this in terms of WANS, it would be like a network architect constructing a computer network without installing gateways (i.e., the computers that sit on the boundaries between two or more networks); it would be like constructing a space without the virtual doorways that allow users access to conversations taking place in the other rooms of our virtual house.

NT theorists should avoid and defer agonistic either/or formulations that would force the conclusion that there is one and only one answer to any question. Instead, we need to adopt a multifaceted Janusian stance that keeps at least one door open to

Other possibilities. I believe we must enable and celebrate the struggle and conflict between competing subject positions and communities, and for this reason I believe we need to knock holes in the walls of Burke's (1973) parlor or at least relocate his parlor analogy in a multiroom house. Like Porter (1992), I believe that Burke's parlor analogy needs to be revised because it is too singular and too monolithic in its approach to discourse communities. Burke's analogy has been useful since it suggests how audiences shape speakers and writers; yet, Burke's model also ends up promoting another agonistic either/or formulation since it suggests that either we enter the *only* conversation in the room or we don't. We either must be inside the conversation or outside it; no other choice is possible. However, in the Porter analogy (1992), rather than offering one, single conversation that we must enter, Porter asks us to imagine that a reception is going on in the parlor and that there are "several groups engaged in discussion" (p. 80). Rather than forcing us to join Burke's singular conversation or remain silenced, Porter's scene suggests that we may move around the room, joining some conversations and backing out of others.

Like Porter's reception analogy, I also believe we need to pluralize Burke's parlor. Indeed, I would problematize the scene further still by asking that we imagine it were possible to move, not only from conversation to conversation, but also from the parlor to the kitchen to the bathroom, carrying with us as we move from room to room our selective and limited memories of those conversations we left behind. In other words, like the Purdue graduate students who were able to leave the various conversations going on in PURTOPOI's virtual space to relocate in another space where it was possible for them to speak comfortably, I imagine a party where it's possible to leave the formal milieu of the parlor and its effects on the conversations there to relocate in the kitchen where that room and the ongoing conversations in it would allow for different kinds of topics and different ways of discussing them, including perhaps comments and observations about those smug, self-righteous snobs in the parlor.

Superimposing this multiroom party analogy on the discussion of the individualistic and constitutive analytical frameworks, I would liken each of these communitarian approaches to a room in the imaginary house: each with its own particular set of furnishings promoting certain kinds of discussion within it; and yet, each unavoidably imbricated in a whole system of other/Other relations by the very walls that make them possible. Each is dependent on the existence of Other rooms for its very existence; each needing, not only walls between them, but also different kinds of furniture on the other side of those walls, distinctions from without that will make the landscapes within meaningful.

This last point (i.e., the differences in the furniture or in the internal landscapes of the different rooms) is particularly significant because it implies that somehow there must be a space, a crack, or a doorway between the walls through which *remembering* subjects may pass. Without doorways that allow remembering subjects to bring their memories of what is *outside* the room to bear on what is *inside* the room, there can be no meaning. Consider, for example, the famous lines from Frost's poem (1973), "The Road Not Taken." The persona of the poem, a hiker, comes to a point where the path splits in two directions and is forced to make a choice between them. S/he surveys the landscape hoping for some sign of Nature upon which to base some reasonable choice between the two paths. Ultimately, finding no natural sign in the landscape yet having made the choice and feeling the need to rationalize that choice, the traveler concludes:

> I shall be telling this with a sigh
> Somewhere ages and ages hence:
> Two roads diverged in a wood, and I—
> I took the one less traveled by,
> And that has made all the difference. (p. 197)

What, we should ask, is the "that" which "has made all the difference?" How can we know that the traveler's choice made any difference at all without having traveled both roads in order to compare them? The point I'm trying to make here is, of course, that we can't. And this is also the case with the rooms in our imaginary house. It is only our knowledge that there are other possibilities or other potential landscapes that gives meaning to the rooms we have left *and* to the room we are entering.

If I may abandon the imaginary house party for the moment to return to Burke's parlor analogy, it should now be possible to see how this binary between the inside/outside confronts communitarian theorists with a difficult dilemma. Since the conversation in Burke's parlor is the only one around, individuals can be located in only one of two places: they either can be inside the conversation or they can be outside it. Consequently, they seem to have the same problem that the traveler in Frost's poem had: how to choose between two paths or places when there are no meaningful signs in the landscape that might serve as foundations upon which to base that decision. To analyze or critique the community, subjects have to be able to stand outside the community where the differences between inside and outside become meaningful, thereby providing subjects with foundations on which to base their choice. And yet, having taken a stance outside, how can subjects also be inside since, by definition, being outside means that they cannot also be inside? That is, if critique depends on the differences between inside and outside, and being outside means that subjects can't be inside, then standing outside the community to offer a critique is impossible since subjects don't have access to the differences of the inside.

The upshot of this rather confusing state of affairs is that theorists are confronted with a dilemma. The binary logic being used here is governed by the "law" of noncontradiction, and this law states that it is not possible for subjects to be both inside and outside at the same time. However, a subject's ability to critique a community depends on being both inside and outside at the same time so that meaningful differences may be observed. Therefore we must conclude either that critique is not possible or that subjects may be both inside and outside at the same time. As it is unacceptable to conclude that critique is not possible, NT theorists must create a space for critique and demonstrate that it is possible for subjects to be both inside and outside at the same time. This can be done through an examination of the logic on which the inside/outside binary depends.

There are two problems with the logic of the binary form. The first is the impression that it is somehow observerless. Binaries don't just happen; they aren't ontological facts fixed in being and time, though some binaries like male/female, madness/reason, or human/nature have become so reified in certain communities they have developed almost the same status as ontological facts. Nevertheless, binaries aren't actual, they're virtual; or to use de Saussure's (1989) term, they are "arbitrary" (p. 116). They are *used* by people in and across time; they require *an observer* immersed in a system of differential social relations to function. Hence, they are as particular and contingent as the subjects who use them. The second problem is that the logic of binaries requires that the observer/user adopt a wholly spatial orientation with respect to the objects being observed. In other words, binaries locate contradictory objects in spatial opposition to each other. Water, for example, occupies the space of liquids; ice, solids. Hence, according to the spatial logic of binaries, since liquids are not solids, water cannot be ice.

The obvious point here is that binaries like the inside/outside or the solid/liquid binary don't take into account the temporal dimension. Consequently, the objects located within a binary's spatial framework assume a timeless and totally unified form. Indeed, the objects of a binary cannot be fragmented *except* across time. The very idea of a fragment is unthinkable and unspeakable within the spatial logic of the binary since, as soon as an object becomes fragmented, each resulting fragment is seen to be a new object in and of itself; it becomes the object of anOther space, radically distinct from the original. Within the timeless spatial logic of the binary then, it is not possible to explain how ice becomes water or how water becomes ice; ice must *be* one thing, water anOther. Similarly, it is this same timeless spatial logic that says that a subject cannot *be* an insider and an outside at the same time.

Of course, we all know that ice certainly can *become* water. But we know this because we are *remembering* subjects and are thus able to take into account the temporal dimension that is lacking in the logic of binaries. As remembering subjects, we exist in and across time and bring a contingent continuity to observation. I say contingent because (as the following discussion of articulatory moment will show) we are still situated *in* time; yet, because we also exist *across* time (which will be discussed further in the notion of the positionality) there is still a degree of continuity. In short, because we exist across time, we can take objects like ice out of their timeless places in binaries and observe how these *same* objects fragment across time, occupying new places.

Returning now to the role of the insider/outsider binary in the individualistic and constitutive approaches to communitarian theory, both these views depended on the timeless spatial orientation of binary logic in their location of subjects. The utopian and pragmatic determinism problematic resulted from the inability of subjects to become both insiders and outsiders at the same time. In the case of the individualistic view, subjects were always outsiders and never insiders because they were always subjected by a transcendent common sense. They could not be subjects inside a community or subjects of a community because their subjectivities always depend on their understanding of an eternal super/sensible realm, a realm quite literally above, beyond, and especially outside the sensible world of contingent communal experience. Hence, because individualistic communitarian subjects were always outside and therefore unable to recognize meaningful differences between inside and outside, their knowledge was predetermined. Constitutive communitarian subjects, on the other hand, always were seen to be insiders and never outsiders. Their subjectivities always were constituted by their location inside communities that they could never escape. This once again led to a form of determinism because there was no way for subjects to position themselves both as insiders and outsiders so that critique and change was possible.

Based on this examination, it's clear that the inside/outside binary is a kind of trap. This binary (and more importantly the timeless spatial logic upon which it depends) can lead to forms of radical determinism and hopelessness. Binary logic alone, without the introduction of the temporal, is (to return to my previous analogy) like building a multiroom house without any doors because there's no way in or out; that is there's no agency for change.

Despite this observation, however, one should not conclude that we must dispense with all binaries. If change is to occur, there is still the need for difference and conflict. To construct objects for examination, we still must establish boundaries between an object we wish to discuss and those other objects from which it differs for, as de Saussure (1989) notes, "no linguistic item can ever be based, ultimately, upon anything other than its *non-coincidence* with the rest" (p. 116, emphasis added). In other words, a house without walls cannot stand. But we also must construct walls and the subjects that inhabit the rooms they create so that individuals can adopt a Janusian stance in the doorway, a stance that allows them to look both inside and outside, both forward and backward at the same time. And to construct these walls and these Janusian subjects, I need to flesh out the notion of contingent continuity that introduces the temporal dimension into the differential logic of binaries. Two concepts need to be added to this discussion: 1) the concept of positionality from feminist standpoint theory that deals with the continuity of subjects and 2) the concept of the articulatory moment from Laclau and Mouffee's (1985) *Hegemony and Socialist Strategy* that deals with why continuity must remain contingent.

POSITIONALITY

The concept of a subject's positionality comes from the recent work of feminist standpoint theorists and their attempts to deal with many of the same problems posed by the inside/outside binary discussed above. Specifically, the concept has been used to explain how it is possible for subjects to be both inside and outside a discourse community at the same time. First coined by Alcoff in a 1988 article, "Cultural Feminism Versus Post-Structuralism: The Identity Crisis in Feminist Theory," the term subsequently has been applied to the problem of resistance and accommodation problem in the field of rhetoric by Bizzell and by Jarratt and Reynolds.

Bizzell (through her examination of antifoundationalist approaches to rhetorical theory [1990]) and Jarratt and Reynolds (through their examination of poststructuralist approaches to rhetorical theory [1990]) argue that the antifoundationalist and the poststructuralist approaches have left rhetoricians with no privileged place from which we can examine the practices of our own discourse communities. As Bizzell (1990) put it, "anti-foundationalist philosophers are preoccupied with the necessity of saying no to foundationalist knowledge. Hence their concern is to simply knock down any authority claims made by others and to offer instead little more than a presumed individual autonomy" (p. 666). Jarratt and Reynolds (1990) similarly argue that, "a theory that reduces all discourse to the play of difference cannot adequately serve the feminist goal of articulating specifically gendered subjectivities in their own historical moments" (p. 2). Clearly then, Bizzell, Jarratt, and Reynolds are confronting the problem of pragmatic determinism that results from the inside/outside binary. The antifoundationalist and poststructuralist approaches "have no positive program" and prevent researchers from making any claims about the value of their observations because what researchers see has been predetermined by what the research community tells them to see (Bizzell, 1990, p. 667). In other words, the antifoundationalist and poststructuralist approaches don't allow researchers to get outside their research communities. Hence, no new contributions can come from within a field because all knowledge is relative to the field.

Positionality offers at least a partial solution to this problem of licentious relativism by enabling what Jameson (1988) calls a "principled relativism" (p. 65). Positionality recognizes that subjectivities are constructed; yet, it also recognizes the importance of being able to occupy different subject positions. Rather than the unified, whole subject that emerges from the timeless spatial logic of the insider/outsider binary, the concept of positionality asks us to view the subject as the fragmented and fluid position of *an individual* moving in and especially across time. Instead of a whole spatial unit that must be entirely located in one and only one place, this fluid view of subjectivity can be explained as:

> A non-essentialist notion of a "nomadic" self that makes itself, interdiscursively, as it moves between various and contradictory

subject positions it encounters (and inhabits or resists or trans-
forms for its own purposes) in the fragmentary course of everyday
life. (Trimbur, 1989, p. 697)

Basically then, the concept of positionality introduces the temporal continuity necessary to allow individuals to be both insiders
and outsiders simultaneously because it drives a wedge between
subject positions and the individual. It says, in effect, that the
subject positions that members of communities inhabit do not
represent the sum total of possible subjectivities or standpoints. It
says that we should not equate the subject with the individual;
rather, we should view members of a community as *subjected individuals*, individuals who belong to numerous discourse communities and who have personal engrams of Other subjugations. As
individuals, we remember who we were at other times.

In sum then, positionality asks us not to view subjectivity as
a state of *being* in the same sense that ice had to *be* a solid.
Instead, it asks us to see subjectivity as a process of individuals
becoming subjected in the same way that ice may *become*
water/fluid or even steam/gas. Furthermore, positionality asks
us to celebrate the differences that result from becoming. Like
the Janus metaphor, it does not reject boundaries between
objects because it recognizes that we desperately need the conflicts they create to resist, re-envision, and revise what we
already know. Rather than nostalgic, petulant yearnings for a
return to a golden "mainstream" that has been left behind by a
new generation of theorists (Hairston, 1990, p. 696) or longings
for the rediscovery of a sincere personal voice that has been
repressed by a "manipulative and insidious form of pedagogical
totalitarianism" (Stewart, 1990, p. 691), positionality and standpoint theory do not ask us to view communities or forums as
peaceful cohabitation. Rather, we should view them as sites of
dynamic struggle and confrontation. The concept of positionality
values and embraces difference and conflict because, as Jaggar
(1985) points out, it recognizes that "a standpoint is a position
in society from which certain features of reality come into promi-
nence and from which others are obscured" (p. 382). Thus, it
promotes polyphony and asks us to actively seek out diverse and
competing positionalities that will open us to "features of reality"
that have been obscured by the discursive practices of the dominant ideology.

Put in these terms, positionality could be defined as an excess
of subjectivity that results from the continuity of the individual.
That is to say, because a particular subject position depends on

the concomitant existence of Other subject positions from which it differs and because individuals have inhabited these Other subject positions across time, the continuous and chronological existence of individuals brings an excess of subjectivity to the subjugation process that occurs within a community. As Smith (1988) has also observed:

> The interpellation of the "subject" into oppressed positions is not complete and monolithic; rather, interpellation also produces contradiction and negativity. The necessary existence of various and different subject-positions in the interpellated "subject" produces resistance to the domination while still being in a sense part of, or a by-product of, that logic. (p. 152)

Because positionality is a celebration of differential logic, it recognizes that a totally sutured, constituted subject cannot exist since the concept of a unified hegemonic subject always must be supplemented by its differential relation to other subject positions in the same way that the meaning of water is supplemented by ice and steam. Furthermore, just as a particular puddle of water can, *across time*, freeze into ice or evaporate into clouds, a particular individual brings an excess of supplementary subject positions into an interpellation process that also occurs across time. Consequently, subjected individuals may thus become outsiders, limited critique becomes possible, and we may move from room to room in our virtual house.

ARTICULATORY MOMENTS

Although the concept of positionality adds the temporal continuity needed to disrupt the spatial logic of inside/outside binaries, it does so by driving a wedge between the individual and the subject. The introduction of the individual is potentially dangerous since it may suggest to some that identity is possible in the individual. In other words, the continuity of the individual could become a retrogress into essentialism and utopian determinism if the individual is viewed as the unified and originary source of identity. Indeed, if the individual is seen as a conscious entity choosing between subject positions, then subjectivities become little more than masks that are donned by a manipulative self, masks that play no role in the formation of consciousness and meaning. Thus, to prevent this from obtaining, it is important to demonstrate how the continuity of the individual is contingent, and I will do so by showing how consciousness is born of what Laclau and Mouffee call the "articulatory moment."

Laclau and Mouffee (1985) define the articulatory moment this way:

> We will call *articulation* any practice establishing a relation among elements such that their identity is modified as a result of the articulatory practice. The structured totality resulting from the articulatory practice, we will call *discourse*. The differential positions, insofar as they appear articulated within a discourse, we will call *moments*. By contrast, we will call *element* any difference that is not discursively articulated. (p. 105)

For Laclau and Mouffee then, articulation is a process that requires a taxonomizing move as a necessary condition of discourse. In other words, the process of creating objects for discourse requires a classificatory act during which the objects are formulated and distinguished by means of differential relationships with other, alterior objects. The meaningful identity of an object thus does not depend on the inviolate form of the thing itself (the object as element); rather, it requires Derridean supplementation from outside, it requires the addition of a system of others from which the object differs and to which it defers. Hence nondiscursive objects or elements are meaningless and unintelligible. Or as Laclau and Mouffee (1985) put it, "Our analysis rejects the distinction between discursive and non-discursive practices. It affirms that every object is constituted as an object of discourse, insofar as no object is given outside every discursive condition of emergence" (p. 107).

The upshot of this analysis is that meaningfulness and intelligibility must occur in the articulatory moment and cannot be the result of an individual operating as a conscious entity outside the contingency of the moment. Hence, an individual may have continuity across time, but *consciousness* occurs *in time*, in the articulatory moment or in what Volosinov (1973) has also called "interindividual territory" (p. 12). According to Volosinov, "Consciousness takes shape and being in the material of signs created by an organized group in the process of its social intercourse" (p. 13). In other words, meaningfulness and intelligibility can come only from what I previously called the subjected individual, a continuity subject to the social contingencies of the articulatory moment. Thus, for Volosinov:

> It is essential that the two individuals be *organized socially*, that they compose a group (a social unit); only then can the medium of

signs take shape between them. The individual consciousness not only cannot be used to explain anything, but, on the contrary, is itself in need of explanation from the vantage point of the social, ideological medium. (p. 12)

From this discussion then, it should be clear that the individual alone cannot serve as a conscious entity able to choose subject positions in his/her own best interests for consciousness emerges in the articulatory moment when subjectivity is formed. Consequently, although the continuity of the individual brings a range of possible subject positions to the articulatory moment, the individual cannot consciously choose which subjectivity will be actualized since the consciousness upon which such a choice must be based presupposes the existence of an already formed subjectivity. Hence, continuity is contingent.

RECOVERING RECIPROCITY

At this point, all the conceptual components needed for an understanding of why it is that electronic forums like PURTOPOI can serve as sites of resistance and change have been assembled. It is now possible to understand why it is necessary for us to have walls in our virtual house and yet how it is also possible for individuals to adopt a Janusian stance in the doorway between those walls.

As the discussion of the articulatory moment and positionality's celebration of difference has made clear, we need walls in our house in order for meaning and intelligibility to emerge. Without the "non-coincidence" of one object to others (de Saussure, 1989, p. 116), we would lack the ability to compare phenomena and to perceive meaningful differences. Without walls, we give up the very consciousness that makes choice possible. The price of this consciousness is contingency, but it is *NOT* determinism, as the discussion of positionality has shown.

Subjected individuals *are* able to resist constitutive communities because they have an excess of subjectivity. It may be that "consciousness becomes consciousness only once it has been filled with ideological (semiotic) content, consequently, only in the process of social interaction" (Volosinov, 1973, p. 11). Nevertheless, as Smith (1988) points out, "where discourses actually take hold of or produce the so-called 'subject' they also *enable* agency and resistance" (p. 40), and they do so because they depend on an excess of subjectivity in order to hail the individual into a particular subject position during the articulatory moment.

Thus, positionality shows that subject positions can never be monolithic, totally sutured entities. Indeed, positionality makes clear that in order to inhabit a subject position at all, individuals must adopt a Janusian stance in the doorway where the noncoincidence between the furniture of the parlor and the furniture of the kitchen is made clear.

Consider, for example, the Purdue graduate students who did not wish to participate in the discussions on PURTOPOI and chose instead to carry on discussions in a different room. If it were possible for the graduate students really to be wholly inside PURTOPOI (i.e., had they really been interpellated into a monolithic, totally sutured subject position created by the discursive practices on PURTOPOI), then we could have expected them to explain their silence on PURTOPOI in terms of the dominant subject position described in the previous chapter. But they did not. They made no mention of PURTOPOI as a collaborative brainstorming effort, as a testing ground for inchoate, unpolished ideas, or as a space where they even could play devil's advocate. Instead, they explained their silence in terms of subject positions that they played outside PURTOPOI. They explained their failure to participate in PURTOPOI's discussions as fears of the effects that PURTOPOI might have in other contexts. In other words, they were unwilling to risk "looking like an idiot," not because they were in a subject position on PURTOPOI that would have made them look foolish, but because they went into PURTOPOI with an excess of other subjectivities. The fact that they knew they could have participated in PURTOPOI was clear when Tammy H. began her posting on PURWCLAS with "I know I should have posted this to PURTOPOI," and indeed some of her classmates had already successfully posted to PURTOPOI and had received responses that suggested that other members of PURTOPOI accepted the appropriateness of their contributions and the authorizing strategies they had adopted.

Consequently, Tammy H. was not silenced on PURTOPOI because she lacked an adequate writing role or credibility, nor because she didn't have personal relationships with others on the list, nor because she chose an inappropriate topic for discussion, nor because she didn't have valid forms of evidence in support of her arguments. Actually, her PURWCLAS message was a discussion of the problems she'd encountered in teaching grammar to freshmen in her composition classes and appeared at the same time that people on PURTOPOI (including some Purdue graduate students) were posting messages that also shared their personal observations about the teaching of grammar. Thus, she easily could have chosen to send her message to PURTOPOI and even was urged to do so by her classmates and by both the PURTOPOI listowners.

Tammy H.'s choice not to post wasn't based on PURTOPOI's dominant discursive practices; instead, it seems to have been based on her desire for reciprocity in contexts other than those on PURTOPOI, in other rooms of the imaginary house. Rather than deciding whether or not to post to PURTOPOI based on her position as an experienced teacher and as a developing researcher in the field of rhetoric and composition, someone with a commitment to sharing and testing out ideas and experiences within a dialogic framework, Tammy H. chose not to participate based on the lack of remuneration she would receive in her positions as a student and as a potential job candidate, subject positions that she brought to PURTOPOI, subject positions made meaningful because of the individualistic concept of reciprocity. From these other subject positions she inhabited as a contiguous individual, she interpreted posting as a risk. What's more, she constructed PURTOPOI's subscribers not as fellow researchers, but as graduate faculty, prelim examiners, dissertation committee members, or job interviewers. From these positions, the risk of "looking like an idiot" outweighed the potential remuneration she might get from PURTOPOI so that reciprocity was not possible for her in that room, and she as a resisting agent chose to enter another.

It is clear that Tammy H. *could have* been interpellated, but this must not be taken to mean that Tammy H. and others like her somehow misinterpreted the role(s) that they were supposed to play on PURTOPOI or that they took subject positions that should not have been taken on PURTOPOI. Such a view would lead back into the agonistic either/or and inside/outside formulations I have sought to avoid. Such a view would, in effect, deny the legitimacy of these writers' historical experiences as individuals, sending us sliding down the nihilistic slippery-slope of poststructuralist indeterminacy and back into pragmatic determinism. Such a view would say, in effect, "You should have let your conscious identities be constructed this way," thus invalidating the very grounds that allowed Tammy H. to experience her oppression and constructing her as an eternal outsider. My point is that Tammy H. is one example of individuals who are able to resist interpellation into one, particular subject position by inhabiting another position that they bring with them. That is, Tammy H. and others rejected the currently dominant subject position on PURTOPOI—that of a developing teacher/researcher who wishes to test unpolished ideas and arguments without fear of damaging her/himself professionally—

because from the position of a graduate student it seems clear that there is a great deal of potential for professional damage. Had Tammy H. and other graduate students not inhabited this other subject position, then they might have never considered the potentially negative consequences of posting. Without a distinct position from which it was possible to re-examine the advantages and disadvantages of posting, graduate students on PURTOPOI might have never *become conscious* of the dangers.

Thus, examining the positionality of an individual allows NT researchers to introduce the individualistic communitarian concept of reciprocity without violating the constitutive communitarian awareness of interpellation and socially constituted subjects. Because contingent continuity recognizes that "'choice' or conscious-calculation is possible only as the by-product of the human agent's negotiation among and between particular subject positions" (Smith, 1988, p. 40), it thus avoids the utopian determinism of individualistic communitarian theories that seek to explain resistance in terms of a transcendent subject located wholly outside the contingent and particular realm of social interaction. On the other hand, because the positionality born of the articulatory moment allows the use of reciprocity to explain the motivation for and mechanism behind resistance, it thus avoids the pragmatic determinism of constitutive communitarian theories that trap subjects wholly inside communities where pre-existing discursive categories and formations determine what may be thought and said.

CONCLUSION: A JANUSIAN SYNTHESIS

In the Introduction to this project, I warned that I would be situating myself in the spaces where the boundaries between electronic publishing and print media play and that this Janusian perspective might seem two-faced to those accustomed to the monological voice of a scholar speaking from the Olympian ground of higher reason. And yet, if I might be allowed a metalinguistic moment for self-conscious self-defense, I would point out that, to the degree that any book can be called a dissertation on some subject, the etymology of dissertation belies the linear treatment of a topic in which the author, from a singular, univocal subject position, marches relentlessly, etiologically toward some inexorable conclusion. Instead, a dissertation (*dis* + *serere*) is literally the undoing or taking apart (*dis*) of objects that have previously been put together, joined, or connected into a series through speech (*serere*). Or an alternative interpretation is that a dissertation is the cutting apart or fragmentation of a theme (*dis*) by means of a series of distinct points or positionalities that like the points or teeth of a serrated knife (*serratus*) saws through the subject.

Whichever of these interpretations we choose to use, the point I wish to make is that dissertators are required to inhabit a number of different positionalities in order to differ from or make intelligible the various propositions they encounter. Hence, I would maintain that, in keeping with the etymological demands of the dissertation genre, I have adopted a fluid, shifting, and unfixed Janusian stance that has allowed me to embrace those multifarious positionalities through which my points or teeth of noncoincidence could emerge.

From a more traditional perspective, this shifting, Janusian perspective may make it appear as though I have sought to occupy apolitical sites from which I could attack other theories without remaining loyal (or being subjected to) any particular theory. It may seem that I have shirked all responsibility in my refusal to privilege either the NT medium over the print (Chapters One and Two), or electronic publishing over traditional publishing (Chapter Three), or individualistic approaches over constitutive (Chapter Four), or rhetorics of accommodation over rhetorics of resistance (Chapter Five), or even those inside PURTOPOI over those outside PURTOPOI (Chapter Six). However, I believe my aim has had continuity, for, in each of the preceding binaries, I sought to show how taking an agonistic stance that invoked the spatial, atemporal logic of the insider/outsider binary leads to forms of radical determinism, determinisms that are antithetical to rhetoric as a means of adjudicating between competing knowledge claims. In other words, for rhetoric to obtain, knowledge never can be certain and universal; there never can be, as was explained in the discussion of theory hope, a general (T)heory. For adjudication and choice to occur, knowledge and theory must be kept probable, local, and contingent. There must always be some doubt, some indeterminacy, some *resistance* to the dominant view.

My constant aim then has been to create a space for resistance within the existing communitarian theories examined here. Thus, I have not sought to eliminate these existing theories by privileging one over the other or by relocating them within some third, alternative, or natural framework. Instead, I have attempted to stand in the doorway, at the interface between inside and outside where meaningful differences may resonate in the same way that a guitar string playing across space and time gives voice to its back and forth oscillations. To eliminate an existing theory would be like cutting the string from its bridge, forever silencing its vacillation by destroying its ability to resist. Hence, I have chosen instead to listen to the vacillation, to celebrate the play of differences, and even to thumb a string when it has fallen silent to hear what explanatory power might be revealed through its voices. It is for this reason that I believe we need binaries and the conflict they represent. We don't need, however, destructive, agonistic binaries based on spatial logics; instead, we need Janusian binaries.

It would be a mistake, however, to assume that, because I have employed deconstructive methods, I have "retreated into the escapism of purely irresponsible textual play" (Smith, 1988, p. 85). Deconstruction without a theory of subjectivity that can account for resistance is irresponsible, for it is destruction without purpose. But this sort of critique for critique's sake should not be our goal. Instead, our goal should be revisionary. I have sought to re-envision the binary between individualistic and constitutive communitarian theory in a way that would allow NT researchers to utilize the individualistic communitarian concept of reciprocity without contradicting the constitutive communitarian's concept of subject formation. I have sought to play the differences between electronic and print publishing in order to better understand *both* what our existing notions of community can say about emerging electronic forums, like PURTOPOI, and what the NT medium can reveal about discursive practices that have been ignored or overlooked in print but that must be consciously renegotiated in NT. In short, I came to these binaries, not to destroy them with deconstruction, but to engage in reconstruction. What's more, when I have employed deconstructive methods, I have done so to resist forms of determinism which, as I stated above, are antithetical to rhetoric.

I lose patience with the argument that embracing the play of differences is meaningless and irresponsible since one of the major findings of this project has been that the vacillation of play is essential to the continued existence of discourse communities. Communities must have discursive practices to maintain group unity. For a community to be identifiable and for its members to have a sense of group unity, some hegemonic forces must be at work that unite members of a community and aim for the realization of total consensus. However, resistance and conflict also are essential to the life of a community precisely because they prevent the community from ever achieving unity. Communities never can be unities because as soon as they become unified, as soon as they realize total consensus, they cease to function as communities. Where all agree, no issue is left for adjudication. Where no issues are left to talk about, there is no communication. And where there is no communication, there is no community since the force that bound the members of the community together is destroyed. Thus, there never can be a community that is completely successful in forcing its members to accommodate its discursive practices, nor can there ever be a community that is completely without hegemonic practices; both resistance *and* accommodation must be present for there to be community.

The resistance resulting from the play between individuals' excess of subjectivity and the interpellative forces of communities and forums is meaningful and does have effect. As I have shown, because individuals bring a contingent continuity to communities and forums, they can and *do* resist interpellation into the dominant subject positions of a group since the very identity of those dominant positions requires differentiation from other noncoincident positions. Thus, interpellation not only hails individuals into dominant subject positions, it concomitantly calls resisting positionalities into existence so that, far from predetermining an individual's identity, the interpellative act actually invites choice. It asks individuals to consider the potential for remuneration from a number of manifold positionalities. In other words, the play of differences in interpellation (and the opportunity for choice that play enables) presupposes that individuals' decisions *will* have meaningful effects in the material world and in the personal histories of those individuals, that choices, such as whether or not to risk "looking like an idiot," are consequential.

Furthermore, the choices individuals make are consequential, not only in terms of their own personal histories, but also in terms of the historical development of particular forums. Just as the traditional "Subject" is not a monolithic, atemporal category produced by the hegemonic interpellation of an individual into discursive formations that never can be escaped and where change has no meaning, a forum is not the singular, uniaccentual manifestation of a community. Forums are like individuals since, as Porter (1992) has pointed out, "Each forum has a distinct history and rules governing appropriateness to which members are obliged to adhere" (p. 108). In other words, a forum is a more or less physical space in which certain kinds of discursive struggle are permitted, and the rules governing what forms of struggle are appropriate change as the distinct history of the forum changes. And in fact, this was just the sort of change occurring on PURTOPOI in the debate regarding the use of signature files. As Chapter Five made clear, PURTOPOI began as a local group of people who had well-established personal relationships because they were all members of the same department, and some of the authorizing strategies that emerged from this were conventions that represented those personal relationships to other members of the group. Yet, as PURTOPOI expanded to include individuals from other universities, people who often lacked such personal relationships, the convention of calling attention to one's professional status in the field began to emerge and long signature files began to be employed. When (from my positionality as listowner) I called attention to the resource-intensive nature of long signature files, many individuals exploded in resistance to the suggestion that use of long signature files be eliminated on the list. Ultimately, the resistance of those individuals did change the historical character and interpellative forces of the forum. Although even today there are still vestiges of the old list (people still refer to each other personally and still argue that the list is a safe place to share unpolished ideas), the introduction of new subject positions changed it from a place where Purdue graduate students like Tammy H. could share their teaching experiences (which was actually the list's original purpose) to a place where they were forced to lurk. Thus, in a sense, the forum has changed so radically that someone subscribing to the list today might never know the forum's original purpose or the subject positions it once promoted.

It is this ability of forums like PURTOPOI to change their rules for appropriate discursive struggle that holds out such revisionary promise for proponents of NT. Although this study has made clear that we cannot assume electronic discussion groups will become sites for the formation of radical subjectivities just because NT is a new medium, neither can we assume that the medium doesn't have an effect on subject formation. If NT is mortgaged to media that have come before, it is also clear that NT is more than simply a more efficient vehicle for the transmission of printed texts. NT does alter the conditions of text production, eliminating for example mediation by publishers in the print medium or physical cues like personal appearance, hand and facial gestures, and the well-timed cough in the oral medium. Simply making the writing process virtually coincident with publication allows the increased interaction and negotiation of competing subject positions in electronic forums. Increasing the degree of connectivity between individuals and access to a means of consuming texts accelerates the process of resistance and consequently the formation of negotiated positionalities. It is in this sense then that NT and electronic forums may serve as a catalyst for contingent change in our society and our classrooms.

appendix a

To date on PURTOPOI, no individual's routine signature file has yet to include more than the items listed here at any one time. However, on other discussion groups (particularly USENET groups), many signature files are so ornate that they even include images produced by the careful arrangement of ASCII characters on the screen. Below are two examples taken from one day's worth of messages posted to the NEWS.HEADLINES group. Note that I have removed the authors' names, addresses, and other personal information.

As these examples clearly illustrate, signature files can become quite elaborate affairs and can convey a great deal of information about an author's background and personality. In fact, such signature files may be interpreted as an attempt to restore the author's loss of physical presence in a virtual space. Indeed, in what has to be my favorite example of a signature file, the author of the signature file below went so far as to include a crude image of himself.

```
===========================================================
    -----------------------------------------------
    |@@@@@@@^^~~``~~~~~~~~~~~~~~~~^^@@@@@@@@|
    |@@@@@@^      ~^  @  @@ @ @ @ I  ~^@@@@@@|
    |@@@@@             ~ ~~ ~I            @@@@@|
    |@@@@'                   '  _,w@<      @@@@|
    |@@@@      @@@@@@@@w___,w@@@@@@@@@  @    @@@|
    |@@@@      @@@@@@@@@@@@@@@@@@@@@@  I    @@@|
    |@@@@      @@@@@@@@@@@@@@@@@@@@*@[  i    @@@|
    |@@@@      @@@@@@@@@@@@@@@@@@@@@[][  |   ]@@@|
    |@@@@      ~_,,_ ~@@@@@@@~ ____~ @      @@@|
    |@@@@      _~ , , '@@@~  _  _'@ ]L  J@@@|
    |@@@@   , @@w@ww+   @@@ww'',,@w@ ][    @@@@|
    |@@@@,  @@@@wwww@@@ @@@@@@@ww@@@@@[   @@@@|
    |@@@@@_|| @@@@@@P' @@P@@@@@@@@@@@[|  c@@@@|
    |@@@@@@@w| '@@P~  P]@@@--, ~Y@@^']@, @@@@@@|
    |@@@@@@@@[   _        _J@@Tk     ]]@@@@@@|
    |@@@@@@@@@,@ @@, c,,,,,,,y ,w@@[  ,@@@@@@@|
    |@@@@@@@@@@ i @w   ====--_@@@@@   @@@@@@@@|
    |@@@@@@@@@@@@',P~ _ ~^^^^Y@@@@@   @@@@@@@@@|
    |@@@@^^=^@@^   ^' ,ww,w@@@@@ _@@@@@@@@@@|
    |@@@_xJ~ ~    ,   @@@@@@@P~ _@@@@@@@@@@@@|
    |@@  @,  ,@@@,_____   _,J@@@@@@@@@@@@@|
    |@@L  ''  ,@@@@@@@@@@@@@@@@@@@@@@@@@@@@@@|
    -----------------------------------------------

===========================================================
```

appendix b

COMMON
NETWORK TERMS

The following is a glossary of technical terms, acronyms and abbreviations often used in this book. It is also intended to serve as a quick reference guide that new networkers may use to become more familiar with some of the key terms and issues in wide-area networking. However, it is important to note that the Internet is dynamic and constantly evolving, so that it is likely that many new terms and software packages will emerge subsequent to the publication of this work. Still, because the only publishing system that can keep up with the Internet is the Internet itself, I hope this list of terms may encourage first-time networkers by serving as a jumping off point for their explorations of the Net. Note that a version of this text was published in the August 1992 issue of *Computers and Composition.*

alias as the term suggests, a word or set of characters that refers to some pre-existing UNIX command or an e-mail address. For example, a user may wish to create a mailing alias for e-mail addresses that are difficult to remember. Thus, rather than typing an entire address like THARON@HUBCAP.CLEMSON.EDU, a user might create an alias called "tharon", allowing him or her to type fewer, more memorable characters to accomplish the same task. A mailing alias also may be created for entire lists of addresses and thus is sometime confused with the following term "list."

anonymous ftp ftp stands for "File Transfer Protocol" (see "protocol") and lets users copy files from a remote site to their local host computer. Usually, ftps are permissible only if users are registered at a site and have passwords allowing them to bypass the computer's security system. However, anonymous ftps are a special type of ftp that allow nonregistered users to access certain public files. Nonregistered users login with the uid "anonymous" (see "uid") and give their e-mail addresses as passwords. Not all sites permit anonymous ftps; many limit the hours when anonymous ftps can be performed, and the process requires packet-switching technology.

ARCHIE a searchable database of software stored at anonymous ftp sites. ARCHIE was developed at McGill University and allows Internet users with ftp access to easily locate and obtain public domain software.

ARPANET Advanced Research Projects Agency Network, U.S. Dept. of Defense; ARPANET was the forerunner of the current Internet.

article USENET users refer to messages or files that have been sent or posted to discussion groups as articles rather than messages.

asynchronous typically used to refer to a type of conferencing system. Asynchronous conferencing systems like LISTSERV, LISTPROC, and USENET groups require users to post a message to a central location where it can be read for a period of days or weeks. Unlike synchronous systems (see "synchronous") that require users to be online at the same time and demand immediate responses from participants, asynchronous systems allow conference participants to read messages at their convenience and to reflect on their responses to messages.

BBS Bulletin Board System (see "bulletin board").

BITFTP@PUCC an ingenious program that allows BITNET users to execute anonymous ftps despite the limitations of their store-and-forward technology. As with LISTSERV software, users interact with BITFTP through mail messages that contain executable commands. For more details about these commands, send a mail message where the first line of the file reads "HELP" to the BITFTP@PUCC address.

BITNET "Because It's There" or "Because It's Time" Network; mainly links university and college computers (see also "CREN"). Currently, most mainframes on BITNET use the CMS/VM operating system, and the network uses store-and-forward technology. Most BITNET addresses have the letters "VM" in them because BITNET computers tend to be IBM mainframes. Networkers conventionally use all uppercase for BITNET addresses and lowercase for Internet.

browser although the term can be used for other systems, a browser is essentially a piece of software that knows how to interpret HTML (see later) files and display them in the appropriate format. A variety of HTML browsers are under development, but two of the first and most popular are MOSAIC and NETSCAPE.

bulletin board a term often erroneously used by neophyte networkers to refer to a LISTSERV list or USENET discussion group. The term refers to computers (usually desktop systems) accessible by modem. Public domain software and document files are usually stored on bulletin boards. Also, many local bulletin board systems have a central theme or organizational agenda and serve as sites where people interested in some subject or members of an organization may share information. Also, public sites like FreeNets or commercial services like America Online, BIX, CompuServe, Delphi, Genie, and Prodigy are actually little more than very large bulletin board systems, though many people confuse them with actual networks.

CAI Computer-Aided Instruction or Computer-Assisted Instruction.

CAC Computer-Assisted Composition.

characters the name that users on a MOO or MUD use during their communications. On many systems, users role-play in their characters, taking on different genders, personality traits, and discursive practices.

chat relay chat programs that support synchronous or real-time conferences (see "conferencing system"). One of the largest and most popular of these is IRC (Internet Relay Chat).

client/server the client/server relationship describes an extremely efficient information transfer system used in many electronic publishing packages. Client usually refers to a piece of software running on the user's local machine (see "browser" for example), though the term also may be used to refer to a user's local machine. When the user issues the appropriate commands, the client software connects to the server where data files are stored. The files are transferred from the server into the active memory of the machine running the client software, and the connection to the server is dropped. The client software then displays the downloaded files in the appropriate format. Because the connections between the client and server are active only when files are actually being transferred, the amount of traffic the network and the server can handle is dramatically increased. Furthermore, because the client rather than the server is responsible for translating the data files and displaying them to the user, the operating systems of the client and server do not have to be the same type. Gopher, WAIS, and WWW are the most popular examples of systems that use the client/server relationship.

CMC Computer-Mediated Communication.

command line interface unlike GUIs (see later) where users use a pointer device to click on an icon, users of command line interface must issue text commands to the software.

commercial network companies like America Online, BIX, CompuServe, Delphi, Genie, and Prodigy are often called commercial networks, even though they are more accurately bulletin board systems.

computer classroom though often confused with "computer lab," a computer classroom is explicitly designed to allow for classroom activities. Rather than focusing on individual workstations where students work independently on different assignments from different classes as in a computer lab, the computer classroom is designed to allow for group interaction and communitarian activity. It usually also has screen-sharing and/or projection facilities enabling instructor or student demonstrations.

computer lab see "computer classroom." Often a room full of stand-alone personal computers, labs tend to be designed for individual, isolated activity.

conference see "discussion group."

conferencing system a software package which allows a group to communicate via computer. Conferencing systems may support real-time or "synchronous" communication such as the talk or chat programs. Or they may support "asynchronous" communication such as the e-mail exchanges on LISTSERV lists.

CREN Corporation for Research and Education Networking; CSNET and BITNET merged to become CREN; however, many users still call the network "BITNET."

cyber-rape the practice of copying messages from someone and then redistributing the messages in other contexts that are either personally or professionally embarrassing to the author. Most often, the cyber-rapist will meet a victim on a chat-relay system and engage him or her in what feels like a casual, oral conversation. Originally, cyber-rapists would steer the conversation toward topics that reveal the sexual behaviors or fantasies of the victim, though the term is now being used to refer to any private and potentially damaging type of information. Because electronic communication is not the same as the oral medium, cyber-rapists are able to save the conversation in a file and then post the file to scholarly or professional discussion groups where the victim's reputation and status is likely to be most damaged.

discussion group a LISTSERV list (see "list"), USENET group, or other collection of people communicating via computer. There appears to be a convention emerging where "discussion group" refers to asynchronous interactions and "conference" is used for synchronous, but the terms are still used interchangeably by many networkers.

DNS Domain Name Server (see "nameserver").

domain name refers to the subnet address on which a user's local machine resides. For example, I work on a machine named "Tigger" that is connected to Clemson University's campus-wide network. The Internet name for Clemson's campus network is CLEMSON.EDU, which is the "domain name" for TIGGER .CLEMSON.EDU.

download the act of transporting a file from a remote computer to one's host computer. Downloads can occur between mainframes or (through protocols like Kermit) between mainframes and personal computers.

e-mail electronic mail; literally, an e-mail message is a file that is copied from one user's account to another's; or, when users are on the same machine, the file never actually moves but is merely renamed and given a new owner.

e-mail address gives the final destination for a mail file. Address syntax is in a state of flux and is an extremely political issue among networkers, but most addresses have three components: a uid, a node, and a network. The typical syntax is UID@NODE.DOMAIN.NETWORK. Networkers conventionally put BIT-NET addresses in uppercase, e.g., "XUCC@PURCCVM," and Internet addresses in lowercase, e.g., "ucc@mace.cc.pur-due.edu." However, as more and more institutions are dropping their CREN memberships, this convention is beginning to lose ground.

emoticon see "smiley face."

e-text electronic text; often a generic term referring to any file containing print characters rather than binary or machine language files used in software. E-text may include e-mail messages; however, it is usually reserved for books, articles, abstracts, and other documents that have been stored in machine-readable databases and archives.

ethernet an early networking system developed by Xerox in the 1970s that uses packet-switching. Ethernets, because of the way they broadcast signals, are limited to distances of not more than one to two kilometers and are thus limited to LANS.

filelist a file indicating to LISTSERV software what documents or other files are available from a list or discussion group. The filelist also tells LISTSERV who can add files to the filelist and who can retrieve them.

flame what networkers call an e-mail message or article that viciously attacks the author or content of a previously posted message. Flames are usually far more emotionally charged than simple disagreements. Typically, one flame produces a series of angry responses, resulting in what networkers refer to as a flame war.

FreeNet a collection of open-access computer systems that receive their software and are organized by the NPTN (see later). Currently, there are five major FreeNet systems: 1) Cleveland, 2) Youngstown, 3) TriState Online, 4) Heartland, and 5) Medina. More FreeNet systems are coming online all the time, but the first, largest, and most interesting of these is the Cleveland FreeNet, which came online in July of 1986. Access to the Cleveland FreeNet is described in the "NPTN" entry. Please note that, though there is currently no usage charge for the FreeNet, visitors may not post to the bulletin boards or send e-mail, and there is a fee to become a registered user.

frownie face see "smiley face."

gateways special computers, also called routers, these serve as bridges or doorways between different networks.

Gopher developed at the University of Minnesota (home of the Golden Gophers), Gopher is an extremely popular electronic publishing system based on client/server architecture (see "client/server").

GUI Graphical User Interface. Rather than requiring users to type in text commands, software packages using GUIs allow users to click on icons to complete tasks.

home page the first document a WWW browser (see "browser") opens when the software is started. A personal home page also is used to refer to an HTML document about an individual user. Many people use these to provide copies of their resumes, to display photos of themselves and their families, and to distribute information and position statements about issues they find important.

host a single computer in a network. "Node" is usually the preferred term; however, when networkers wish to designate a site where a particular program or user exists, they will often use the term host. For example, PURCCVM is the host computer for the PURTOPOI discussion group because it exists only on the PURCCVM machine.

HTML HyperText Markup Language. HTML uses a set of embedded tags in a file that WWW browsers (see "browser") use to display text in the correct font or to locate files on other systems. An example of tagged text in an HTML document is "<B>sample text</B>". The <B> tells the browser to turn on the boldface font, and the </B> tells it to turn off boldface. Other HTML tags tell browsers to display images, audio clips, video clips, or to connect to gopher servers, ftp sites, etc.

HTTP HyperText Transport Protocol. A set of standards used to transport HTML documents on the World Wide Web (see "protocol"). HTTP was invented by Tim Berners-Lee at CERN, the European Particle Physics Laboratory, in 1989.

interface the bridge between the human user and the computer agent.

internet an internet (with a lowercase "i") is a kind of metanetwork or any network of smaller networks and should not be confused with the Internet (with a capital "I").

Internet Often called the information superhighway, this network replaced the original ARPANET and is being replaced by the high-speed NREN. Originally funded by the Dept. of Defense, it also receives funding from the NSF and other government agencies. The Internet is a national internet or metanetwork of smaller, usually regional networks. A large proportion of computers on Internet use the UNIX operating system, and the network itself employs packet-switched technology. Internet addresses usually end in ".edu," ".com," or ".gov" and, by convention, are all printed in lowercase.

IRC Internet Relay Chat. This is a synchronous conferencing system where users enter channels (similar to a channel on a CB radio) where other users are having real-time conversations. Because many people (particularly system administrators) regard the communication that occurs on IRC channels as both trivial and resource intensive, many sites prohibit access to IRC servers.

IP address machines connected to networks using the "Internet Protocol" are assigned numerical network addresses. For example, the numerical IP address for the NCTENet gopher server is 130.127.38.103. (See also "nameserver").

IT Instructional Technology or Information Technology.

LAN Local-Area Network; usually a collection of desktop computers connected together and using packet-switched technology. LANs differ from WANs in that LANs are typically limited to a single room, building, or campus. However, LANs are often able to access WANs.

LANS Local-Area Networking System; refers to the technology rather than the networks or "LANs" themselves. LANS typically use packet-switched technology like ethernet.

list literally, a file listing addresses and names of people or even other lists. The list also contains directions telling the LISTSERV or LISTPROC software how to add new people to a list, how to manipulate messages sent to the list, whether the list is open to the public or confidential, etc.

listowner the person(s) responsible for maintaining a LISTSERV list; also called a "sysop" or system operator. Listowners are often little more than participants in open group discussions, though on some lists they function as editors, deciding what messages will or will not be posted to the list.

LISTPROC a UNIX-based software package that emulates the commands and functionality of LISTSERV software (see "LISTSERV").

LISTSERV a software package written by Eric Thomas that enables large groups of individuals to communicate efficiently. LISTSERV is capable of performing a number of tasks, but its basic function is to distribute e-mail or other files to members of a list. In effect, it allows an individual to send a message to one address and then have that message distributed to every other individual on the list.

lurker an individual who consumes the messages produced by a discussion group but does not actively participate in the discussion by contributing messages of his/her own.

MAJOR-DOMO a UNIX-based program that redistributes e-mail messages to a list of subscribers in much the manner as the LISTSERV software (see "LISTSERV").

MILNET Military Network, links computers at various U.S. military installations around the world. MILNET computers cannot legally store classified information and are linked to Internet.

moderator the USENET equivalent of a listowner. Moderators can take an active role in screening and editing articles posted to USENET groups; however, they usually step in only when a discussion turns particularly vituperative (see "netiquette").

MOO Multi-User Dimension, Object-Oriented. MOOs are text-based virtual worlds where many users from all over the network can meet and conduct real-time, synchronous communications. Typically, MOOs have virtual rooms with objects in them that users can manipulate. Users (called "characters") move through the rooms in a MOO and talk to other characters or even programs (called bots) that respond to certain specific words or phrases.

Mosaic Occasionally confused with the WWW itself (see later), Mosaic is actually a WWW browser that was developed by Mark Andreeson and a project team at the National Center for Super Computing Applications.

MUD Multi-User Dimension. Originally, MUDs began as a network version of the famous game Dungeons and Dragons. Most MUDs are still games where many users from all over the network compete with each other in real-time. Because MUDs are games and because they tie up network resources, many sites prohibit users from connecting to them.

nameserver a specific machine on a network that translates numerical IP addresses into alphabetical names. For example, the numerical address for NCTE.CLEMSON.EDU is 130.127.38.103. This information is stored on the primary nameserver for the CLEMSON.EDU domain so that networkers both inside and outside the CLEMSON.EDU domain can address NCTE.CLEMSON.EDU by name rather than numerical address.

NCTENet National Council of Teachers of English Network; the NCTENet is really not a "network" at all. It is a loose collection of Internet services such as LISTPROC discussion groups, a gopher server, and a WWW server that were developed by the NCTE's Committee on Instructional Technology to provide the NCTE membership with opportunities to learn and to use instructional technologies. Users with gopher clients should connect to NCTE.CLEMSON.EDU. E-mail users should send mail to NCTE-TALK@ITC.ORG.

netiquette Network Etiquette; a highly political area of discussion, netiquette deals with appropriate and inappropriate uses of networks. Netiquette rules may vary radically from network to network and even from discussion group to discussion group. Potential netiquette issues can range from complex legal and ethical questions to simple typographical conventions.

Netscape like Mosaic, Netscape is a WWW browser (see "browser"). Although a number of software companies are developing their own browsers, currently Netscape is the most popular browser on the Internet and sets the standards for HTML tagging.

Netnews a software package developed at the University of Pennsylvania allowing BITNET users access to USENET discussion groups.

network a collection of computers linked together by satellite, telephone line, radio packet, fiber optics, copper wire, or some other means that are able to exchange data because of some shared protocol such as the TCP/IP or OSI. The large, public networks tend to use either packet-switched or store-and-forward technology.

network cloud networkers often use a cloud metaphor to refer to the connections on networks because of the complexity of routers, gateways, and other switching systems in networks and because of the unfathomable number of connections that exist. A message sent through a network is like a plane flying through a cloud; it's visible only when it goes into the cloud and when it comes out the other side.

networkers people who use the networks; also called users.

NIC Network Information Center; as its name suggests, an NIC provides information about networks for users. Networkers can retrieve documents such as RFCs (see "RFCS"), network charters, usage statistics, policy documentation, routing tables, etc., from NICs.

nickname file basically the CMS/VM equivalent of an alias file in UNIX (see "alias").

nodes a single computer in a network of computers; each node has its own name or network address and can support a number of individual users simultaneously. A node is sometimes called a "host" in certain contexts.

NPTN National Public Telecomputing Network; the NPTN operates on the same principle as National Public Radio, except that computers are used to provide the public with information rather than radio stations. Originally begun by Dr. Tom Grundner in 1984 at Case Western University, the NPTN is now managed by a seven-member Board of Directors. Currently, there are five "FreeNets" in the NPTN system with several others under development (see "FreeNet"). To receive more information or to join the NPTN, connect to the Cleveland FreeNet. For 300, 1200, or 2400 baud modem access, dial (216)368-3888. Internet access is available via telnet at FREENET-IN-A.CWRU.EDU (129.22.8.82). Once connected, either via modem or telnet, login as a visitor, type "go admin," and select the menu entries for NPTN.

NREN National Research and Education Network; a five-year, $2 billion project, NREN is to replace the overburdened Internet in 1996 and, when completed, will enable users to send 100,000 pages of text per second across the network. Although the NREN is technically a different network in terms of its funding, technologies, and management, it seems likely that it will continue to be called the Internet or the information superhighway.

NSFNET National Science Foundation Network; the NSF is one of the major funding organizations for the Internet, and, although transparent to most users, the NSFNET serves as a major back-bone for the Internet.

NT Networked Text.

packet-switched a type of network technology that breaks data strings into short chunks that are stuffed into packets or envelopes. Each packet or envelope is then stamped with an address and sent on to its destination where the envelopes are unpacked and reassembled into data strings. This technology is very fast and allows for a wide variety of interactive user services.

post a message sent to a discussion group; the activity is referred to as posting.

postmaster postmasters are one step above listowners in the LISTSERV hierarchy on BITNET systems. They are responsible for maintaining the LISTSERV software for their particular sites, though they do not actually manage the lists themselves. Typically, postmasters are also the system administrators for their sites as well (see "sysop" and "superuser").

postnews a common utility that allows users to "post" or send a file to USENET discussion groups.

Prodigy a commercial network; users pay a fee for connection to the system. Currently, Prodigy is a closed network, and e-mail traffic between Prodigy and Internet or BITNET is not possible.

protocol suite a collection of programs, called a suite, that allows computers to share data. Protocol suites are the common languages and standards computers use to exchange data. In packet-switched networks for example, protocols tell computers how to break data strings into packets and how to reassemble packets into usable data strings. Without protocols, networks could not exist.

RFCs Request For Comments; RFCs are e-texts that are stored at network information centers (NICs) and are used by network architects to negotiate and/or document network conventions. One of the most famous of these, for example, is RFC 822 which outlined the standards for e-mail formats on the Internet.

remote login as its name implies, a remote login or "rlogin" allows users to access files and execute programs on a remote computer without having to leave the users' host computer or, more importantly, without having to travel to the remote computer's physical site.

rn (or readnews) one of the more common utilities used to read articles posted to USENET discussion groups.

.sig file (or signature file) a signature file is a text file that is automatically appended to the ends of e-mail messages or articles. Signature files usually give the user's name and return e-mail address(es). However, some .sig files are quite ornate and may even include pictures and designs.

smiley face made by typing a colon, followed by an open parentheses, and is usually followed by a space to make it easier to read. This combination of characters produces what looks like a smiling face tipped on it side—e.g., :) . By convention, networkers place smiley faces after texts that they intend to be interpreted as humorous or facetious. In addition to humor, networkers can use similar techniques to express other emotions. Irony uses a "winky face"—e.g., ;-) —and sadness uses a "frownie face"—e.g., :-(. In fact, this sort of code can be used even to express physical characteristics of an individual. For example, 8-<) could be interpreted to mean that the author wears glasses and has a mustache.

spam when a networker "spams" a message, he or she posts it to a large number of different discussion groups. The result is that networkers who subscribe to several groups receive multiple copies of the same message. As a result, spamming is generally considered an annoyance, but it is tolerated when the contents of the message are of interest to a broad group of users—e.g., a call for papers or conference announcement.

store-and-forward a type of network technology where files are sent from one node in the network to the next. Each node stores the file and then forwards it to yet another node until the file reaches its final destination. This technology is much slower than packet-switched and does not support telnet's remote logins, anonymous ftps, or other interactive resource sharing utilities. It's used by BITNET and USENET.

subscriber a member of a list, discussion group, or conference.

superuser usually the person or persons responsible for administration and operations at a site. Superusers can create accounts; change passwords; and read, delete, or alter any file on a system.

synchronous usually refers to a conferencing system that supports (seemingly) real-time communication between users. Some examples of synchronous systems include MOOs, MUDs, and IRCs (see "asynchronous").

sysop System Operator or System Administrator; a confusing and often abused term, "sysop" initially referred to a person who operated a system, though that person may not have been the person responsible for the system's administration. However, the term has been expanded through time to include superusers and system administrators.

TCP/IP Transmission Control Protocol/Internet Protocol; protocol suite used by the Internet.

telnet a utility that lets a user on one machine connect to another machine on the network and execute programs.

tn3270 like "telnet," this utility allows a user on one system to connect, in this particular case, to an IBM 3270 system.

uid User Identification; on mainframe computers capable of supporting a number of users simultaneously, individuals are allocated portions of the computer's memory and other resources. Each allocation, account, or space has a specific address known as the "uid." The ownership of files can be transferred from one uid space to another, and this transfer is what enables e-mail exchanges.

UNIX an operating system developed by Bell Labs.

upload the transporting of a file from a host computer to a remote computer. Uploading is the same process as downloading, only reversed (see "download").

URL Uniform Resource Locator; a notation system used on the WWW to indicate where a WWW browser can find some resource.

USENET "User's Network"; a global volunteer network begun in 1979 using store-and-forward technology. USENET does not support e-mail; instead, "articles" are "posted" to discussion groups where they may be read by anyone; personal messages are thus discouraged. However, since USENET directors are elected and the network is voluntary, development and enforcement of network policies is problematic.

UUCP "UNIX to UNIX Copy Program"; the UUCP network is one of the oldest networks and is primarily populated by commercial companies. On UUCP, a host computer dials the number of the remote computer, and a direct connection is established for file transfers and remote logins; hence the name "UNIX to UNIX." As a general rule, academics mainly will encounter UUCP addresses and networkers via USENET discussion groups.

viewer sometimes also referred to as helpers, these are programs that allow a client (see "client/server") to display a particular type of file. For example, many versions of Gopher for Macintosh systems required that users have a program called JPEG VIEW stored on their systems in order for them to have image files displayed on their systems.

virtual reality or space a "virtual space" is a way of referring to the lack of a physical presence in electronic media and is perhaps best understood when contrasted with actual space.

Historically, the term virtual emerged as a way of describing a space in a computer's memory that was configured to behave as though it were an actual piece of hardware. For example, a "virtual disk drive" is not an actual piece of hardware but, instead, is a portion of the computer's memory that has been instructed to behave as though it were, in reality, an actual disk drive. The metaphor has become extremely popular among networkers and has been applied to almost every aspect of NT and networking. For example, the LISTSERV software package signs its notification messages "Virtually Yours" as a way of indicating that the message was produced by a computer program rather than an actual human being.

VM/CMS Virtual Machine/Conversational Monitor System; an operating system that is often used on IBM mainframe computers.

WAIS Wide-Area Information Server; a WAIS system is essentially a collection of databases that can be searched via the network. WAIS clients differ significantly from operating system to operating system, but most offer very powerful search engines.

WAN Wide-Area Network; these differ from LANs in that they cover large geographical areas such as regions, countries, and continents. WANs may be connected to LANs or other WANs, forming huge global internets. In many cases, these interconnections or "gateways" are transparent to end-users.

WANS Wide-Area Networking Systems; refers to the systems or technologies used by WANs rather than the networks themselves. There are a number of different WANS, but the two major types are "packet-switching" and "store-and-forward."

whispers what networkers call messages that occur outside a discussion group. They are messages that discuss topics raised by the group, but rather than being distributed to the whole group, are sent directly to a few individuals. For example, individual members of a group often send whispers directly to a listowner, complaining about the topics being discussed or about other subscribers.

WWW World Wide Web; originally created in 1989 by Tim Berners-Lee of CERN, the European Particle Physics Laboratory, the WWW was intended to be a gigantic hypertext that would link physicists around the world. Interest in WWW was limited until the introduction of the NCSA MOSAIC GUI-based browser in 1993 when the interest in the Web exploded because of its ability to display images, videos, audio clips, and a variety of text fonts, and also because it allowed users to connect to sites all over the world through a point-and-click interface.

REFERENCES

Alcoff, L. (1988). Cultural feminism versus post-structuralism: The identity crisis in feminist theory. *Signs 13*, 405–36.

Allen, R. (Ed.). (1987). *Channels of discourse*. Chapel Hill: University of North Carolina Press.

Althusser, L. (1971). Ideology and ideological state apparatuses. *Lenin and philosophy and other essays* (pp. 127–186), (B. Brewster, Trans.). London: Monthly Review Press.

Aristotle. (1954). *Rhetoric* (W.R. Roberts, Trans.). New York: Random House.

Aumente, J. (1987). *New electronic ways*. Beverly Hills: Sage.

Barlow, J. P. (1992, Nov.). The great work. *EFFector Online* [Online Serial], 2(2). Available E-Mail: EFF-NEWS-REQUEST@EFF.ORG.

Barthes, R. (1972). *Mythologies* (A. Lavers, Trans.). New York: Noonday.

Bartholomae, D. (1985). Inventing the university. In M. Rose (Ed.). *When a writer can't write: Studies in writer's block* (pp. 134–165). New York: Guilford.

Barton, B. & Barton, M. (1984). Communication models for computer-mediated information systems. *Journal of Technical Writing and Communication 14(4)*, 289–306.

Bazerman, C. (1979). Written language communities: writing in the context of reading. ERIC Document, ED 232 159.

Bazerman, C. (1980). A relationship between reading and writing: The conversational model. *College English 42*, 656–661.

Bazerman C. (1981). What written knowledge does: Three examples of academic discourse. *Philosophy of the Social Sciences 11*, 361–387.

Bazerman C. (1983). Scientific writing as a social act: A review of literature of the sociology of science. In P. Anderson, J. Brockman, & C. Miller (Eds.). *New essays in technical and scientific communication* (pp. 156–184). Farmingdale, NY: Bagwood.

Bazerman C. (1984). The writing of scientific non-fiction: Context, choices, constraints. *PRE/TEXT 5*, 39–74.

Bazerman C. (1985). Physicists reading physics. *Written Communication 2*, 3–23.

Bazerman C. (1988). *Shaping written knowledge: The genre and activity of the experimental article in science*. Madison, WS: University of Wisconsin Press.

Bazerman C. (1990). Comments on "A common ground: The essay in academe." *College English 52*, 329–330.

Benveniste, E. (1971). *Problems in general linguistics* (M. Meek, Trans.).
Coral Gables: University of Miami Press.

Berlin, J. (1982). Contemporary composition: The major pedagogical theories. *College English 44*, 765–777.

Berlin, J. (1987a). Revisionary history: The dialectical method. *PRE/TEXT 8*, 47–61.

Berlin, J. (1987b). *Rhetoric and reality: Writing instruction in american colleges, 1900–1985*. Carbondale, IL: Southern Illinois University Press.

Berlin, J. (1988). Rhetoric and ideology in the writing class. *College English 50*, 477–494.

Bitzer, L. (1968). The rhetorical situation. *Philosophy and Rhetoric 1*, 1–14.

Bitzer, L. (1978). Rhetoric and public knowledge. In D. Burks (Ed.). *Rhetoric, philosophy, and literature* (pp. 67–93). Lafayette, IN: Purdue University Press.

Bizzell, P. (1978). The *ethos* of academic discourse. *College Composition and Communication 29*, 351–355.

Bizzell, P. (1982a). Cognition, convention, and certainty: ... *PRE/TEXT 3*, 213–243.

Bizzell, P. (1982b). College composition: initiation into the academic discourse community. *Curriculum Inquiry 12*, 191–207.

Bizzell, P. (1986). Foundationalism and anti-foundationalism in composition studies. *PRE/TEXT 7*, 37–56.

Bizzell, P. (1990). Beyond anti-foundationalism to rhetorical authority: Problems defining "cultural literacy." *College English 52*, 661–675.

Bolter, J. (1991) *Writing space: The computer, hypertext, and the history of writing*. Hillsdale, NJ: Lawrence Erlbaum Associates.

Bourdieu, P. (1982). *Outline of a theory of practice* (R. Nice, Trans.). Cambridge: Cambridge University Press.

Bourdieu, P. (1984). *Distinction: A social critique of the judgment of taste* (R. Nice, Trans.). Cambridge, MA: Harvard University Press.

Bowers, C. A. (1988). *The cultural dimensions of educational computing: Understanding the non-neutrality of technology*. New York: Teachers College Press.

Brent, D. (1991, Nov). Oral knowledge, typographic knowledge, electronic knowledge: Speculations on the history of ownership. *EJournal* [Online Serial] *1*(3), Available E-Mail: EJRNL@UACSC2.ALBANY.EDU.

Brodkey, L. (1989). Transvaluing difference. *College English 51*, 597–601.

Bruffee, K. (1972). The way out. *College English 33*, 457–470.

Bruffee, K. (1983). Writing and reading as collaborative or social acts. In J. Hays (Ed.). *The writer's mind* (pp 159–69). Urbana: NCTE.

Bruffee, K. (1984). Collaborative learning and the "conversation of mankind." *College English 46*, 635–652.

Bruffee, K. (1986). Social construction, language, and the authority of knowledge. *College English 48*, 773–790.

Bruffee, K. (1987). Letter to the editor. *PMLA 102*, 216–217.

Bruffee, K. (1990). Comments on John Trimbur's "Consensus and difference in collaborative learning." *College English 52*, 692–694.

Burke, K. (1973). *The philosophy of literary form*, 3rd ed. Berkeley, CA: University of California.

Burnham, D. (1984). *The rise of the computer state*. New York: Vintage Books.

Campbell, G. (1968). *The philosophy of rhetoric*. In J. Golden & E. Corbett (Eds.). *The rhetoric of Blair, Campbell, and Whately* (pp. 145–272). New York: Holt, Rinehart & Winston.

de Certeau, M. (1984). *The practice of everyday life* (M. Randall, Trans.). Berkeley, CA: University of California.

Chase, G. (1988). Accommodation, resistance and the politics of student writing. *College Composition and Communication 39*, 13–22.

Cixous, H. (1986). The laugh of the medusa. In H. Adams & L. Searle (Eds.). *Critical theory since 1965* (pp. 309–321) Tallahassee: Florida State University Press.

Connolly, F. et al. (1991a). A bill of rights for electronic citizens, Part one. *EDUCOM Review 26*(2), 37–41.

Connolly, F. ct al. (1991b). A bill of rights for electronic citizens, Part two. *EDUCOM Review 26*(3/4), 53–57.

Connors, R. (1990). Foreword. In G. Clark. *Dialogue, dialectic, and conversation: A social perspective on the function of writing* (pp. ix–xi). Carbondale, IL: Southern Illinois University Press.

Cooper, M. & Selfe, C. (1990). Computer conferences and learning: authority, resistance, and internally persuasive discourse. *College English 52*, 847–869.

Corlett, W. (1989). *Community without unity: A politics of derridian extravagence*. Durham, NC: Duke University Press.

Crane, D. (1972). *Invisible colleges: Diffusion of knowledge in scientific communities*. Chicago: Chicago University Press.

Cronkite, W. (1983). Foreword. In D. Burnham. *The rise of the computer state* (pp. iv–viii). New York: Random House.

Crowley, S. (1984) On post-structuralism and composition. *PRE/TEXT 5*, 185–195.

Crowley, S. (1990). Jacques Derrida on teaching and rhetoric: A response. *Journal of Advance Composition 10*(2), 393–396.

Culler, J. (1980). Literary competence. In J. Tompkins (Ed.). *Reader-Response criticism* (pp. 101–117). Baltimore: Johns Hopkins University Press.

Culler, J. (1988). *Framing the sign: Criticism and its institutions*. Norman, OK: University of Oklahoma Press.

Daly, B. (1990). The effects of computer-mediated communication on inductive learning by groups. Dissertation. University of Illinois.

DeLoughry, T. (1994, Nov. 23). Gatekeeping on the Internet. *Chronicle of Higher Education*, A21–A22.

Derrida, J. (1987). *The truth in painting* (G. Bennington & I. McLeod, Trans.). Chicago: University of Chicago Press, 1987.

Derrida, J. (1990). Jacques Derrida on rhetoric and composition: A conversation. With Gary Olsen. *Journal of Advanced Composition 10*(1), 1–21.

Deward, R. & Rheingold, H. (Eds.). (1988). *Electronic citizenship.* San Francisco: Pacific Bell.

Doheny-Farina, S. (1989) A case study of one adult writing in academic and non-academic discourse communities. In C. Matelene (Ed.). *Worlds of writing: Teaching and learning in discourse communities at work* (pp. 17–47). New York: Random House.

Earnest, C. (1992). Happily modeming to school. *Online Access 7*(1), 6–8.

Eco, U. (1979). *The role of the reader: Explorations in the semiotics of texts.* Bloomington: Indiana University Press.

Ede, L. & Lunsford, A. (1984). Audience addressed/audience invoked: The role of audience in composition theory and pedagogy. *College Composition and Communication 35*, 155–171.

Effrat, M. (1974). *The community: Approaches and applications.* New York: Free Press.

Elbow, P. ((1982). Preface 4: The doubting game and the believing game. *PRE/TEXT 3*, 339–351.

Elbow, P. (1987). Closing my eyes as I speak: An argument for ignoring audience. *College English 49*, 50–69.

Eldred, J. (1991). Pedagogy in the computer-networked classroom. *Computers and Composition 8*(2), 47–61.

Faigley, L. (1992). *Fragments of rationality: Postmodernity and the subject of composition.* Pittsburg: University of Pittsburg Press.

Farrell, T. (1976). Knowledge, consensus, and rhetorical theory. *Quarterly Journal of Speech 62*, 1–15.

Fish, S. (1980a). Interpreting the *Variorum.* In J. Tomkins (Ed.). *Reader-Response criticism* (pp. 164–184). Baltimore: Johns Hopkins University Press.

Fish, S. (1980b). *Is there a text in this class? The authority of interpretive communities.* Cambridge, MA: Harvard University Press.

Fish, S. (1980c). Literature in the reader: Affective stylistics. In J. Tomkins (Ed.). *Reader-Response criticism* (pp. 70–100). Baltimore: Johns Hopkins University Press.

Fish, S. (1985). Consequences. In W.J.T. Mitchell (Ed.). *Against theory: Literary studies and the new pragmatism* (pp. 106–131). Chicago: University of Chicago Press.

Fiske, J. (1987a). British cultural studies and television. In R. Allen (Ed.). *Channels of discourse* (pp. 254–290). Chapel Hill: University of North Carolina Press.

Fiske, J. (1987b). *Television culture.* London: Methuen.

Flores, M. (1990). Computer conferencing: Composing a feminist community of writers. In C. Handa (Ed.). *Computer and community: Teaching composition in the twenty-first century* (pp. 106–117). Portsmouth, NH: Boynton/Cook.

Fontaine, S. (1988). The unfinished story of the interpretive community. *Rhetoric Review 7*, 86–96.

Fortune, R. (1991). Visual and verbal thinking. In G. Hawisher & C. Selfe (Eds.). *Evolving perspectives on computers and composition studies: Questions for the 1990s* (pp. 43–64). Urbana: NCTE.

Foucault, M. (1972). *The archaeology of knowledge and the discourse on language* (A.M. Smith, Trans.). New York: Pantheon.

Foucault, M. (1977). *Discipline and punish: The birth of the prison* (A. Sheridan, Trans.). New York: Pantheon.

Foucault, M. (1981). The order of discourse. In R. Young (Ed.). *Untying the text: A post-structuralist reader* (pp. 48–78). Boston: Routledge & Kegan Paul.

Freed, R. & Broadhead G. (1987). Discourse communities, sacred texts, and institutional norms. *College Composition and Communication 38*, 154–165.

Freire, P. (1985). *The politics of education* (D. Macedo, Trans.). South Hadley, MA: Bergin Garvey.

Frey, D. & Adams, R. (1990). *!%@:: A directory of electronic mail addressing and networks*. Sebastopol, CA: O'Reilly & Associates.

Frey, O. (1990). Beyond literary darwinism: Women's voices and critical discourse. *College English 52*, 507–526.

Frost, R. (1973). The road not taken. In R. Ellmann & R. O'Clair (Eds.). *The Norton anthology of modern poetry* (pp. 196–197). New York: W.W. Norton.

Fulwiler, T. (1990). Looking and listening for my voice. *College Composition and Communication 41*, 214–220.

Gadamer, H. (1988). *Truth and method*. New York: Crossroad.

Geertz, C. (1983). *Local knowledge: Further essays in interpretative anthropology*. New York: Basic Books.

Gerrard, L. (1983). Computers and compositionists: A view from the floating bottom. *Computers and Composition 8*(2), 5–16.

Giroux, H. (1983). *Theory and resistance in education*. South Hadley, MA: Bergin & Garvey.

Gore, A. (1989, May 18) National high-performance computer technology act of 1989. *Congressional Record*, S5689.

Gorgias. (1960). Fragments and testimonia. In P. Wheelwright (Ed.). *The presocratics* (pp. 248–258). Indianapolis: Bobbs-Merrill.

Haas, C. (1989). Seeing it on the screen isn't really seeing it: Computer writers' reading problems. In G. Hawisher & C. Selfe (Eds.). *Critical perspectives on computers and composition instruction* (pp. 16–29). New York: Teachers College Press.

Habermas, J. (1970). Towards a theory of communicative competence. *Inquiry 13*, 360–375.

Hairston, M. (1990). Comments on John Trimbur's "Consensus and difference in collaborative learning." *College English 52*, 694–696.

Halliday, M. (1973). *Explorations in the functions of language*. London: Edward Arnold.

Hall, S. (1991). The four stages of national research and education network growth. *EDUCOM Review 26*(1), 18–25.

Harris, J. (1989). The idea of community in the study of writing. *College Composition and Communication 40*, 11–22.

Harris, R. A. (1991). Rhetoric of science. *College English 53*, 282–307.

Hartsock, N. (1983). The feminist standpoint: Developing ground for a specifically feminist historical materialism. In S. Harding & M. Hintikka(Eds.). *Discovering reality: Feminist perspectives on epistemology, metaphysics, methodology and philosophy of science* (pp. 283–310). Dordrecht: D. Reidel.

Hawisher, G. (1992). A meeting of the minds: The dynamics of undergraduate electronic discussion. Paper presented at Conference on College Composition and Communication, Cinncinati.

Hawisher, G. & Selfe, C. (Eds.). (1991a). *Evolving perspectives on computers and composition studies: Questions for the 1990s.* Urbana: NCTE.

Hawisher, G. & Selfe, C. (1991b). The rhetoric of technology and the electronic writing class *College Composition and Communication 42*, 55–65.

Hillery, G. (1955). Definitions of community: Areas of agreement. *Rural Sociology 20*, 111–123.

Hillery, G. (1959). A critique of selected community concepts. *Social Forces 37*, 237–242.

Hiltz, S. & Turoff, M. (1978). *The network nation.* Reading MA: Addison-Wesley.

Hodge, R, & Kress, G. (1988). *Social semiotics.* Ithaca, NY: Cornell University Press.

Howard, B. (1994, Sept. 13). Free e-mail can be costly. *PC Magazine 13*(15), 107.

Howard, T. (1993, June). Intellectual property issues in e-mail research. *Bulletin of the Association for Business Communication 54*, 40–41.

Howard, T. (1992). WANS, connectivity, and computer literacy: An introduction and glossary. *Computers and Composition 9*(3), 41–57.

Howard, T. & Dedo, D. (1989). Cultural criticism and esl composition. Paper presented at National Council for Teachers of English Conference, Baltimore.

Hymes, D. (1980). *Language in education: Ethnolinguistic essays.* Arlington, VA: Center for Applied Linguistics.

Internet statistics: A terabyte here—A terabyte there. (1992, Mar.). *Boardwatch Magazine*, 43, 45.

Iser, W. (1980). The reading process: A phenomenological approach. In J. Tompkins (Ed.). *Reader-Response criticism* (pp. 50–69). Baltimore: Johns Hopkins University Press.

Jaggar, A. (1985). *Feminist politics and human nature.* Totowa, NJ: Rowman & Allanheld.

Jameson, F. (1988). History and class consciousness as an unfinished project. *Rethinking Marxism 1*, 49–72.

Jarratt, S. & Reynolds, N. (1990). The splitting image: contemporary feminisms and the ethics of *ethos.* Paper presented at Rhetoric Society of America Conference, Arlington, TX,.

Kant, I. (1988). *The critique of judgment* (J. Meredith, Trans.). Oxford: Oxford University Press.

Kaplan, N. (1991). Ideology, technology, and the future of writing instruction. In G. Hawisher & C. Selfe (Eds.). *Evolving perspectives on computers and composition studies: Questions for the 1990s* (pp. 11–42). Urbana: NCTE.

Karis, W. (1989). Conflict in collaboration: A burkean perspective. *Rhetoric Review 8*, 113–126.

Kiesler, S. Zubrow, D. Moses, A. & Geller, V. (1985). Affect in computer-mediated communication: An experiment in synchronous terminal-to-terminal discussion. *Human-Computer Interaction 1*, 77–104.

King, T. (1991). Critical issues for providers of network-accessible information. *EDUCOM Review 26*(2), 29–33.

Kinneavy, J. (1991). I won't teach without computers again. Paper presented at Conference on College Composition and Communication, Boston.

Kirsch, G. (1987). Audience awareness and authority: A study of experienced writers composing for contrasting audiences. Dissertation. University. of California, San Diego.

Kirsch, G. (1989, Spring). Authority in reader-writer relationships. *Reader 21*, 56–67.

Kirsch, G. (1990). Experienced writers' representations of audience: The case of three writers. In G. Kirsch & D. Roen (Eds.). *A sense of audience in written communication* (pp. 318–339). Newbury Park, CA: Sage.

Knapp, S. & Michaels, W.B. Against theory. In W.J.T. Mitchell (Ed.). *Against theory: Literary studies and the new pragmatism* (pp. 11–30). Chicago: University of Chicago Press.

Kneupper, C. (1980). Rhetoric, argument and social reality: A social constructivist view. *Journal of the American Forensic Assocation 16*, 173–181.

Kneupper, C. (1981, Spring) Argument: A social constructivist perspective. *Journal of the American Forensic Association 17*, 183–189

Kuhn, T. (1970). *The structure of scientific revolutions*. 2nd ed. Chicago: University of Chicago Press.

Kuhn, T. (1977). *The essential tension*. Chicago: University of Chicago Press.

Labov, W. (1970). The study of language in its social context. *Studium Generale 23*, 66–84.

Laclau, E. & Mouffe, C. (1985). *Hegemony and socialist strategy: Towards a radical democratic politics* (W. Moore & P. Cammack, Trans.). Thetford, Norfork: Thetford Press.

LaQuey, T. (1990). *The user's directory of computer networks*. Bedford, MA: Digital.

Lassner, P. (1990). Feminist responses to rogerian argument. *Rhetoric Review 8*, 220–33.

Latour, B. (1987). *Science in action: How to follow scientists and engineers through society*. Cambridge, MA: Harvard University Press.

Latour, B. & Woolgar, S. (1979). *Laboratory life: The social construction of scientific facts.* Beverly Hills, CA: Sage.

Laurel, B. (1993). *Computers as theatre.* Reading, MA: Addison-Wesley.

Lentricchia, F. (1985). *Criticism and social change.* Chicago: University of Chicago Press.

Lipnack, J. & Stamps, J. (1986). *The networking book: People connecting with people.* New York: Routledge & Kegan Paul.

Lynch, C. & Preston, C. (1990). Internet access to information resources. In M. Williams (Ed.). *Annual Review of Information Sciences, Vol. 25* (pp. 263–312). Amsterdam: Elsevier Science.

Mailloux, S. (1989). *Rhetorical power.* Ithica: Cornell.

Marvin, C. (1988). *When old technologies were new: Thinking about electric communication in the late nineteenth century.* New York: Oxford University Press.

McLeod, S. (1990). Cultural literacy, curricular reform, and freshman composition. *Rhetoric Review 8*, 270–278.

McLuhan, M. (1972). *The gutenberg galaxy: The making of typographic man.* Toronto: University of Toronto Press.

McLuhan, M. & Fiore, Q. (1968). *War and peace in the global village.* New York: Bantam Books.

Miller, S. (1989). *Rescuing the subject: A critical introduction to rhetoric and the writer.* Carbondale: Southern Illinois University Press.

Miller, S. (1990). Comments on "A Common ground: The essay in academe." *College English 52*, 330–334.

Mirel, B. (1988). The politics of usability. In S. Doheny-Farina (Ed.). *Effective documentation* (pp. 277–297). Cambridge, MA: MIT Press.

Mitchell, R. Crawford, M. & Madden, R. (1985). An investigation of the impact of electronic communication systems on organizational communication patterns. *Journal of Business Communication 22*(4), 9–16.

Moi, T. (1985). *Sexual/Textual politics: Feminist literary theory.* New York: Methuen,.

Mortensen, P. (1989) Reading authority, writing authority. *Reader 21*, 35–55.

Mulkay, M. (1977). Sociology of the scientific research community. In I. Spiegel-Rosing & D. deSolla Price (Eds.). *Science, technology, and society: A cross-disciplinary perspective* Beverly Hills: Sage.

Murray, D. (1985). Conversation for action: The computer terminal as a medium of communication. Dissertation. Stanford University.

Myers, G. (1985). The social construction of two biologists' proposals. *Written Communication 2*, 219–245.

Myers, G. (1985). Text as knowledge claims: The social construction of two biology articles. *Social Studies of Science 15*, 593–630.

Myers, G. (1986a). Reality, consensus, and reform in the rhetoric of composition teaching. *College English 48*, 154–174.

Myers, G. (1986b). Writing research and the sociology of scientific knowledge: A review of three new books. *College English 48*, 595–610.

Myers, G. (1988). Review essay—books on the sociology of knowledge. *College Composition and Communication 39*, 465–474.

North, S. (1987). *The making of knowledge in composition: Portrait of an emerging field*. Porsmouth, NH: Boynton Cook/Heinemann.

Nystrand, M. (1982). Rhetoric's "audience" and linguistic's "speech community": Implications for understanding writing, reading, and text. In M. Nystrand (Ed.). *What writers know* (pp. 1–27). New York: Academic.

Nystrand, M. (1990). Sharing words. *Written communication 7*, 3–24.

Oakeshott, M. (1962). The voice of poetry and the "conversation of mankind." *Rationalism in politics* (pp. 196–247). New York: Basic Books.

Ohmann, R. (1985). Literacy, technology, and monopoly capital. *College English 47*, 675–689.

Ong, W. S. J. (1977). *Interfaces of the word: studies in the evolution of consciousness and culture*. Ithaca: Cornell University Press.

Ong, W. S. J. (1982). *Orality and literacy: The technologizing of the word*. London: Methuen.

Overington, M. (1977). The scientific community as audience: Toward a rhetorical analysis of science. *Philosophy and Rhetoric 10*, 143–164.

Paine, C. (1989). Relativism, radical pedagogy, and the ideology of paralysis. *College English 51*, 557–570.

Perelman, C. (1982). *The realm of rhetoric* (W. Kluback, Trans.). Notre Dame, IN: University of Notre Dame Press.

Perelman, C. & Olbrechts-Tyteca, L. (1969). *The new rhetoric* (W. Kluback, Trans.). Notre Dame, IN: University of Notre Dame Press.

Phelps, L. W. (1991). Practical wisdom and the geography of knowledge in composition. *College English 53*, 863–885.

Plato. (1974). *The republic* (G.M.A. Grube, Trans.). Indianapolis: Hackett.

Porter, J. (1986). Intertextuality and the discourse community. *Rhetoric Review 5*, 34–47.

Porter, J. (1990). *Divisio* as em-/de-powering topic: A basis for argument in rhetoric and composition. *Rhetoric Review 8*, 191–205.

Porter, J. (1992). *Audience and rhetoric: An archaeological composition of the discourse community*. Englewood Cliffs, NJ: Prentice Hall.

Poster, M. (1990). *The mode of information: Poststructuralism and social context*. Chicago: Chicago University Press.

Quarterman, J. (1991). *The matrix: Computer networks and conferencing systems worldwide*. Bedford, MA: Digital.

Rafoth, B. (1988). Discourse community: Where writers, readers, and texts come together. In B. Rafoth & D. Rubin (Eds.). *The social construction of written communication* (pp. 131–146). Norwood, NJ: Ablex.

Rafoth, B. (1990). Descriptive and explanatory adequacy in the concept of discourse community. In G. Kirsch & D. Roen (Eds.). *A Sense of Audience in Written Communication* (pp. 140–152). Newbury Park, CA: Sage.

Randall, D. (1992, 28 Jan.). Purtopoi. Electronic mail message.

Rawls, J. (1971). *A theory of justice*. Oxford: Oxford University Press.

Reither, J. (1985). Writing and knowing: Toward redefining the writing process. *College English 47*, 620–629.

Rheingold, H. (1988). Case history: Town hall on a desktop. In R. Deward & H. Rheingold (Eds.). *Electronic citizenship* (pp. 6:3–11). San Francisco: Pacific Bell.

Rheingold, H. (1991a, Apr.). Standing at the fork in the road. *Publish*, 37–38.

Rheingold, H. (1991b, July). The thought police on patrol. *Publish*, 46–47.

Rheingold, H. (1993). *The virtual community: Homesteading on the electronic frontier.* Reading, MA: Addison-Wesley.

Rickard, J. (1994, Oct.). Internet stats for first half of 1994. *Boardwatch*, 70–71.

Rickard, J. (1995, Feb.). US House of Representatives: Thomas system on the web. *Boardwatch*, 40–42.

Ritchie, J. (1989). Beginning writers: Diverse voices and individual identity. *College Composition and Communication 40*, 152–173.

Romaine, S. (1982). What is a speech community? In S. Romaine (Ed.). *Sociolinguistic variation in speech communities* (pp. 13–24). London: Edward Arnold.

Ronald, K. (1988). On the outside looking in: Students' analyses of professional discourse communities. *Rhetoric Review 7*, 130–149.

Rorty, R. (1979). *Philosophy and the mirror of nature.* Princeton: Princeton University Press.

Rorty, R. (1985). Philosophy without principles. In W.T.J. Mitchell (Ed.). *Against theory: literary studies and the new pragmatism* (pp. 132–138). Chicago: University of Chicago Press.

Rose, L. (1995, July). The many interfaces of freedom. *Boardwatch*, 100–103.

Rosenzweig, S. (1991, Nov.). How do I get to carnegie hall? *Publish*, 10.

Sandel, M. (1982). *Liberalism and the limits of justice.* Cambridge: Cambridge University Press.

Sanderson, D. (1993). *Smileys.* Sebastopol, CA: O'Reilly.

de Saussure, F. (1989). C. Bally & A. Sechehaye (Eds.). *Course in general linguistics* (R Harris, Trans.). La Salle, IL: Open Court.

Scholes, R. (1984). Is there a fish in this text? *College English 46*, 653–664.

Selfe, C. (1990). Technology in the English classroom: Computers through the lens of feminist theory. In C. Handa (Ed.). *Computers and community: Teaching composition in the twenty-first century* (pp. 118–139) Portsmouth, NH: Boynton/Cook.

Selfe, C. (1992). Testing the claims for on-line conferences: Where do we go from here? Paper presented Conference on College Composition and Communication, Cinncinati.

Selfe, C. & Selfe, R. (1994). Politics of the interface. *College Composition and Communication 45*, 480–504.

Shannon, C. & Weaver, W. (1949). *The mathematical theory of communication.* Urbana: University of Illinois Press.

Silverman, K. (1983). *The subject of semiotics.* New York: Oxford University Press.

Sims, B. (1992). Electronic mail and composing: A study of electronic mail users. Paper presented Conference on College Composition and Communication, Cinncinati.

Smith, P. (1988). *Discerning the subject.* Minneapolis: University of Minnesota Press.

de Sola Pool, I. (1983). *Technologies of freedom.* Cambridge, MA: Harvard University Press.

Spafford, G. (1990). The USENET In T. LaQuey (Ed.). *A user's directory of computer networks* (pp. 386–390). Bedford, MA: Digital.

Spellmeyer, K. (1989). A common ground: The essay in the academy. *College English 51,* 262–276.

Stamm, K. (1985). *Newspaper use and community ties: Toward a dynamic theory.* Norwood, NJ: Ablex.

STC's BBS: An invaluable resource. (1991, Nov.). *STC Intercom,* 8.

Stewart, D. (1988). Collaborative learning and composition: Boon or bane? *Rhetoric Review 7,* 58–83.

Stewart, D. (1990). Comments on John Trimbur's "Consensus and difference in collaborative learning." *College English 52,* 689–691.

Stuckey, E. (1991). *The violence of literacy.* Portsmouth, NH: Boynton.

Sullivan, P. (1991). Taking control of the page: Electronic writing and word publishing. In G. Hawisher & C. Selfe (Eds.). *Evolving perspectives on computers and composition studies: Questions for the 1990s* (pp. 43–64). Urbana: NCTE.

Taylor, M. (1982). *Community, anarchy, and liberty.* Cambridge, MA: Cambridge University Press.

Tehranian, M. (1988). *Technologies of power: Information machines and democratic prospects.* Norwood, NJ: Ablex.

Teilhard de Chardin, P. (1961). *The phenomena of man* (B. Wall, Trans.). New York: Harper & Row.

Thomas, G. (1986). Mutual knowledge; A theoretical base for analyzing audience. *College English 48,* 580–594.

Tompkins, J. (1987). Me and my shadow. *New Literary History 19,* 169–178.

Tompkins, J. (1988). Fighting words: Unlearning to write the critical essay. *Georgia Review 42,* 585–590.

Trimbur, J. (1989). Consensus and difference in collaborative learning. *College English 51,* 602–616.

Van Houweling, D. (1992, March 12). Testimony of Douglas E. Van Houweling, Merit Network, Inc. Paper presented Hearing on the National Science Foundation Network, US House of Representatives Subcommittee on Science.

Vitanza, V. (1987). "Notes" towards historiographies of rhetorics; or, rhetorics of the histories of rhetorics: Traditional, revisionary, and sub/versivc. *PRE/TEXT 8*(1/2), 63–125.

Vitanza, V. (1990). "Clarity"; or, what's at stake in writing histories of rhetorics. Paper presented Conference on College Composition and Communication, Chicago.

Volosinov, V. N. (1973). *Marxism and the philosophy of language* (L. Matejka & I.R. Titunik, Trans.). Cambridge, MA: Harvard University Press.

Wahlstrom, B. (1989). Desktop publishing: Perspectives, potentials, and politics. In G. Hawisher & C. Selfe (Eds.). *Critical perspectives on computers and composition instruction* (pp. 162–186). New York: College Teachers Press.

Welsh, G. (1992). Developing policies for campus network communications. *EDUCOM Review* 27(3), 42–45.

Wilson, K. (1988). *Technologies of control: The new interactive media for the home.* Madison, WS: University of Wisconsin Press.

Winsor, D. (1989). An engineer's writing and the corporate construction of knowledge. *Written Communication* 6, 270–285.

Winterowd, W.R. (1990). *The rhetoric of the "other" literature.* Carbondale, IL: Southern Illinois University Press.

Woolgar, S. (1988a). *Knowledge and reflexivity: New frontiers in the sociology of knowledge.* London: Sage.

Woolgar, S. (1988b). *Science: The very idea.* London: Tavistock Publications.

Young, R. (1981). *Untying the text: A post-structuralist reader.* Boston: Routledge & Kegan Paul.

Ziman, J. (1968). *Public knowledge: An essay concerning the social dimension of science.* Cambridge: Cambridge University Press.

Zuboff, S. (1988). *In the age of the smart machine.* New York: Basic Books.

Author Index

Subject Index

A

Access to electronic texts, 48–53

Analytical frames, 6–7, 8, 10, 60, 110, 150, 164

Anti-Foundationalism critique, 92–94, 96, 156

ARPANET (Advanced Research Projects Agency Network), 16–19, 172, 177

Articulatory moment, 12, 23, 149, 154, 158–160

Authorizing strategies
  concept of, 130–131
  used in e-mail, 131–142

B

BBS (bulletin board systems), 48–49, as political force, 172

Bruffee's four tenets of social construction, 88–94

C

Censorship, 2, 17, 28, 50–55

Classrooms, effect of WANS on 7, 30, 52–55, 114

CMC or "computer-mediated communication", 2–3, 16, 22, 174

Cognitive engineers, 108

Common sense, 27, 31, 45–46, 78–80, 84, 109

Conn/unix vs. *Com/munus*, 69–70

Communitarian theorist, 11, 64–68, 75, 76–78, 81

Constitutive theory of community, 11, 70–73, 75–76, 80, 87, 94, 101, 115–116, 130–147, 149–150, 154–155, 160, 163, 165

Contingent continuity, concept of 154, 155, 158–160, 163

Coproduction of text, 42–44, 131

Cyber–rape, 3, 125, 174

D

Democracy, representative, 46–48

Determinism, *see also* Utopian and Pragmatic determinism, 11, 12, 59, 75–76, 80, 84, 86, 96, 99, 109, 155, 160, 164

Desert Storm, 15

Discourse community, 62–63, 101–103

Desktop publishing
  history, 33–35
  vs electronic publishing, 36–38

E

E-journals, 43–44

Electronic citizenship, 8–9, 50, 111–112

Electronic communities, 111–116

Electronic discussion groups, 22–23, 24, 71, 104, 111–112, 115–118

Electronic Frontier Foundation, 55–56

Electronic photocomposition, 36–37

Electronic publishing
  vs. electronic writing, 36–38
  vs. desktop publishing, 36–38
  how readers interpret, 33–45